"What an excellent resource! Here is a call to prayer that understands the prophetic; a call to intercession that understands the importance of Israel; a call to supplication that understands the Spirit. Jim Goll is one of the few leaders in the Body today who could write such a book, let alone do it with passion, biblical grounding and balance. This is highly recommended reading."

—Dr. Michael L. Brown, President, Brownsville (Fla.)
Revival School of Ministry

"I personally can attest to the intercessory grace on Jim Goll's life and his passion for Jesus, because I have walked with Jim for the past fifteen years. *Kneeling on the Promises* will add needed ammunition to the prayer arsenal to inspire effective, fervent prayer from the heart."

—Mike Bickle, Ministry Director, Friends of the Bridegroom;
Senior Pastor, Metro Christian Fellowship of Kansas City

"Jim Goll has done it again! Few can put it together like Jim in concept and application. Touch this work and you will be touched."

—Jack Taylor, President, Dimension Ministries

"Jim Goll is a man God has used to give my life prophetic direction and definition. Jim is sold out to God. He has been used to bring healing and encouragement to me and the church I lead in Iowa."

—Francis Frangipane, River of Life Ministries

"In this intensive study of the Bible, Jim Goll has uncovered a host of ways people prayed that worked. If one method failed to get the desired answer, God would lead them to a new level, using a different approach. Learn from the mighty heroes of faith—as Goll introduces them to us—both from the Bible and from history, those who moved God for great miracles.

"This volume could and should revolutionize your own life as you discover and put to use the means God has provided to answer your own prayers. If you are a minister, a teacher, a leader, a parent, share this exciting revelation of praying prayers that work. This is a timely, much-needed book, as God looks for and no doubt wonders where the intercessors are (Isaiah 59:16). It's high time for the world changers to arise as the nations move into uncertain waters. God has the answer!"

—Freda Lindsay, Chairman of the Board Emeritus, Christ for
the Nations, Inc.

"If the Lord eternally titled His own house as a 'House of Prayer,' there must be incredible depths and dimensions of prayer we have yet to discover. One who could show us such profound and prophetic revelation would need to be a humble seeker, a desperate travailer and a warring prevailer. I know of no man more qualified to take us on that journey than Jim Goll."

—Dr. Ché Ahn, Senior Pastor, Harvest Rock Church, Pasadena

"Not only does Jim Goll have an excellent prayer and prophetic ministry; he also has an ability to teach and equip the Body of Christ with excellence."

—John Arnott, Senior Pastor, Toronto Airport Christian Fellowship

"I have a prescription for every believer who needs vitality in his or her prayer life. Devour this book! For those who want to intercede for family, friends and the nation, Jim Goll gives a blueprint for action in the Spirit realm. It places within your hands God's battle plan for victory. Jim gives not just an understanding of the theology of intercession, but how the principles apply in your daily life.

"I remember well the testimony of healing from barrenness that this book vividly describes, because I was used by the Lord as a tool of mercy in the Master's hands. As a result, not only do the Golls have four children today, but Jim and Michal Ann have entered into a depth of prayer and are able to impart these truths to the lives of believers. I encourage every believer in every church to allow the Holy Spirit to weave the great truths contained in *Kneeling on the Promises* into the fabric of their lives."

—Mahesh Chavda, Founder and Senior Pastor, All Nations Church, Charlotte, North Carolina

"I highly recommend this book by my friend Jim Goll. It is an excellent work, refreshing and unlike any other approach to this subject. It challenges us to embrace the positive promises of God as 'kneeling Christians,' that we may stand upon them daily as strong believers. I am more hungry for God after reading this book."

—Paul Cain, Shiloh Ministries

"The last thing the Body of Christ needs is another gimmicky book on prayer. Jim Goll hasn't given us one. Instead, he speaks of the kind of biblically informed intercession that transformed the age of Wesley, set ablaze the meadows of Cain Ridge and, as in Wales and Zambia, shaped the course of nations. If it is true, as Jonathan Edwards said, that 'when God determines to give His people revival, He sets them a-praying,' then this book is as much a hopeful sign as it is a fresh unveiling of God's ways."

—Stephen Mansfield, Senior Pastor, Belmont Church, Nashville

KNEELING
ON THE
Promises

Other Books and Materials by Jim W. Goll

The Lost Art of Intercession

Encounters with a Supernatural God

Twelve complete study guides on subjects such as *Prayer and Intercession, Prophetic Ministry* and *Empowered Ministry Training*

Hundreds of audio teaching tapes and numerous videotapes

KNEELING
ON THE.
Promises

Birthing God's Purposes
through Prophetic Intercession

JIM W. GOLL

Foreword by Cindy Jacobs

Chosen Books

A Division of Baker Book House Co
Grand Rapids, Michigan 49516

© 1999 by Jim W. Goll

Published by Chosen Books
A division of Baker Book House Company
P.O. Box 6287, Grand Rapids, MI 49516-6287

Fourth printing, September 2000

Printed in the United States of America

Library of Congress Cataloging-in-Publication Data

Goll, Jim W.
    Kneeling on the promises : birthing God's purposes through prophetic intercession / Jim W. Goll ; foreword by Cindy Jacobs.
        p.   cm.
    Includes bibliographical references (p.   ).
    ISBN 0-8007-9268-8 (pbk.)
    1. Intercessory prayer—Christianity. I. Title.
BV215.G65   1999
248.3'2—dc21   98-54809

For current information about all releases from Baker Book House, visit our web site:

http://www.bakerbooks.com

This book is dedicated to my almost perfect wife, Michal Ann Goll, and mother of our four, great, miracle children. You are my best friend and supporter and the best team member I have ever had. You are an example of character and gifting brought together in one unique combination! Thanks for fighting for our children! I love and need you.

CONTENTS

Contents

FOREWORD

This morning I arose early and went into my prayer room. There is a little, old-fashioned couch in a corner of the room that is my "kneeling spot." Each day when I am at home, I like to rise early and meet God in that quiet place. Some days, like this morning, I wrap a blanket around myself because it is very cold. There is snow on the ground in my city of Colorado Springs, Colorado.

From that small spot on the floor I travel around the world praying, doing exactly what Jim Goll describes in this book. I am aware, however, that I am not alone in my travels in prayer. All over the world voices are joining mine in many languages—the harmony of God's children calling out to Him in intercession.

This prayer movement has grown throughout the 1980s and '90s. Whereas many churches did not have prayer rooms and ministries when we started teaching on intercession, there are numerous ones today. That is why this book, *Kneeling on the Promises*, is so strategic in its importance. It deals with prophetic intercession—praying God's will into the earth.

While some books like my own *Possessing the Gates of the Enemy* touch on this subject, none covers it as well as this one. Jim Goll is extraordinarily gifted to write on the subject of intercession and prophetic intercession with humor, integrity and deep insight. He plumbs deep wells of understanding that others have given us only a light drink from.

The Body of Christ needs this book. It is a next step in the mentoring of a prophetic group of intercessors who fight as warrior brides. You will want to read each chapter again and again because each time you do, you will receive fresh insight and understanding.

I invite you to take a journey into the realm of intercession with my friend Jim Goll that you have never traveled. Open the pages of this book and drink deeply of its revelation. You will come away from it refreshed, encouraged, challenged and nearer to God than you have been.

Cindy Jacobs, co-founder
Generals of Intercession
Colorado Springs, Colorado
December 1998

ACKNOWLEDGMENTS

It seems that I have labored over this book for years. Whenever you work on something for a protracted period of time, you have a volume of people you need to thank! So it is with this one.

First I want to acknowledge the two main intercessory tutors the Lord has put in my life. Thanks to Dick Simmons of Men for Nations for his relentless cry for mercy, which I have observed firsthand. Thank you, Dick. You have impacted my life beyond measure. Then I wish to acknowledge my dear friend Mike Bickle, with whom I was blessed to serve in Kansas City for years. What an example you have been to me of reminding God of His Word and of keeping prayer central amid the swirl of many good things to do. Bless you, Dick and Mike!

I also want to acknowledge others who have lent their teaching expertise to help fill in my gaps—people like Avner Boskey of Final Frontiers and Pat Gastineau of Word of Love Ministries. I also owe a great debt to the teaching ministry of Derek Prince, from whom I have learned more over the years than from any other teacher in the Body of Christ.

I wish to acknowledge my prayer partners, Richard Glickstein and David Fitzpatrick. Thanks for walking with me. May many more Holy Ghost excursions transpire! Thanks also to Bob and Terry Bailey, who head up our Prayer Shield, and Sue Kellough, who acts as a watchman, keeping her eyes open for us. Bless you!

Then I want to thank all the past and present staff of Ministry to the Nations, who have helped me in this journey. You have been such a blessing!

Last I wish to thank Jane Campbell, the editor of Chosen Books, for seeing in me a diamond in the rough and being willing to tutor me in the creative ways of writing. Thank you so much!

ONE

CULTIVATING A HEART
FOR PRAYER

ON BENDED KNEE

"It's a boy!" our doctor declared as our first-born came forth. It was the Day of Atonement, October 4, 1983, at Johnson County Memorial Hospital in Warrens-burg, Missouri. A time of a new beginning had finally arrived as Justin Wayne emerged weighing eight pounds six ounces.

It seemed as though my wife and I had waited an eternity for this blessed event. We had shed blood, sweat and tears in our first years of marriage. But finally, in our seventh year of union, the circumstances of barrenness in the natural realm turned into fruitfulness with the opening of Michal Ann's womb.

You see, it took a miracle. We could not have children.

What does our personal testimony about healing from barrenness have to do with a book called *Kneeling on the Promises*? Everything! The true life story of our supernatural healing paints a graphic picture of the ways of God in joining the revelatory gifts of the Holy Spirit, the realm of the prophetic and intercessory prayer. Our circumstances screamed into my wife's and my faces, *No way!* But with God there *is* a way.

So hold onto this thumbnail sketch of our personal testimony, and I will fill in the blanks in the next chapter, "Birthing a Promise: Our Personal Journey." But first let me share with you some of my beginnings in this walk, why I have written this book and what you can expect as you devour the full-course meal set in front of you.

A Place of Beginning

Hey, we all start somewhere! I began the Christian walk by singing the songs of the Church. Before I even started elementary school I was singing anthems from my brownish-red Cokesbury hymnal as loudly as I could.

I grew up in a Midwest rural community where they probably added the number of dogs and cats in the town to come up with the grand population of 259. I was raised in church and it seems I lived my life there. It helped that Dad was treasurer of the board, Mom the president of Women's Society of Christian Service, and both cleaned the building, mowed the lawns and did a whole lot of other tasks. Why, we spent so much time there that I was a church mouse, a regular fixture.

In my growing-up years in Missouri, I did all the usual things kids do in church—made paper airplanes out of the bulletins, tried to listen to those things called sermons and watched the older folks nod off and wondered how that head could stay on that stem of a neck when it bobbed so much! I also loved to sing the hymns of the Church. Today I have a T-shirt that says, *Real Men Sing Real Loud.* That's me. I think I must have sung before I walked! As I look back on the Cowgill Methodist Church, I am grateful. Some good, old-fashioned cement was poured into me in those foundational years.

I have since learned that many of the great anthems of the past contain wonderful deposits of rich Church history and doctrinal understanding. But there is one hymn I would tweak a bit if I could. Now hold onto your hat. It is "Standing on the Promises":

> Standing, standing,
> Standing on the promises of God my Savior;
> Standing, standing,
> I'm standing on the promises of God.[1]

Hey, I know these words are biblical. After all, the apostle Peter wrote that God "has granted to us His precious and magnificent promises" (2 Peter 1:4). And Paul, the beloved apostle, penned: "Put on God's complete armor, that you may be able to resist and stand your ground on the evil day [of danger], and having done all [the crisis demands], to stand [firmly in your place]. Stand therefore—hold your ground . . ." (Ephesians 6:13–14, Amplified). We are called to stand our ground and not give an inch to the devil.

Yes, I do love that great hymn and have sung it many times with all my heart. Also, like you, I have been taught that I must put on the full armor of God. But before you flip out, let me tell you how I would adjust that marvelous hymn "chiropractically":

> Kneeling, kneeling,
> Kneeling on the promises of God my Savior;
> Kneeling, kneeling,
> I'm kneeling on the promises of God.

Whew! I think you are still with me. In fact, I hope that by the time you finish reading this book, you will be humming right along with me.

Now let me fill you in on some secrets of this book ahead of time.

An Overview of This Book

Why another book on prayer? Haven't there already been a number of old classics and new manuals brought forth? Well, you will see as you read that this is not just another book on prayer. It is about the merging of the priestly and prophetic ministries joined at the point of prayer. Actually, I know of no other book to date given to this subject.

In this first section, "Cultivating a Heart for Prayer," we gaze at the importance of kneeling before our Father. "Wait a second," you say, "A heart for prayer? What's that?" Each of us New Testament believers in the Lord Jesus Christ is called to be "a royal priesthood" (1 Peter 2:9), priests unto our Lord. This is our birthright, the reason we have been born again. In the Old Testament the priest represented the people before God, while the prophet represented God to the people. As New Testament priests we are called to offer freely the sacrifices of praise, prayer, worship and intercession before our glorious Lord. As our job description we are blessed with the highest of privileges: ministering to the King of the universe.

But this is not just some ceremonial task we perform and then say, "Been there, done that—even got the T-shirt." It is the prayer of the heart to which the Lord responds. In this first chapter we will see how worship *precedes* petition and how we can become worshipful watchers. Then we will study the four biblical definitions of intercession and be challenged to step forth into this calling as intercessory warriors.

In the second chapter we see how the Lord Jesus, who "is the same yesterday and today, yes and forever" (Hebrews 13:8), changed the pronouncement of barrenness and enabled Michal Ann and me to bring forth four fine arrows in our quiver. In chapter 3 we proceed to the question "What moves the hand of God?" Here we take special note once again that it is the prayer of the heart that is heard from on high. We will also look at the forgotten place of the prayer of tears. (Shall I tell you more or just keep it a secret until then?) And we close out this first section by studying intense forms of prayer from the Scriptures and Church history that are often termed *travail*.

The pivotal second section, "Cultivating a Heart for the Prophetic," raises the question, "What *is* prophetic prayer?" I will leave that thought hanging in your heart and mind for now, and entice you righteously to continue on.

The unusual material in this second section starts off with a clarion call, "Wanted: A Generation of Prophetic People," and hinges on the crucial sixth chapter, "The Prophetic Intercessory Task." From there I blow a bullhorn, "Calling All Watchmen," and develop our understanding of men and women standing guard on the walls of our cities, churches and nations. Next we investigate the subject of "Reminding God of His Word," with a corresponding appendix in the back of the book full of hundreds of Bible verses to help you in your task of Scripture praying. Finally we glue all these concepts together—intercessory prayer, the realm of the prophetic and the Scriptures—with a historical overview of the founding of the nation of Israel and several good Holy Ghost stories thrown in to whet your appetite. In Appendix 2 I have prepared an outline of Scriptures to help you pray aright on the important subject of the regathering and restoration of the Jewish people to their homeland, and Scriptures to pray for their salvation.

Finally we turn the corner in our final section, "Applications for Prophetic Priests." What are prophetic priests? Not some new cult group! They are simply believers in Jesus graced with the revelatory gifts of the Holy Spirit in their lives—a word of wisdom, a word of knowledge, discerning of spirits and the gift of prophecy—who respond to these

19

giftings by praying the insight back to God. Here we take courage from the life of Amos and his tenacious, bold intercession that thwarted the judgments of God in his day. I will also give powerful illustrations of crisis intervention that have occurred in my own life and invite you to do that for which *you* were created: help to write history through praying God's promises and making a difference for Christ's sake.

In chapter 11, "Wisdom Issues for Intercessors," is material that could just save your life from the perils and pitfalls that often seem to hit frontline intercessors. And in the final chapter I close out our pilgrimage together by telling you about an awesome encounter I had in May 1989. The Lord is searching for "gatekeepers of His presence."

Before you shut the last page of the book, be sure to take a look at Appendix 3, a helpful "Glossary of Terms" with simple definitions of different words I use throughout the book, to help bring clarity. Since each of us has a different background, experience and understanding, I hope this will help you grasp these terms and get us onto the same page.

Why "Kneeling"?

I think I just heard someone ask, "Why this title? Aren't you taking this concept a bit far—kneeling versus standing? What's the big deal, anyway?" Let's consider this for a moment.

I do not think I am just splitting hairs. Ponder it with me for a moment. Kneeling is a picture of dependency. Kneeling is a posture of humility and brokenness. Kneeling is a sign of reverence and honor. Kneeling is the act of worship that precedes petitioning.

Prayer leader Dick Eastman stated in his first book, *No Easy Road*, that "those who learn to kneel in humility and weakness will soon feel God's supernatural power. The man of prayer is the man of power." Eastman went on to quote some beautiful lines by Richard Chenevix Trench that deliver a simple message:

> We kneel—and all about us seems to lower;
> We rise—and all, the distant and the near,
> Stands forth in sunny outline, brave and clear.
> We kneel, how weak! We rise, how full of power![2]

Kneeling is an outward expression of an inward work of grace. In fact, before Paul ever tells us in Ephesians 6:13–14 about the value of standing, he frames out for us the privilege of kneeling: "For this reason [seeing the greatness of this plan by which you are built together in Christ], I bow my knees before the Father of our Jesus Christ . . ." (Ephesians 3:14, Amplified). Isn't that awesome? Now, I am not trying to impose another ritualistic routine for you to have to obey. I am simply focusing a magnifying glass on a heart issue that each of us needs to see. Some of us today are taught to stand and shoot at the devil before we are taught to kneel before our Father. If we reversed the order, maybe our aim would be better!

I have a simple question: What is the most commonly used position for giving birth around the world? I will give you a hint: It is not lying flat on your back! Why, even in good old North America, hospitals are starting to get smart. Birthing chairs are being used in certain places to bring into account the pull of gravity. The most ordinary position is squatting—or kneeling, you could say. Kneeling is the posture of giving birth.

Sooner or later we are all going to kneel. Philippians 2:9–10 portrays this picture graphically:

> Therefore [because He stooped so low], God has highly exalted Him and has freely bestowed on Him the name that is above every name, that in (at) the name of Jesus every

knee should (must) bow, in heaven and on earth and under the earth.

Philippians 2:9–10, Amplified

If all of us at the end of the age are going to end up in the same posture anyway, we might just as well learn it sooner than later!

The Act of Worship

What is authentic worship? What does it look like? Worship is an act of giving ourselves to God wholeheartedly, with our entire being—spirit, soul and body. Twelve different Hebrew and Greek words in the Bible are translated *worship*. All four of the Hebrew words, and especially the primary word, *shachah*, mean "to depress, prostrate (in homage to royalty or God)—bow down, crouch, fall down (flat), humbly beseech, do (make) obeisance, do reverence, make to stoop, worship."[3] One Greek word for worship is *proskuneo*, which means to kiss (as a dog licks his master's hand); to prostrate oneself in homage; to do reverence; to adore.[4]

The first mention of the word *worship* is found in Genesis 22, after the Lord asks Abraham to offer his son Isaac before Him on Mount Moriah. Abraham rises early the next morning, saddles his donkey and launches out in obedience to present his son before God. After three days of travel, Abraham's eyes rest on the site of sacrifice.

And Abraham said to his young men, "Stay here with the donkey, and I and the lad will go yonder; and we will *worship* and return to you."

verse 5, emphasis added

We connect worship with music and sometimes make them synonymous. But there is no mention of music here.

The only instruments listed are wood, fire and a knife, and I don't think Abraham had in mind to whittle a flute and play a tune. All he offered was sacrifice, obedience and faith. This is worship in its highest form—a life prostrate before God. Worship is about bending the knee.

Throughout Scripture expressions of worship and prayer are emphasized continually (see 2 Chronicles 7:14; Ezekiel 22:30; John 4:23; 1 Timothy 2:1, 8). Both prayer and expressions of worship are mentioned as integral elements in the early Church (see Acts 13:1–3; 16:25; Philippians 4:4–6; 1 Timothy 2:1–2, 8; 2 Timothy 1:3–4; Philemon 1:4–6). Let's briefly consider three New Testament accounts of how people approached the Master. We quickly find a trend: *Worship precedes petition.*

First, in Matthew 8:2–3, we are given the account of the leper whom Jesus cleansed:

> Behold, a leper came to Him, and bowed down to Him, saying, "Lord, if You are willing; You can make me clean." He stretched out His hand and touched him, saying, "I am willing; be cleansed." And immediately his leprosy was cleansed.

Before the man brought forth his petition in tremendous desperation, he bowed before the Lord. No wonder the healing virtue of God came forth so quickly!

In another awesome demonstration of the mercy of God, we find prostration once again coming before petitioning. I do not believe this was just cultural and ethnic protocol. I am convinced that resurrection power proceeded in response to faith, humility and true worship:

> Behold, there came a synagogue official, and bowed down before Him, saying, "My daughter has just died; but come and lay Your hand on her, and she will live." And Jesus rose and began to follow him, and so did His disciples. . . . And when Jesus came into the official's house, and saw

the flute-players, and the crowd in noisy disorder, He began to say, "Depart; for the girl has not died, but is asleep." And they began laughing at Him. But when the crowd had been put out, He entered and took her by the hand; and the girl arose.

Matthew 9:18–19, 23–25

The third example comes from the Syrophoenican woman with the daughter who was cruelly demonized. The woman came forth with persistence, shouting and crying out, "Have mercy on me, O Lord, Son of David" (Matthew 15:22). The Lord did not answer her a word in order to test her and see how desperate she really was. But she continued in her urgency and would not take no for an answer:

She came and began to bow down before Him, saying, "Lord, help me!" . . . Then Jesus answered and said to her, "O woman, your faith is great; be it done for you as you wish." And her daughter was healed at once.

verses 25, 28

Oh, for those results today! But did you notice? Take another look. The Amplified Bible renders verse 25: "She came and kneeling, worshipped Him, and kept praying, 'Lord, help me!'" Yes, she got what she came for. But she, too, first came on bended knee.

Does Jesus deserve anything less?

Four Biblical Definitions of the Intercessory Task

Before we proceed any further, let's check our foundation of what it means to be an intercessor. Many teachers of prayer credit S. D. Gordon with the following statement: "The greatest thing anyone can do for God and man is pray. You can do more than pray after you've prayed. But you cannot do more than pray until you've prayed." Isn't that awesome? Intercession is the right to shape and make history, and each of us gets to step up to the plate as part of our calling as priests before the Lord.

To lay the foundation properly, let's look at four major Scriptures, two from the book of Isaiah and two from Ezekiel. As we do, we will draw four overlapping yet distinct definitions of the task of priestly intercessor.

1. Being God's Secretary

Want a good job? I have one for you. God always has the need for good secretaries. There is plenty of work waiting just for you. Here is our first biblical definition of the task of priestly intercession:

> On your walls, O Jerusalem, I have appointed watchmen; all day and all night they will never keep silent. You who remind the LORD, take no rest for yourselves; and give Him no rest until He establishes and makes Jerusalem a praise in the earth.
>
> Isaiah 62:6–7

An intercessor is one who reminds the Lord of promises and appointments not yet met and fulfilled.

What is the job of a good secretary? A secretary is an assistant who keeps track of the appointments on the boss' calendar. This capable assistant lays out the calendar, reminds the boss of his appointments and prepares the material needed so the job can be completed properly.

The intercessor, like the secretary, does the same type of task. The person of prayer searches through the divine calendar, the Bible, and finds the promises and appointments and commitments that have not yet been met. After locating these appointments, we remind our Boss, the Lord of hosts, that it is time for Him to fulfill His Word. It works something like this:

"Sir, on Your calendar it says You are going to pour out Your Spirit on all flesh. Your Word says You are going to bring forth a deluge of Your presence on the old, the young, the male, the female, those living in free nations and even those among the supposedly closed nations. Now I make an appeal to You. The time has come. According to Your divine calendar, it is time to have mercy on Your people. I ask You, Sir, to remember Your holy appointments with mankind and act."

I will expound more thoroughly on this vital subject in chapter 8, "Reminding God of His Word."

2. Taking Up the Cause of Justice

For our second glance at the fascinating job description of these priestly intercessors, let's turn once again to Isaiah:

> Yes, truth is lacking; and he who turns aside from evil makes himself a prey. Now the LORD saw, and it was displeasing in His sight that there was no justice. And He saw that there was no man, and was astonished [appalled] that there was no one to intercede.
>
> Isaiah 59:15–16

The second definition of the great task of a priestly intercessor highlights for us another key principle. *Justice* is the key word to understanding this verse. A brief, distinct definition based on this Scripture is as follows: *An intercessor is one who takes up the cause of justice before God on behalf of another.*

In this awesome priestly position, we stand in the gap before the Lord for others in great need or distress, lifting a cry to Him, the Judge of all. Take the unborn, for example. It is said that the most dangerous place for a person to live these days is in his or her mother's womb—statistically a more vulnerable locale than even the inner city!

We must intercede, standing in the gap on behalf of those who stand alone and lifting our voices for those in need of holy intervention: "Father, we plead the case of the unborn [or the lost, lonely, homeless or those ravaged by war, sickness or Satan] and bring them before Your holy presence. Kind Father, remember them and show mercy to them."

An intercessor is one who takes up the cause of justice before almighty God for another in distress. Let's not let God's evaluation of our day be the same as it was for Isaiah's. You can change things. Take your place. Don't let a caring Father God be astonished and appalled because we are a bunch of pathetic, weak, half-cold, almost comatose bodies! Let the zealous new man called the Body of Christ arise and cry out to the Lord. Take your place, O royal priesthood. Get in His face!

3. Building Up the Wall

Now we get to be masons. I am not talking about joining Freemasonry or any other false organization attempting to substitute for the living Church of Jesus Christ. I am talking about laying bricks of protection around the corridors of our families, churches and cities. Let's turn to Ezekiel to see this picture:

> "O Israel, your prophets have been like foxes among ruins. You have not gone up into the breaches [*breaks in the wall*, NIV], nor did you build the wall [*hedge*, KJV] around the house of Israel to stand in the battle on the day of the LORD."
>
> Ezekiel 13:4–5

From this Scripture I catch another glimpse of the defining purpose of the priestly intercessor. In this one the Lord calls us to stand. (Remember, you have the strength to stand only once you have knelt.) *An intercessor is one who makes up the hedge, who builds up the wall of protection in a time of battle.*

This is, after all, a day of battle. Satan is "like a roaring lion, seeking someone to devour" (1 Peter 5:8). Spirits of darkness want *you* for their next meal! So here Isaiah releases an exhortational cry against the prophets of his day. They were not doing their jobs, which meant the enemy could do his. Prophetic intercessors are needed to build up the walls of protection to keep the enemy out so that Israel (and the Church) can stand in that day.

Part of our problem is that we have not had watchmen on the walls surveying the schemes of the devil to stand against his game plans. Satan and his cohorts have had free rein in many of our cities to do as they please. No guards—no protection.

The sad state of affairs is that the enemy has been so much in our midst, and our discernment level has been so weak, that many of us call the wiles of religious spirits "godliness," and the licentiousness of compromising demons "biblical freedom." Right now we need not only watchmen on the walls to keep the enemy out, but a wholesale cleansing of the Body of Christ, because the enemy is within.

But praise the Lord, things are changing! Let's call for the standards of God to be restored. "Lord, build up the wall!" is a cry that can actually be heard in our day. We are to be like Nehemiah and Ezra of old, taking a stand for righteousness and rebuilding the walls of protection around our cities. This is intercessory activity. Through it we are taking a firm stand against the powers of darkness and commanding them to vacate the premises they have entered deceitfully.

4. Standing in the Gap

So far we have seen that our high priestly calling of intercession involves being God's secretary (reminding God of His Word); taking up the cause of justice (having a courtroom hearing with the Judge); and building up the walls (keeping the enemy out). But if this is the case, what could the phrase *standing in the gap* mean? Isn't that the same as building up the wall?

Let's take another peek at Ezekiel to get a clue:

> "I searched for a man among them who should build up the wall and stand in the gap before Me for the land, that I should not destroy it; but I found no one. Thus I have poured out My indignation on them; I have consumed them with the fire of My wrath; their way I have brought (poured) upon their heads," declares the LORD God.
>
> Ezekiel 22:30–31

Watch closely for our fourth and last definition of the privilege of the priestly prayer warrior, or you will miss the impact of it. In the previous definition we saw that we are called to build up a wall to keep the enemy out. Most of us understand this angle rather well. But look at this verse, which comes from the life of Ezekiel, with a longer lens. It is not just another rendition of the same thing. The prayer warrior has another task: to fend off God's wrath.

We are to take our position between God and His people and between God and the world. People of prayer are called to build up a wall, all right—but this time it is between us and Him.

We are given good news, though: God is waiting for someone to persuade Him not to pour out His indignation. Amazing, isn't it? Who knows? Perhaps our incense (see Exodus 30:34–36; Psalm 141:2; Revelation 5:8; 8:3–5) of holy argumentation will cause the judgment due to be averted or postponed. Our prayers can be used to cut short, lessen or delay God's righteous judgments. We can be shareholders in the time clock of God and purchase seasons of mercy.

From here we derive our fourth definition of the intercessory calling: *An intercessor is one who stands in the*

*gap between God's righteous judgments that are due and
the need for mercy on the people's behalf.*

We are called to stand in the gap at various times for different reasons. We need to be involved consistently in reminding God of His Word; to be His secretary on the earth. Some are given a particular mandate to carry the burdens of others; to argue the case for justice on behalf of those who are weak and helpless. The clarion call also goes forth beckoning us to build up the walls in the day of battle to keep the enemy out. But we have also been invited into a holy wrestling match with God Himself. The Almighty searches for a people who will hold His judgments at bay, standing in the gap between His righteous judgments, which are due, and the people's need for mercy.

Worshipful Watchers

The Holy Spirit is looking for worshipful intercessors and interceding worshipers. These two "gracelets" are being merged into the seamless garment of the royal priesthood. We must learn both aspects to be victorious.

In January 1998 I was blessed to participate in a prayer tour of Israel with Don Finto and his Caleb Company ministry, on whose board I serve. Don is the former senior pastor of Belmont Church, a 3,500-member, cell-based church in the heart of Nashville, where our ministry is presently based. The Caleb Company leadership team went to Israel to pray and meet with the messianic leaders of the indigenous church emerging there. Like most groups we visited historic sites and stopped for prayer at different locations.

One of the places we stopped on our prayer tour was the very brook at the spring of Harod where the Lord sifted through the 32,000 warriors Gideon had amassed and chose just three hundred to fight the Midianites (Judges 7:2–8). I was thrilled because the life of Gideon is one of my favorite portions of the Bible. I relate to him and his need to see himself as God saw him—a "valiant warrior" (Judges 6:12). Like Gideon I have often felt my head turn and wondered who the Lord was talking to when He called me (just as He has called you) one of His valiant warriors!

Eight of us reenacted the choosing of Gideon's mighty men. We knelt at the clear, winding brook—not on both knees, only on one—and lapped the water like dogs. Awesome!

What was the Lord searching for that day when He selected three hundred soldiers fit to fight against their strong enemy? He was looking for worshipful watchers. He instructed Gideon to accept only those who lapped the water "as a dog laps" (Judges 7:5). Ever watch a dog eat his food or lap his water? He keeps one eye on the food bowl and the other on whomever is approaching. Ninety-seven hundred of the men who remained dropped quickly to both knees and knelt to quench their thirst. All they could see were their own reflections in the water. But three hundred other soldiers, with one knee bent, were symbolically acknowledging and worshiping their King. With hands cupped to their mouths, they were watching to see what was about to appear on the scene—a prophetic picture of worshipful watchers.

Today the Lord is looking for the same. He seeks those on bended knee who are watching and praying, acknowledging that God is the strength of their lives. They are intercessory watchmen kneeling on the promises of protection and guarding against enemy attack.

I'm Kneeling, Kneeling . . .

In times of corporate praise and worship, my wife and I often step forth into singing what we call the "prophetic song of the Lord" (see Zephaniah 3:17; Hebrews 2:12). We both have a long personal history of ministering to and for the Lord in song, and doing so has been one of the delights of our lives over the years as husband and wife. At times we launch out, not knowing where we are going, and trust the wind of God, the Holy Spirit, to direct the words, melody and end result. Sometimes we sing out of the overflow of our hearts. At other times we take a Scripture passage and retell it in song. Many of these songs are actually prayers put to spontaneous tunes, petitioning the Lord of the harvest for revival and the outpouring of His promised Holy Spirit.

One afternoon, as Michal Ann and I stood before a congregation at a conference, I was catapulted into a spiritual vision and began to put lyrics to the vision I was receiving— a vision of the end-time army of God coming forth. These warriors were marching forward in unity. I saw the troops top a hill with resolve in their hearts. They were broken vessels in the Lord's hands. The Holy Spirit seemed to indicate that they were "the velvet warriors" or "the velvet army." As the Spirit of prayer was upon them, they were taking territory in the Lord's great name.

Michal Ann joined me in singing and we took turns weaving a beautiful song describing how this army was invading the enemy's camp. They were proceeding more slowly than they had hoped—but march they did! In the vision, you see, they were coming forward marching on their knees.

Yes, we are kneeling on the promises of God our Savior; kneeling on the promises of God!

God's end-time army will have an outstanding characteristic. Their strength is not in themselves. All their strength is in Him. Yes, we are the fighting bride, the worshiping army of God. The Lord is searching for His dependent warriors. His eyes are scouring the earth to mark those who weep over their Jerusalems, to find those who know how to worship Him in Spirit and in truth.

Stop. Pause right now at the beginning of this adventure. Join with me in asking Him to delight in *your* life:

Let Your eyes rest here, Lord. Let them light right now on Your little servant, and anoint me to be part of Your velvet army. I sign up for Your calling on my life. I volunteer to be a priest ministering unto Your holy name. I want to see Your purposes fulfilled, Your Kingdom come to my community, state and nation. Give me the Spirit of prayer and supplication and make me one of Your worshiping warriors. In Jesus' name. Amen.

That is what this book is about. It is a picture depicting each of us—first as individuals in humility before our Father, and then collectively as the bride of Christ—marching forward, kneeling on God's promises. The lessons contained in this book have come from the trenches of life experience. The story of Michal Ann's and my healing from barrenness, which I recount in the next chapter, represents a prophetic parable of Jesus' desire to heal His bride and bring her into fruitfulness. The brief replay of our family testimony is intended to build a bridge of history with you. Michal Ann and I learned in travail of soul the heart of a Father who cares and the effective power of compassionate, prophetic intercession.

This is not just a theological textbook, then, filled with ideas of how things are supposed to turn out right. It is filled with lessons from Scripture, Church history and contemporary adventures of real people today in their lives with God. First comes the natural and then the spiritual (see 1 Corinthians 15:46). So it has been in my life. May the Lord impart truth and inspiration into *your* life as you ponder the treasure He has given us.

So let the journey begin!

PRACTICAL APPLICATIONS—MAKING IT REAL!

- In your quiet time before the Lord, incorporate worship before proceeding into prayers of petition.

- Try posturing yourself on bended knees in dependency, humility, brokenness and worship before the Lord.
- In your prayer group, ask the Lord to lay foundational principles of the four distinct tasks of an intercessor:

    Reminding God of His Word;

    Taking up the cause of justice before God on behalf of another;

    Building up the walls to keep the enemy out;

    Fending off God's wrath.
- Encourage the spontaneous prophetic song of the Lord in your personal life, small group or church.
- Join with me in asking the Lord to anoint us to be His velvet warriors—those who come forth in unity and brokenness, on bended knees, resolved in their hearts to take territory for the King.

RECOMMENDED READING

Love on Its Knees by Dick Eastman (Chosen, 1989)
Prayer: Finding the Heart's True Home by Richard J. Foster (HarperSanFrancisco, 1992)

2

BIRTHING
A PROMISE

Our Personal Journey

Life has some interesting twists and turns!
What keeps us going forward is our proper response to the
circumstances that come our way.

Maybe you have a dream that came from God. You know
for sure that you did not make it up or pick out the goal
yourself, but its fulfillment keeps slipping through your fingers. Does this relate? Take courage! We have to yield to
the power of brokenness and then get right back up and
fight. Remember, first we must kneel before our Father so
we will have the strength to stand against the enemy.

This is part of what my wife and I have learned. As you
read our saga in this gutsy chapter—a ride through history
on the Goll Family Express!—maybe some tidbits along the
way will help you continue in your fight to see your own
dream come to pass.

Who Turned On the Lights?

I grew up in a Methodist home in rural, out-of-the-way Cowgill, Missouri. I was given a love for God and for the Church at an early age. My parents, Wayne and Amanda, were already proud of their two daughters, Sandra and Barbara, and wanted a son. Tragedy came when my mother miscarried a baby boy. But, as I have been told the story, she cried out to the Lord and said, "If You will give me another son, I will dedicate him to Christ's service." I was born one year later to the day—July 3, 1952.

I do not remember a day when Jesus was not my close Friend. Sometimes comically I say, "When I was born, I came out of my mother's womb, waved my hands and said, 'Hallelujah!'" I know that sounds kind of bizarre, but Jesus is all I have ever known.

Growing up with a country setting for a backdrop, I loved to go on long walks on the railroad tracks, singing with all my heart and talking with God, who was up there somewhere in the clouds. I just wanted to know and serve Him.

I was given three prayers in my youth that I often prayed—from the inspiration of Sunday school lessons, I guess. I would start out and ask the Lord to give me wisdom beyond my years, like Solomon. Then I would ask Him to raise up His Joseph counselors to the Pharaohs of our time, as He did in days gone by. My last prayer was that God would give me a heart of purity, that I might walk with Him all my days. These great prayers could only have come from heaven above! I still pray them today.

In grade school and high school I gave myself to academics, singing, the 4-H Club and church. I may have been respected but I did not always fit into the pop scene of the topsy-turvy '60s generation. After high school, while studying at Central Missouri State University, I attended Explo '72 in Dallas sponsored by Campus Crusade for Christ. On the last night Billy Graham spoke at the Cotton Bowl on commitment. I, along with thousands of others, stood to my feet to declare I was volunteering for full-time Christian service. That night was one of the demarcations of my life. I was going for it—God and nothing else!

This is where I first ran into the Jesus People in a powerful way. Quite a culture shock for a country Methodist kid! But they had something that drew me to them. On a purely human level I was uncertain at times, even repulsed. But my inner being was intrigued. I wanted more of God. I wanted whatever it was they had.

My little black-and-white Christian screen changed in a major way. (Today we call it a paradigm shift.) Life quickly went from black and white to color as I was filled with the Holy Spirit in the fall of 1972 and—lights, camera, action! Things changed and I changed. Today my kids would say, "Who turned on the lights?" God did. This skinny kid was now on fire and growing like a weed for Jesus. All I wanted to do was go to prayer meetings, read my Bible and get others immersed in the Spirit as I was. I was now one of the Jesus People. I had finally found my place of belonging. I loved every minute of it.

A little band of on-fire Christians was given use of a vacated fraternity house right in the middle of the campus. This sore spot was now turned into a hot spot, transformed by zealous believers into the "Jesus House." Everything seemed new. Life was an adventure!

The Plot Thickens

Young ladies? Well, of course, I still had my eyes open. But now my sights were set primarily on Him who died for me and had risen from the dead. Jesus was the passion of my life.

By God's grace I graduated from CMSU in 1974 with a degree in social work. I went to work for the summer at the local Johnson County Memorial Hospital as a male nurse's aid. This is where I met Ann Willard.

She was a joyful, kind and pretty young woman who had just graduated from Warrensburg High School that spring. The nurses tried putting us together, but I would not think of such a thing. After all, she was only eighteen and I was now a college grad! To top it off, she was dating a young man at seminary who was studying to be a pastor. But we took our breaks together, did Bible studies, prayed and had great talks. As the summer unfolded she taught me how to make hospital beds the right way and I talked to her constantly about the power of the Holy Spirit.

When summer came to an end, we went our separate ways. She started college and I leap-frogged into full-time campus ministry and another round of adventures with my best friend, the Holy Spirit.

That was September 1974. I did not see Ann (as I called her then) for nearly a year. But one Sunday morning the following May, I went on one of my favorite long walks, talking with the Lord. I remember the conversation extremely well.

I said out loud, to myself and to God, "Well, who's for me?"

I was surprised when I heard an answer back: *Ann Willard.* It sounded clear, just as if someone were right there talking with me.

"Who?"

The response came a second time: *Ann Willard.*

I had not been expecting that kind of answer! So I asked the question a third time: "Who?"

Ann Willard.

Then I got really serious. "Well, the last I knew, she was practically engaged to some man studying to be a Methodist pastor. Who?"

Ann Willard. Not only that, but you will be outwardly engaged by September and married on the following May 15.

Even though I had not anticipated this kind of answer, the words settled down inside of me and I accepted them as true. And by the way, I liked what I heard!

After a couple of months, I tried to reach Ann by phone. I did not know her phone number and prayed one of those "Holy Spirit, lead me" type of prayers. Sure enough, I got the right Willard (there were only four) and asked her to accompany me to a Christian function being held at the university campus. She accepted. And that was the start of things that forever changed our lives.

Yes, the word that came that spring morning had been the voice of the Lord. We got engaged in September and were married the following May 15, 1976.

A Promise in the Night

At the end of our first year of marriage, Ann graduated from CMSU with a degree in child development. I was already full steam into Christian outreach ministry as a campus minister at the university. It was now time for us to consider starting our family. Little did we know the difficulties that lay ahead.

If ever I had met a woman destined to be a great mother, it was my wife. She did not have extraordinary goals set for her life. She simply wanted to love the Lord her God with all her heart, mind, soul and strength, someday be a godly mom and pass the heritage on.

Ann had been reared on a farm in rural Missouri, fifteen miles in all directions from the nearest town. She thrived in that setting even though her three older siblings were all boys! She was taught the fear of the Lord at an early age from her grandparents and parents and a dear old saint she fondly called Mr. Tyler. Her family and their nearby country Methodist church—totaling eighteen people when they all showed up!—served her well. Her best friend was her Bible, and she loved spending hours with that dear companion.

But what a paradox seemed to unfold after we got married! The one thing she wanted the most, to be a mom, appeared out of our grasp.

We did everything we knew to do. Year by year we had the same results—nothing. We consulted doctors, took classes in natural family planning and received prayer from the spiritual Who's Who of the 1970s. We attended so many meetings in which the power of the Holy Spirit was present that it started to get embarrassing! We would get ministry but always leave the same way—with no apparent change.

Many trials and tests of endurance came our way those first few years. But we continued on our journey of fulfilling our desire, even though the sentence of barrenness was being pronounced over us. Desperation grew month by month in our hearts and souls. Ann and I were investigating all our options—natural family planning, medical tests, exploratory surgery, adoption and anything else you can think of.

One night in the spring of 1980, in our little home east of Warrensburg, Missouri, I had one of those short dreams—the kind you wake up out of and remember. It was simple. The Holy Spirit spoke clearly to me and said, *You will have a son and his name will be called Justin.*

When Ann awakened in the morning, I shared the dream with her. Since we had been trying to have children for several years, it was welcome news. God said we were going to have a son and He even gave me his name. What could be better than that? All right! We believed the good report.

I know it may seem unusual that I would not question the message that came in the dream. But I felt total assurance that it was from God. A peace and gentle spirit of faith seemed to rest on Ann and me. In fact, through the revelation that came through this simple dream, we felt rearmed for the battle. Sure enough, we were going to have a son! After all, we carried promises of fruitfulness and healing from the written Word of God—promises like Deuteronomy 28:2, 4, 11; Psalm 103:3; Isaiah 53:4–5; and 1 Peter 2:24. We had praying people around the country standing with us. And now we had a revelatory spoken word—a three-strand cord. What a combination!

But circumstances did not change immediately, despite this clear little dream from heaven, and we began to analyze it. As we pondered the word I had been given—*You will have a son and his name will be called Justin*—we realized it did not tell us *how* we would have this son. We wanted to respond with humility to the promise, yet stand firm and believe God. Now we were left with an odd mix of faith and uncertainty on how to go forward. Things had still not changed in our world. In fact, circumstances were screaming right in our faces! Could it be that we would be given this son through adoption? We were not ruling anything out at this point. We wanted our own children, yet knew we must be open to whatever way the Lord wanted to fulfill the dream.

That summer of 1980 we were already scheduled for an interview with a church adoption agency in St. Louis. But things took a peculiar twist.

We made the four-hour drive on a hot, humid July day and were sitting in the waiting room of the agency headquarters with about eight other couples. Ann and I looked around the room and at one another, wondering what to do. Each of these couples wanted children just as badly as we did. Apparently they could not produce their dream either. Our names were called first. It was time for our appointment. But instead of going in for the interview, we asked if we could have a few minutes as we went on a walk in downtown St. Louis. We needed to talk things over one more time on that hot summer day.

After a heart-to-heart conversation and some serious internal wrestling, we decided to yield our right to having a child by adoption so that another deserving, caring couple could find their dream fulfilled. After all, we had been

41

given hope, and knew whom we were trusting—not just a dream, but the God of the dream. So instead of signing up that day, we went back into the office and told the agency directors that we did not believe we should go through with the adoption procedures.

We drove the four hours home, and the quiet peace of God was with us.

Before the Light Came Darkness

Have you ever noticed that in creation, before the light, came darkness? How else would we know when it became day? Well, the path for Ann and me got darker. We were about to walk through what Christians of old have called the "dark night of the soul." Circumstances had not budged an inch. Though we still believed the message of the dream, we were beginning to tire from the roller coaster ride.

A year had passed. It was now the summer of 1981. Although we had closed the door to adoption, we had continued on our search to understanding, through prayer and the medical profession, what path God intended for us. So we submitted to a long series of medical tests to determine the obstacles to achieving our goal. The further we went, the more difficult and complicated things became. As Ann underwent a laparoscopy and other tests, our infertility specialist (tops in the Midwest at that time) found a condition he had never seen in any of his patients. Not only were my wife's normal female cycles anywhere from six weeks to six months in length, but the surgeon found a condition he had never seen before. Ann's uterine cavity was five to six times the normal size and the lining was not viable enough to sustain life. There were other complications as well, all adding up to the reality that it was not possible for us to have children.

I can still see him coming out of the operating room, telling me he could not solve the problem through surgery or any other medical means. He could do no more. The long and the short of it? We had no more alternatives. In fact, the whole medical profession could do nothing more for us. The situation was dark indeed. We faced obstacles, numerous complications and no more options. We needed a creative miracle.

Well, at least now we had hard facts—detailed information of organs that were not shaped right, did not work right and *could* not work right! But we turned that detailed diagnosis into persistent prayer: "God, You gave us Your holy Word. You gave us a dream. We have believing people of prayer agreeing with us. We cannot perform this thing ourselves. We are totally dependent on You to bring it to pass. Fulfill the dream You gave us. Give us a miracle, in the great name of Jesus!" Then we would pronounce the promises of healing from the Scriptures with a declaration of faith and command life over our bodies. We fought the good fight of faith, as Paul told Timothy to do (1 Timothy 1:18–19), by using the Word of God as a weapon of war. (We will talk more about this kind of battle in chapter 8.)

As the months unfolded we were given many valuable lessons in God's class on "Prayer 101." Through the trials of it all, we continued to trust Him who held our hands. With gutsy determination, great brokenness and total dependence on God, we persisted in prayer, crying out to the Lord to intervene.

The battle raged. Ann's body went through hard tremors and shaking, as though rejecting life from being formed. As days turned to weeks and weeks turned to months, we saw no sign of change. It was distressful and difficult. At times all the "why" questions bombarded our minds.

One fall evening in 1981, as Ann's body was convulsing, I could take it no longer. I prayed for her but nothing changed. In frustration I darted out of the house and went on a walk to straighten out my head and have a good talk with the Man upstairs.

As I was out walking, the Holy Spirit dealt with Ann. As she described it later, she told the Lord, "I won't like it, but I yield to You my right to have children."

Immediately the God of all comfort answered, *I appreciate your attitude, but I am not requiring this of you. I say to you, You must fight for your children.*

Ann remembers it this way:

> As soon as I heard the Lord say those words, I was filled with the knowledge that the Lord was feeling my pain and that He longed for me to have children more than I did! I knew He was pulling for me! In a moment I became aware that I had been blaming God that I was childless. I realized very clearly that the blame really belonged to Satan. So I took a stand and made a proclamation that day. I said, "From this day forward, I'll no longer blame God for my barrenness. I take the blame off God my Father and put it squarely where it belongs—on the devil!" Suddenly it was as though a breakthrough had come, and I knew that significant damage to the works of darkness had been done. I was filled with new hope and with a courageous, fighting spirit.

So with new, holy boldness and armed with fresh faith, we continued in our battle to believe the impossible and fight for our dream to come true.

In the summer of 1982 it looked as though we had achieved our long-awaited goal. Signs seemed to indicate that Ann was expecting. But right at that season tragedy came hard and fast to Ann's family. Not only did her dear mother and best friend, Dorris, become severely sick, but Ann began to have problems of her own. She had to spend the next four weeks either in bed or on the couch. Our specialist, on his long summer vacation, was out of reach. On his return we rushed to the medical center, only to find out that maybe, maybe not, we had been pregnant. A sac was present, but that was all, so a dilation and curettage was in order. Sadness filled our hearts as once again we came home emptyhanded.

Let me turn to Michal Ann (as she goes by today) and ask her to share her thoughts with you about that period of time:

> We depleted every option we could think of in our search for an answer to our complex circumstances. Most of all we prayed. We asked God and asked God; then we turned and rebuked our barrenness and declared God's Word over our bodies. We did everything we knew to do—physically, medically and spiritually. Yet in spite of all of this, after six years, all attempts ended up in the same place—with no fruit.
>
> Let me tell you, it was incredibly painful. Jim and I were part of a small church in a university setting at the time. We spent those years praying and counseling with a lot of college students. They would fall in love, ask Jim to perform their wedding ceremonies and then, not long after, ask us to pray over their children as they dedicated them to the Lord. Meanwhile, our house remained empty.

In the fall of that year Dorris' battle with cancer heightened. She was a woman who deeply loved her Lord. One time she phoned Michal Ann, her only daughter, and asked her to visit. When Michal Ann arrived at the farmhouse, Dorris had a present for her, a complete surprise. Dorris had made a precious baby blanket for us! It was a beautiful yellow afghan designed after the original McCoy family pattern (Michal Ann's mother's maiden name). Although Dorris' days were numbered and her strength was fading, she had made the baby blanket in faith that we would have a miracle of our own.

What a sacrifice and what a gift!

A Touch from God

After serving as a campus minister for eight years at Central Missouri State University, I assumed the senior pastor role of our small congregation, Harvest Fellowship Church. One evening in November 1982 we were pleased to have a healing evangelist, Mahesh Chavda, visit and minister at our small church. I had met Mahesh some years before and we had become friends. He had also prayed twice for Michal Ann and me for healing from barrenness. He was especially sensitive to the moving of the Holy Spirit and was often used in the gifts of healing and workings of miracles. Every year he went on two forty-day periods of prayer and fasting, and as a result had seen Jesus do wonderful and unusual things.

As the special evening service came to an end, Mahesh began to release words of knowledge for healing. He gave expression to each impression that the Holy Spirit brought to his mind. Things were going great. The power of the Spirit was present and people's lives were being touched.

Michal Ann and I, sitting in the congregation that night, were as eager as the next person to receive from the Lord. But to be honest with you, I felt both excitement and uncertainty. *What are we to do?* I remember wondering. *Are we supposed to go up at the end of the meeting and be prayed for again?*

Mahesh was approaching the close of the service. He gave out two more words of knowledge pertaining to specific healing needs. Then he gave a final word—for barren women to come forward. What were Michal Ann and I to do? Not only had we prayed and fasted and been to scores of meetings, but we had been prayed over twice by Mahesh himself.

Then, with the encouragement of some friends, a streak of holy stubbornness rose up inside of me and propelled me out of my analytical mind and into a heart cry of desperation. I grabbed Michal Ann by the arm and said something like, "Well, what do we have to lose?!" The next thing we knew we were standing on the platform and were next in line to be prayed for.

Our dear, gentle friend Mahesh moved closer to us. He seemed to be caught away, looking elsewhere for a moment. Then he said to Michal Ann, "Oh, I see you as a joyful mother of three children."

The power of the Holy Spirit came on us and, at the same moment, we fell like timber to the floor. The presence of the Lord Jesus was so strong and tangibly powerful that we were unable to stand to our feet.

Or perhaps we dropped to the floor out of shock. We had been trying to believe God for one child. Now Mahesh said he saw three!

Time would tell if it was just another good meeting, since the proof was in the pudding. But one thing we knew for sure. We had been touched by the living presence of our Master, Jesus.

Over the next few mornings, when Michal Ann awakened, she told me she felt warmth in her midsection. She actually felt pulling and stretching in her stomach region. It seemed as though she were coming out from under spiritual anesthesia.

As Thanksgiving approached, Dorris took a serious turn for the worse. For the next few weeks Michal Ann, along with her brothers and other family members, remained at the side of her dying mom.

When we all gathered at her family's farmhouse for what was to be our last Christmas together, Dorris displayed what some call intuition. Someone in the room, she remarked, was expecting.

Well, John had not yet married and David and Cindy knew it was not they. That left Paul and Sarah and Michal Ann and me. And frankly, even though we had just had a powerful experience after being prayed for by Mahesh, having a baby was not on our "functional screen" at the time, especially as my dear wife and her family were nursemaiding their dying mother almost every night. So no one knew what to do with the comment. Michal Ann and I definitely felt it could not refer to us.

Dorris graduated to heaven right after Christmas that year. She had been a godly wife, mother, friend, schoolteacher and ambassador of Christ. Michal Ann's heart was heavy. She had lost not only her mother but her best friend.

Right after the first of the year, just after we had buried her mom and were in a time of grief, Michal Ann caught the flu. Was she ever sick! I prayed for her and she got even sicker. I would say, "Come out! Leave her!" And boy, did it ever! Get the picture? This continued for days. I did not seem to be a man of any profound gifting. Instead of the Midas touch, it seemed I had the bad touch! The more I prayed, the sicker she got.

Finally one day I said to Michal Ann, "I'm taking you to the doctor. We're going to find out what this thing is."

So off we went to the doctor. He knew our case inside out, plus the fact that Michal Ann's mom had just passed away from cancer and that Michal Ann was her only daughter. He did some typical tests, then returned to the examination room.

"I have some news for you," said the pious-faced doctor. "This is the kind of sickness that's not going to leave for a long time." He paused soberly, then took a deep breath. "This is the real thing."

What was he trying to say?

Then he added with a twinkle in his eye, "You're going to have a baby."

We were both elated and shocked. I think our jaws dropped to the floor.

It was true. The following Day of Atonement, October 4, 1983, our firstborn son, Justin Wayne, came into the world.

I know the angels sang that day. I know *we* did! And in heaven Dorris was peering over the banister and saying, "I knew it! That's my grandson!"

Remember the baby afghan? Sure enough, as proud parents we wrapped our sweet little son in that baby blanket about one year to the date from when Dorris gave it to us. Holding him in that family treasure, we dedicated Justin to the Lord.

Interpreting Our Life's Journey

May I give you one more update in the Goll family saga? Even though the Lord had spoken to Michal Ann's heart that she must fight for her children, the touch we received from the Lord did not, for whatever reasons, fix all the plumbing permanently. We had to continue to kneel on the promises and then rise up in faith and fight for our inheritance. Each one of our promised three children, Justin, GraceAnn and Tyler, came as a result of prayer, fighting the enemy and supernatural acts of God's power.

But then number four came along! When Michal Ann became pregnant with Rachel, she went to Mahesh and said, "You said, 'I see you as a joyful mother of three children.'"

Mahesh just grinned.

"You must understand," he said. "In the prophetic you see in part and you prophesy in part. I was seeing only three-fourths of the part!"

It was yet another lesson. And today we are blessed beyond measure with four fine arrows in our quiver.

From the Curse to the Blessing

I might have confused you along the way, calling my wife "Ann" part of the time and then "Michal Ann." Let me explain. In these last few years the Holy Spirit has helped my wife and me understand that we have been walking through a prophetic parable for the Church.

Michal Ann was named after King David's first wife, Michal. Do you remember what happened to that daughter

49

of Saul? She mocked David for dancing energetically in the streets as the Ark of the Covenant was being restored to its proper place and was struck with barrenness (see 2 Samuel 6:23). She was mentioned only one more time in the Scriptures.

A few words about barrenness. Deuteronomy 28:18 states, "Cursed shall be the offspring of your body," or it can be rendered, "Cursed shall be the fruit of your womb." Several other verses in that chapter, speaking of curses, mention that they may take the form of a lack of fruitfulness or productivity (see verses 23–24, 30, 38–41). In my understanding this surely includes barrenness—the inability to bring forth life or the tendency to lose life through multiple miscarriages—as a curse. One thing we know for sure: It is not a blessing.

But God will change the curse into a blessing. The name *Ann* means "grace." Our life story involves, in part, the power of God to change this curse into a blessing by His great grace. And guess what? The name *Michal* actually means "stream or brook." Today, instead of being barren, the circumstances of our lives have been changed to become a stream of grace for other people. So now my fighting bride graciously goes by her whole name—Michal Ann.

The prophetic parable based on the testimony of our lives is also a message to the corporate Church. We could have stopped at any point along the way, thrown up our hands and said, "We quit! This just isn't fair!" But by His grace we continued to believe our dream, even when obstacles loomed right in our faces. My fighting bride, Michal Ann, modeled herself after the warrior brides who had gone before: "By faith even Sarah herself received ability to conceive . . . since she considered Him faithful who had promised" (Hebrews 11:11).

Today God wants to heal other barren women just as He healed my dear wife. This in itself becomes a prophetic picture for us of His great desire to heal, change and empower the greatest woman of the Bible—the bride of Christ. He will arouse our love and plant the seed of His Word within our womb and bring forth the miraculous from the conception of intimacy. He will put "the Spirit of grace and of supplication" on us (Zechariah 12:10) so that the dream called revival—a stream of grace—will flow across the globe.

The Spirit of Prayer

During the roller coaster ride and the trials, something was imparted to Michal Ann and me. The spirit of prayer and the power of travail (remember the "Glossary of Terms" on page 301) were put into our souls. I know for sure that God is faithful and that He answers prayer. I get the awesome opportunity to watch miracles in front of my eyes every day. You cannot take that away from me! Our Father God is faithful and He answers prayer.

Now do you understand why I want to infect you with this holy, contagious disease and hope you never recover? I want to see the velvet army of God arise on the scene. Remember, worship comes before petition. The task of intercession involves being a secretary and reminding God of His Word; taking up the case of justice in a courtroom hearing; building up the walls to keep the enemy out; and standing in the gap with a cry for mercy, mercy, mercy!

It is never time to quit or give an inch to the devil. God's Spirit works in and through us "both to will and to work for His good pleasure" (Philippians 2:13). It is not about us; it is all about Him in this path of learning to cultivate a heart of priestly prayer.

Can You Learn the Tune?

I love the joy of speaking back into the heart of the Father what His Word and will declare. Mingling the incense of prayers with the harp of David, when the Spirit of revelation flows freely, is a unique and wonderful instrument in God's hand. What a joyful sound! I think I can hear it now. Listen in. Maybe you are learning this tune, too. Yes, we are kneeling on the promises of God!

Do you want to see revival in your church or city? Do you hunger for Jesus to receive the rewards of His suffering? Are you satisfied with your Christian life or do you want more of Him? Do you want to be the little donkey, the beast of burden Jesus is looking for right now?

If you answer yes to any of these questions, come and let His presence sit on you, and receive the spirit of prayer. Then continue with me on this journey. Let's walk together through these next pages and learn a few lessons on how to birth God's purposes through the power of intercession. As we turn the corner to the next chapter, we will spot another signpost along the way: what it takes to move the hand of God.

PRACTICAL APPLICATIONS—MAKING IT REAL!

- Continue to seek the Lord to open the way for supernatural healings even in your barrenness.
- Ask the Lord to activate dreams while you are sleeping so you can receive from Him.
- Invite the Holy Spirit's presence right where you are, and enjoy Him!
- Read Lamentations 3 and such Psalms as 13, 22, 35, 42, 43, 55, 60 and 69 to give you an idea of the dark night of the soul and God's promises to see you through such a journey.
- Go to a conference where power healings are taking place and expect God to touch you or move through you.

RECOMMENDED READING

Only Love Can Make a Miracle by Mahesh Chavda
(Servant, 1990)

Power Healing by John Wimber (HarperSanFrancisco,
1987)

THE
DESPERATE PRAYER
OF THE HEART

As we proceed on our course of cultivating a heart for prayer, I have a pop quiz for you: What moves the hand of God?

This important question has been asked throughout the ages, with a great variety of responses. Ponder it for a while. I am sure there are many right answers to the question; faith is a correct one, for sure! Purity, compassion and integrity would be other good answers to this simple yet profound question. But let me cast light for a moment on one strategic quality the Lord looks for: desire.

Webster's defines the noun form of *desire* as "a wish or craving; sexual appetite; a request; anything desired." The often-quoted teaching of Jesus on the subject of faith states, "Therefore I say unto you, What things soever ye *desire*, when ye pray, believe that ye receive them, and ye shall have them" (Mark 11:24, KJV, emphasis added).

What do you desire? What is your passion? What do you want so badly that you can hardly live without it? James 4:2

says, "You do not have because you do not ask." This verse could easily be rendered, "You ask for nothing because you desire nothing." What you want motivates you! Do you have a deep craving within you that results in passionate pursuit? Do you want more of God? Do you hunger to see Him move in the earth? Desire is the beginning of the desperate prayer of the heart.

Maybe we need to back up a bit and ask another simple yet profound question: What is prayer? Ultimately prayer is nothing more than desire expressed to God. One proper definition of intercession is "the act of making a request to a superior." So we could say that prayer, in its many forms, is the act of expressing a deep-seated yearning to our one and only superior, God, for things to change. You have heard people say, "I'm so desperate I'll do anything!" Well, how about reaching the end of ourselves to the point that we intercede as if there is no other option left?

Prayer and intercession are the cry of desperation for things to change.

An Encounter to Remember

My dear friend Mahesh Chavda and I held a crusade in Haiti in January 1987. We conducted five consecutive nights of outdoor meetings in this impoverished yet beautiful Caribbean nation. On the first night Mahesh preached a salvation message and invited people to come to the front to dedicate their lives to Jesus. Gently and quickly Mahesh laid his hands on the heads of each of the hungry souls. As the anointing of the Holy Spirit touched them, many collapsed to the ground under the power of God.

While Mahesh preached, I remained on the platform of a flatbed truck nearby, interceding. We had amassed a wonderful team of tenacious prayer warriors doing 'round-the-clock intercession and spiritual warfare for this event. As

Mahesh preached, I wept. It seemed as though some invisible hand was gripping my heart inside my chest and squeezing with great might. Night after night my heart actually ached inside my chest as I seemed to be carrying the pain and suffering of these lovely people who had been ravaged by the deceitful works of the enemy. The other intercessors and I were crying for their deliverance from sin, sickness and Satan.

On the first night of the crusade, a girl not ten years old ushered an older woman to the front in response to the invitation to salvation. There they stood, straight and tall, like soldiers volunteering for duty. Then, as Mahesh laid his hand softly on the older woman's head, she sank to the ground. Later, when she arose, her companion checked her out, seeming to find that she was the same as she had been before. Did I detect disappointment?

The next night my brother in Christ preached about being filled with the Holy Spirit and again welcomed anyone to the front to receive the Spirit's power. One of the first in line was the same young girl with her elderly friend. Mahesh proceeded down the lines of waiting people, as before, with the same results. When the older woman got up, the girl looked her over, to find once again that she appeared to be the same as before. Again, she looked disappointed.

The following night the sermon was on healing; the night after that, on the breaking of curses. Each time the youngster escorted her elderly friend forward, with the same results. What was this little girl checking for? It was starting to get embarrassing!

On the fifth and last night of the meetings, the crowd was larger, and anticipation filled the air. News had spread across the island that these meetings were challenging the kingdom of darkness.

Mahesh preached that night on deliverance from evil spirits, and exhorted those present to renounce the powers of darkness and to receive prayer to be set free. Sure enough, there was the tenacious girl standing eagerly with the old lady. Mahesh came by and prayed the prayer releasing the anointing, and as he did, many dropped to the ground.

But this time something was different. The next thing we knew, this old lady was standing on the flatbed truck with her arms in the air, shouting over the loudspeaker system in her Creole language, "Praise the Lord!"

We found out that this woman, who was 77 years old, had been blind from birth, that her young companion was her eight-year-old granddaughter, and that the old woman could now see!

There are many lessons we can learn from this event. We can look at the value of stubborn faith—not taking no for an answer. How about the 'round-the-clock prayer going on behind the scenes? We can also look at the accumulation of the anointing of the Holy Spirit releasing a breakthrough. The power of God was working through my brother Mahesh. I was used as a "breaker of intercession" as I wept profusely. (More on this in the last chapter.) Indeed, there are many angles to consider. And we can all learn from the persistence of a 77-year-old woman coming back night after night.

But think about the eight-year-old-girl. Something was alive within her. Desire was paramount. This little girl was desperate. She had a deep-seated longing for God to change the circumstances of her grandmother's life. She wanted Grandma to see! Because the youngster was desperate, her heart was bursting for God to break loose. Praise the Lord, for the Father of mercy appeared on the scene!

"Jesus Christ is the same yesterday and today, yes and forever" (Hebrews 13:8).

What Is Prayer Passion?

I am convinced that the last days battle is a battle of passions. The world flaunts her lustful passions daily across the stage of life full blown with no shame. But the Church has often been anemic in this arena. It is time for the bride of Christ to be filled with passion for her Bridegroom and perform extravagant displays of lavish love. What better place to exhibit boundless zeal and holy passion than in the place of prayer? Prayer is the bridal chamber of intimacy with our Master.

I think I hear you saying something like, "This sounds interesting. Tell me more about this thing you are calling prayer passion."

R. A. Torrey writes, "The prayer that prevails with God is the prayer into which we put our whole soul, stretching out toward God in intense and agonizing desire. . . . If we put so little heart into our prayers, we cannot expect God to put much heart into answering them."[1]

Having read many different great authors on prayer, and having logged a few hours under my belt in the trenches of intercession, I would like to share with you some common ingredients for the recipe of true prayer passion. The following thoughts of mine have been shaped by the writings of Dr. Wesley Duewel of OMS International:

1. Prayer passion is incubated in a heart of love.
2. It increases out of holy desire.
3. It may be a special gift of God empowering you for the precise moment He wants to use you in prayer.
4. It often springs forth from a new vision of a need as your eyes are opened.
5. It may escalate in your life from a gradually deepening conviction of the urgency of that need and God's willingness to meet that need.
6. It grows within you as you continue to give yourself to intercession.
7. It will revitalize and strengthen your faith.

Finney advised, "If you find yourself drawn out in mighty prayer for certain individuals, exercised with great compassion, agonized with strong crying and tears, for a certain family or neighborhood or people, let such an influence be yielded to."[2]

Some subjects are best defined by considering what they are not. Let's flip the coin and look at the other side of this issue:

1. Prayer passion is not synonymous with loud, demonstrative praying. At times it may be quiet or even silent prayer. Many warriors of prevailing prayer have agonized silently in the night hours as others slept nearby, knowing nothing about it.
2. It is not synonymous with physical exertion. The effectiveness of our spiritual wrestling in prayer cannot be judged by our physical activity or stance. Prayer passion is not necessarily produced by standing, kneeling, lying prostrate on the floor, lifting the hands, waving the arms, walking back and forth or any other active or passive posture or action.
3. We must also realize that at times the use of such various postures is fitting, and can harmonize with and give expression to the cry of our souls—humility before God, desperate pleas to Him, waiting in His presence, spiritual determination and urgency. Many desperate prayer warriors have become soaked with perspiration from the anguish of their souls during prevailing prayer, just as Christ sweat drops of blood in Gethsemane. (But whatever you do, don't try to work up spiritual intensity by your own human effort. That does not help you or God.)
4. Prayer passion is not synonymous with immediately answered prayer. Many prayers are heard and responded to instantly without protracted praying, and many prayer desires of the heart are answered as you simply "delight yourself in the LORD" (Psalm 37:4).

5. Prayer passion is not a form of works earning you better status with the Father. It does not win you salvation or any other of God's blessings. The place of fervency in priestly intercession is an outworking of the Spirit's ministry of grace within you.

Prayer passion begins when we bask in the awesome love the Father has for us, His children—the supreme object of His affection. When you are in love, you will do anything to get near that person. One song puts it this way: "Ain't no mountain high enough . . . to keep me from you." It might not be the current tune on the world's pop chart, but it is the song the Son of God sings over His bride. A revelation of bridal love makes your communion more passionate than anything I know.

Consider the words of E. M. Bounds: "Prayers must be red hot. It is the fervent prayer that is effective. . . . It takes fire to make prayers go. Warmth of soul creates an atmosphere favorable to prayer. . . . By flame prayer ascends to heaven."[3] The vital ingredient is what we call prayer passion—the characteristic necessary to fan desire into a full flame.

Expressions of the Heart beyond Words

Has your heart ever been bursting with love for your spiritual Husband, the Lord Jesus, so much that words cannot express what is inside of you? Sometimes when I am overwhelmed by the loveliness of His great presence, words seem inadequate. When I am captivated by the qualities of this Man Christ Jesus, my heart aches and yearns with the desire to know Him and to embrace His ways. This is when prayer passion is in full bloom. Out of the abundance of the heart the mouth speaks.

But sometimes love speaks a strange language. First and foremost, you see, it is a language of the heart.

The Language of Compassionate Weeping

I think I hear you pondering another question: "Do you mean to say there are prayers of desperation that go beyond the articulation of words?" Yes, sir! Let's consider the power of compassionate weeping.

Several Salvation Army officers in the last century asked General Booth, "How can we save the lost?" Booth stated simply, "Try tears."[4] Today church growth seminars are held across the nation. Techniques and methodologies are discussed at great length on how we can have successful, growing churches. Cookie-cutters can be passed out, too! But a heart for God is forged only through the crucible of the cross.

The weeping prophet Jeremiah bore his heart:

> Their heart cried out to the Lord, "O wall of the daughter of Zion, let tears run down like a river day and night; give yourself no relief; give your eyes no rest. Arise, cry out in the night, at the beginning of the watches; pour out your heart like water before the face of the Lord. Lift your hands toward Him for the life of your young children, who faint from hunger at the head of every street."
>
> Lamentations 2:18–19, NKJV

Jeremiah 9:1 records, "Oh, that my head were waters, and my eyes a fountain of tears, that I might weep day and night for the slain of the daughter of my people!" (NKJV). Jeremiah knew the power of the language of tears.

From the Trenches of Those Who Knew

I love Church history and going to the places where heaven has touched earth. I have been privileged to participate in meetings in the very location in Wales where a great revival took place under the leadership of Evan Roberts. Evan Phillips was an eyewitness to the Welsh revival of 1904. He tells the following about those blessed days and the presence of the Lord that was with the young revival leader, Evan Roberts:

> Evan Roberts was like a particle of radium in our midst. Its fire was consuming and felt abroad as something which took away sleep, cleared the channels of tears, and sped the golden wheels of prayer throughout the area. . . . I have wept now until my heart is supple. In the midst of the greatest fearfulness I have found the greatest joy. Now the bed belongs to the river and Wales belongs to Christ.[5]

One of the most famous of all the great English pulpiteers was Charles H. Spurgeon. Consider this thought from a man of the tearful trenches:

> Let us learn to think of tears as liquid prayers, and of weeping as a constant dropping of importunate intercession which will wear its way right surely into the very heart of mercy, despite the stony difficulties which obstruct the way. My God, I will "weep" when I cannot plead, for Thou hearest the voice of my weeping.[6]

Saint Bernard of Clairvaux said, "The tears of penitents are the wine of angels."[7]

King David petitioned, "Be merciful to me, O LORD, for I am in distress; my eyes grow weak with sorrow, my soul and my body with grief" (Psalm 31:9, NIV). Again: "I am weary with my crying; my throat is dry; my eyes fail while I wait for my God" (Psalm 69:3, NKJV).

Our beloved Paul, the apostle and writer of many epistles, wrote: "For three years I did not cease to warn everyone night and day with tears" (Acts 20:31, NKJV). And: "Out of much affliction and anguish of heart I wrote to you, with many tears . . ." (2 Corinthians 2:4, NKJV).

The heart of God for the prophetic purposes of the city of Jerusalem is revealed through the Messiah. Luke 19:41

states: "As [Jesus] approached Jerusalem and saw the city, he wept over it" (Luke 19:41, NIV).

George Fox experienced a similar place in God for his generation: "I saw the harvest white, and the seed of God lying thick in the ground, as ever did wheat that was sown outwardly, and none to gather it; and for this I mourned with tears."[8]

The Gift of Tears

One of the prophetic statesmen of our day is Paul Cain of Shiloh Ministries in Kansas City, Missouri. Our dear brother Paul acts as a contemporary bridge to the move of God of past generations to enlighten us about the costs and ways of God for our present generation. Let's look at what this broken warrior has to say about the gift of tears:

> What if all of us were called upon to accept God's gift of tears before He would ever consider giving His gift of revival? Would you apply for the gift? Would you seek of the gift? Would you beg for the gift? If you really want revival, I believe you would. Let's try tears.
>
> I tell you, there will be no public reaping without some public weeping. The greatest reapers are the greatest weepers. Ministry in the last days is worth everything. It will cost everything. Are you willing to pay the price in much tears, in much prayer and supplication? We need to pray as Jesus prayed, with strong crying and tears.[9]

May we dig again the trenches of the prayer of tears! May we learn to "weep between the porch and the altar," as the prophet Joel pleaded (Joel 2:17). Let's follow in the footsteps of the revivalists of old and call forth these seemingly forgotten ways of brokenness as a prayer language of the heart. Let the power of compassionate weeping lay hold of *you*, and may you be used to break open the heavens in behalf of another.

A Desperate Prayer That Called Forth Life

I have been blessed to travel to many nations across the world, to learn from others and to bring the light of prayer and the prophetic to many peoples. I have often had the blessing of ministering in the Czech Republic and knowing many leaders of the "living Church" there. Let me share with you a true-life story about the awesome power of an "eruption of compassion" in intercession that was used to call forth life.

In my travels a few years back I met a fiery revivalist named Evald Rucky of Libreac. The following report comes from conversations I had with Evald and his best friend, Peter.

During the latter years of Communism, Evald Rucky was a pastor in the northern region of Czechoslovakia (now the Czech Republic) in a small Moravian congregation in the city of Libreac. The totalitarian rule over that nation had just lifted, and a fresh wind of the Holy Spirit was beginning to blow across the congregation and in many places. Opportunities for ministry abounded, and Evald was one of the laborers the Lord was thrusting forth into the newly opened fields of harvest.

Evald had been running hard and fast, with great results. Then, on a missions trip to Sweden, he was hospitalized with a serious heart problem. He slipped into a coma and lay between life and death. There were few signs of encouragement for his wife, who had traveled from Libreac to be by his side. His congregation, as well as believers across Czechoslovakia, were praying for the now-fragile life of their beloved pastor.

Evald's best friend and associate pastor, Peter, also came to Sweden to pray for him. In Peter's words: "It seemed as though I was carrying with me the prayers of the saints. I was the point of the spear and they were the shaft."

As Peter visited his friend lying seemingly lifeless in a hospital bed, the Lord let Evald escape to experience heaven for a three-day period. Evald was shown some wonderful promises concerning God's purposes for the nations. While his consciousness was heavenward, he forgot his earthly circumstances and simply enjoyed God and all the beautiful surroundings.

Peter, back in the hospital room, stood over Evald's body lying in bed. He had come to pray but could not compose a prayer in any natural language. So he began to weep.

As his tears dropped onto his friend's body, Evald—in heaven that very moment—suddenly became aware that he was a husband, father and pastor and that his work was not yet complete. He realized he had a decision to make. The next thing he knew, he found his spirit soaring through the heavens and joining his body lying in the hospital bed. Instantly this Czech pastor was healed and reunited with his wife and best friend. The doctors declared it a miracle and released him without even requiring payment for any of the medical expenses!

Rejoicing broke out in Evald Rucky's home, congregation and region as a result of this modern-day miracle. A new beginning had come and an authentic apostolic call received. What called him forth? I believe it was the eruption of the power of compassionate weeping—the desperate prayer of the heart.

The Spirit Helps Our Weakness

Psalm 56:8 poetically describes a heavenly reality: "Thou hast taken account of my wanderings; put my tears in Thy bottle; are they not in Thy book?" The answer to that last question, of course, is a resounding yes! God hears. God knows. God rewards. But I have a thought for you to ponder: What does God do with our tears? What comes of all of these "compassion eruptions," as I often call them?

We are given a hint in Psalm 126:5–6: "Those who sow in tears shall reap with joyful shouting. He who goes to and fro weeping, carrying his bag of seed, shall indeed come again with a shout of joy, bringing his sheaves with him." Sounds as though there is a connection between sowing in tears and reaping an abundant harvest.

Maybe desperation is a tool used to break up the hard soil of the hearts of men and women. Maybe, just maybe, our tears of desperation fill bottles in heaven, and the Judge of all pours them back out as rain of mercy on a dry and parched land. Who knows? Maybe a bottle of *your* tears will be poured out to help create the next outpouring of God's latter rain!

With this background of the language of the heart, let's consider the familiar passage of Romans 8:26–27:

> In the same way the Spirit also helps our weakness; for we do not know how to pray as we should, but the Spirit Himself intercedes for us with groanings too deep for words; and He who searches the hearts knows what the mind of the Spirit is, because He intercedes for the saints according to the will of God.

The language of prayer, you see, is a language of the heart and the heart is not limited to the vocabulary of the mind. I have often paraphrased this passage in Romans 8 like this:

> Often we do not know what or how to pray effectively, as we should. But as we admit our limited abilities and yield to the direction of our Helper, the Holy Spirit, God will give Him the language of perfect prayer through us that is too deep for the articulation of natural speech.

This is my description of how the prayers of *sighing* and *groaning* work. And they do work!

The heart cry of the Holy Spirit is just too deep for human words. At times the depths of the Holy Spirit's praying become groanings within our hearts that express a prayer desire so infinite that it is incapable of being expressed totally in man's natural language.

About now some of you are thinking, "Well, maybe I can handle this weeping stuff. But you're going over the edge with all this moaning and groaning!" Hold on. I understand. I used to think the same thing. But hang in there with me and consider the words of the evangelical prayer leader Wesley Duewel from his powerful book *Mighty, Prevailing Prayer:*

> Our knowledge is limited, so we do not know what is best to pray for in each situation. The Spirit's very definite and infinitely deep desire must be expressed in groanings rather than in our words, since our words are inadequate. Spirit-born groaning is always in accord with God's will. The Spirit could desire nothing other. But God can translate these groanings into His fullest understanding and do "immeasurably more than all we ask or imagine, according to His power that is at work within us" (Ephesians 3:20).
>
> God the Father understands the Spirit's meaning as He groans within us (Romans 8:27). Our weakness (8:26) is that our human words cannot adequately and fully articulate the depth of divine longing, just as our personality cannot experience the fullness and depth of the Spirit's longing. We can express it truly, but not totally. We are finite; He is infinite.[10]

Praying Payson of Portland was one who prevailed mightily in prayer. After his death he was found actually to have calloused knees. By the side of his bed, where he wrestled in prayer day after day, were two grooves worn into the hard boards as he moved back and forth on his knees in prayer. Payson used to say that he pitied the Christian who could not experience the meaning of the words *groan-ings which cannot be uttered.*[11]

Yes, God chooses to involve us in His intercession. He has chosen to prevail through our intense prevailing. Martin Luther wrote, "Nor is prayer ever heard more abundantly than in such agony and groanings of struggling faith."[12]

One of the wonderful comrades the Lord has given Michal Ann and me is our friend and intercessory teacher Pat Gastineau of Word of Love Ministries in Roswell, Georgia. Let me summarize some of the understandings we have come to mutually concerning the subject of groaning.

Each of us has walls of resistance toward God that we neither know about nor understand how to break down on our own. Groaning is used to bring deliverance by pushing back the pressures of darkness. Groaning pushes us through tight, distressful places into the larger places of the Spirit. Groaning comes from deep within us and can be a tool preparing us for the utter abandonment to our task that God requires. But this kind of prayer is higher than our understanding, for it bypasses our minds and allows the Holy Spirit to move us into the purposes of God according to His will and not our own.

Groaning is not for those who understand what they want to pray. It is for those who desire to reach beyond what they know or understand, the ones who "do not know how to pray as [they] should." Those who are self-satisfied will have difficulty groaning; those who are desperate will have great difficulty *not* groaning.

Not only does the Holy Spirit have a deep love language that He will express through us, but He will arise at times with the indignation of God and wage war through His people. This is the intercessory and spiritual warfare posture. Obstacles stand in the way of God's purposes and will being accomplished through His Church. But the Holy Spirit will step to the plate and pronounce the will of God through His

yielded vessels, using a language that goes beyond the articulation of natural words.

The Prayer Passion of Jesus

The writer of Hebrews gives us a peek into the passionate prayer life of the Son of God. He penned that Jesus
"offered up both prayers and supplications with loud crying and tears to Him who was able to save Him from death,
and ... was heard because of His piety" (Hebrews 5:7). Read
it again slowly. Did you catch the intensity and desperation
with which Jesus let His heart be known? He "offered up
both prayers and supplications with loud crying and tears."
Yeshua was not afraid to let His emotions show. "Big boys
don't cry" was not true of the Son of Man!

In an amazing comment found in Hebrews 7:25, we are
told of the ongoing ministry in which Jesus engages continuously: "He always lives to make intercession for [those
who draw near to God]." Amazing! For three years Jesus
did miracles among His people on earth, but for hundreds
and even thousands of years, He lives to make intercession.
Striking, isn't it? Profound! Startling! I wonder what God is
trying to say to us? However you analyze it, Jesus lives for
prayer.

May the Father put in us the same relentless, pulsating
heartbeat of persistent intercession.

The Epitome of Desperation

I have often wondered how many friends Jesus had.
Whom did He just talk with, hang out with, go for a walk
with, beyond the pull of the ministry? And I marvel at the
writings of John concerning the emotional agonizing of
Jesus when His friend Lazarus had "fallen asleep" (John
11:11). This chapter uniquely portrays the humanity of Jesus
and the deep care of His heart.

Lazarus had a unique relationship with the Son of God: They were friends. Let's paint the scene of this awesome encounter.

Jesus was with His disciples—probably across the Jordan River—some distance from the city of Bethany, where Lazarus had fallen sick. Mary and Martha, Lazarus' two sisters, sent word for Jesus to hurry and come to his aid. But the Lord waited two more days before He began His journey. The disciples could not figure this one out! But Jesus had sought the Father and learned that this sickness was to promote the honor and glory of God and that the Son of God would be glorified through it (verse 4).

By the time the Messiah and His disciples showed up on the scene, Lazarus had been in the tomb four days. No one could understand what was going on. But Jesus had His own agenda when He came into town that day. He had come to change the spiritual atmosphere—to fulfill the Father's will.

Word of Lazarus' death had spread quickly from Bethany, which was only two miles from Jerusalem, and many Jews had gone out to Martha and Mary to console them over the death of their brother. Emotions were running high when Jesus finally arrived and was greeted by the grief-stricken Martha.

With anguish Martha cried out, "Lord, if You had been here, my brother would not have died" (verse 21). Then she raced back to the house and called her sister Mary, who had remained in the house. Now, in response to Martha's whisper, she, too, went running to meet Jesus, and the Jews who were there consoling her followed. Everyone was in a turmoil. A frantic atmosphere of shock and disbelief prevailed. A swirl of spiritual warfare was at its apex.

On finding Jesus, Mary threw herself to the ground at His feet. Can you hear her say between deep sobs, "Lord, if You had been here, my brother would not have died" (verse 32)?

Let's read what happened next:

When Jesus saw her sobbing, and the Jews who came with her [also] sobbing, He was deeply moved in spirit and troubled. He chafed in spirit, and sighed and was disturbed. And He said, Where have you laid him? They said to Him, Lord, come and see. Jesus wept. The Jews said, See how tenderly He loved him! But some of them said, Could not He, Who opened a blind man's eyes, have prevented this man from dying?

Now Jesus again sighing repeatedly and deeply disquieted, approached the tomb. It was a cave—a hole in the rock—and a boulder lay against [the entrance to close] it. Jesus said, Take away the stone. Martha, the sister of the dead man, exclaimed, But Lord, by this time he [is decaying and] throws off an offensive odor, for he has been dead four days! Jesus said to her, Did I not tell you and promise you that if you would believe and rely on Me, you should see the glory of God? So they took away the stone. And Jesus lifted up His eyes and said, Father, I thank You that You have heard Me. Yes, I know You always hear and listen to Me; but I have said this on account of and for the benefit of the people standing around, so that they may believe that You did send Me—that You have made Me your Messenger.

John 11:33–42, Amplified

We know the final outcome. Jesus spoke with authority to the deceased, decaying body of His friend Lazarus, and life came forth out of death. It gave undisputed testimony that Jesus is the resurrection and the life. Darkness was overcome and light prevailed.

What Was the Prayer the Father Heard?

But how did events move from the chaos of uncertainty to the Kingdom of God being manifested on earth as it is in heaven? Was there a bridge that carried them from one point to another?

Notice the phrase "Father, I thank You that You have heard Me." The NASB translates this, "I thank Thee that Thou heardest Me." Whatever way you put it, it comes out the same. The terminology refers to a past-tense prayer—something that had already taken place. Was there some form of intercession that carried them like a bridge from the chaos of darkness to a heavenly intervention?

For a long time I could find no recorded prayer that Jesus offered up. Then I began to look more deeply into the language used and began to ponder deeply on this passage.

John 11:33 (Amplified) begins with, "When Jesus saw [Mary] sobbing, and the Jews who came with her [also] sobbing, He was *deeply moved in spirit and troubled. . . .*" The NKJV states that "He groaned in the spirit and was troubled." According to Vine's *Expository Dictionary*, the Greek word for "groaned," *embrimaomai*, signifies "to snort with anger, as of horses."[13] *The American Heritage Dictionary* defines *snort* as "a rough, noisy sound made by breathing forcefully through the nostrils." Wow! Jesus was overcome with compassion and responded to the circumstances in the natural realm, and to the powers of darkness in the spiritual realm, by sighing, sobbing, groaning or in some way audibly releasing the weapons of Holy Spirit–birthed intercession.

As you look more closely, you can find at least three waves of the Spirit's presence moving upon and through the Messiah. He identified with the pain and sorrow of the people. As He did so, a wave of compassion hit Him and He stopped, sighed, groaned and expressed His heart's cry of desperation to the Father.

Others standing nearby wanted to take Jesus to see the tomb of His friend Lazarus. As they started to direct Him there, another wave of emotion struck Him and He wept openly. He stopped, and giant-sized tears wet His face and probably His garments.

Once again Jesus attempted to approach His beloved friend's place of burial. As He did, He became deeply troubled and stirred within. Like an animal snorting when it is angered—and with the likelihood of mucus coming out of His nose—Jesus, the Son of Man, sighed repeatedly and groaned in the Spirit. Jesus was desperate. But in His time of desperation, He resorted to the Holy Spirit's enabling, and to prayers going beyond the articulation that any earthly known language could ever express.

Finally, as this compassion eruption subsided, Jesus lifted His head and eyes with confidence and said, "Father, I thank You that You have heard Me." What was the prayer the Father heard? I believe it was the desperate prayer of the heart.

The Invitation Is Extended

So what does all this mean? Simply that we have an invitation to enter into the intercession of Christ that goes beyond our limited knowledge. In no way does our experience compare with the depth of Christ's substitutionary, intercessory act of the cross. That has already been accomplished! Nonetheless, the invitation is given to us to enter the depths of the heart of Jesus, and let sighs and groans too deep for the articulation of man's natural vocabulary surface, whether to express the sorrow of God, to resist the enemy or to lift a cry that we make more room for God in our lives, congregations and cities. Whatever the distinctive purpose of these ancient forms of intercession—just yield. Let Him do it.

With the close of this chapter we are rounding third base and heading toward home plate in the last chapter of this first section, "Cultivating a Heart for Prayer." Let's take Michal Ann's and my personal testimony on the healing of barrenness, wed it with these concepts from "The Desperate Prayer of the Heart," and finally ponder for a while on our final subject in this section, "Travail, the Prayer That Brings Birth."

It looks to me as if we are becoming extremely dependent on God through the power of prayer—just another way of humming the tune we are learning together, the song of dependency and the song of grace. Now how does it go?

> Kneeling, kneeling,
> Kneeling on the promises of God my Savior;
> Kneeling, kneeling,
> I'm kneeling on the promises of God.

PRACTICAL APPLICATIONS—MAKING IT REAL!

- A desperate life ignites desperate prayers. Ask the Lord to give you a heart of desperation, hunger and brokenness in your life before Jesus.
- What does it mean to be broken before God? Ask the Lord to begin the work of the cross in your life so you will become a clay vessel broken before Him.
- Intimacy with the Father is an essential ingredient in your prayers of fervency. Cultivate intimacy in your desperation. Ask the Lord to tenderize your heart.
- In a group setting, listen and wait for the Holy Spirit's burden, then join Him as He groans through you for the coming forth of the sons and daughters of God.
- Pray and ask the Lord to give you a compassionate burden for an individual or church or nation, to feel His heart and tears for His people.

RECOMMENDED READING

Time to Weep by Stephen Hill (Harvest, 1996)

The Power of Brokenness by Don Nori (Destiny Image, 1992)

TRAVAIL

The Prayer That Brings Birth

While Michal Ann was giving birth to our third child, Tyler Hamilton, I got a graphic understanding of what real, live travail is all about.

Do you remember her conversation with the Lord in the fall of 1981? She had said, "I won't like it, but I yield to You my right to have children." The voice of God spoke back to her instantly within her being: *I appreciate your attitude, but I am not requiring this of you. I say to you, You must fight for your children.* The Lord was speaking about our natural children, of course. But these lessons also apply (as we have been learning) to spiritual children and giving birth to the promises of God.

The Lord's words on that strategic day have marked Michal Ann's and my lives ever since. We did fight for our natural children and continue to do so. But on July 7, 1988, as we were in the labor room, we faced another major lesson about what it means to fight for our children.

Now, I don't mean to offend anyone, but may I get a bit graphic to explain the situation? The birthing process had been proceeding fairly well. Dilation was one centimeter away from completion so that birth could occur. The short but painful part of labor called "transition" was now in gear.

We knew what to expect. After all, this was not our first experience of childbirth; it was our third. Michal Ann's pain level began to intensify greatly, and I kept reassuring her, "The end is in sight!" But my sweet, cool, collected darling of an almost-perfect wife was losing her cookies. The pain was not just intense—it was almost unbearable. Instead of continuing to make progress in the final stage of dilation, the opening began to become smaller. The contractions, instead of pushing the baby down the birth canal, began to clamp down and enclose the child. My dear wife was now caught in transition for more than an hour of gripping, intense labor.

Let me tell you, my own efforts were of no help. I had been trying to comfort her but I did it all wrong. She began to scream out, to my shock, "I can't do it! I can't take this any longer!"

We had no choice, of course. We could not decide this late in the game not to have our baby after all. We were fighting for this child's life. A completely different level of spiritual warfare now centered around this child's birth and the destiny of God on his or her life. All we knew to do was cry out to the Lord with all our might.

Intense is the only word to describe the battle Michal Ann and I underwent. It was called *travail!* Finally, when there seemed to be no more strength left in Michal Ann, something took over. Dilation occurred rapidly and the transition was over in an instant. Out came Tyler Hamilton so fast that the doctor had to run over to the table to catch him as he emerged.

Since the natural realm is often a mirror to the spiritual, what lessons can we learn through the anguishing cry of travail? If travail precedes natural birth, does it precede spiritual birth as well?

When They Cried to the Lord

"At God's counter there are no 'sale days,' for the price of revival is ever the same—travail!"[1] This statement came from a man who knew God's ways in revival—Leonard Ravenhill, the English evangelist and author of *Why Revival Tarries*. Many felt he was a modern-day Simeon, given a promise that his eyes would not close until he had seen the fulfillment for which he had labored. Leonard Ravenhill graduated to heaven in November 1994, right at the season when a fresh wind of the Holy Spirit began to blow across the nations, particularly in places like Toronto, Canada, and Pensacola, Florida. Indeed, Ravenhill's tenacious daily prayers, as well as those of others, have helped pave the way for a time of new beginnings in the Body of Christ.

The fabled nineteenth-century evangelist Charles Finney said:

> Why does God require such prayer—such strong desires, such agonizing supplications? These strong desires mirror the strength of God's feelings. They are God's real feelings for unrepentant sinners. How strong God's desire must be for His Spirit to produce in Christians such travail—God has chosen the word to describe it—it is travail, torment of the soul.[2]

Matthew 11:12 says it this way: "The kingdom of heaven suffers violence, and the violent take it by force" (NKJV). Sounds rather intense, don't you agree? This kind of understanding, let alone experience, seems superseded by our fast-food approach to God in modern-day Christendom. But hold on. This, too, is subject to change.

God's Responses in Scripture

We find many accounts, biblically and historically, of God's response to agonizing cries of intercession.

As I have studied, the Lord has directed me to numerous Scripture passages on the subject. Let's look at His responses when men and women cried out to Him. (All the following are taken from the NIV.)

> The Israelites groaned in their slavery and cried out, and their cry for help because of their slavery went up to God. God heard their groaning and He remembered His covenant with Abraham, with Isaac, and with Jacob. So God looked on the Israelites and was concerned about them.
>
> Exodus 2:23–25

> Again the Israelites did evil in the eyes of the LORD, and for seven years He gave them into the hands of the Midianites. . . . Midian so impoverished the Israelites that they cried out to the LORD for help.
>
> Judges 6:1, 6

> [Samuel] cried out to the LORD on Israel's behalf, and the LORD answered him.
>
> 1 Samuel 7:9

> They were helped in fighting them . . . because they cried out to [God] during the battle.
>
> 1 Chronicles 5:20

> In you [God] our fathers put their trust; they trusted and you delivered them. They cried to you and were saved; in you they trusted and were not disappointed.
>
> Psalm 22:4–5

> Put on sackcloth, O priests, and mourn; wail, you who minister before the altar. Come, spend the night in sackcloth,

you who minister before my God. . . . Summon the elders and all who live in the land to the house of the LORD your God, and cry out to the Lord.

Joel 1:13–14

During the days of Jesus' life on earth, he offered up prayers and petitions with loud cries and tears to the one who could save him from death, and he was heard because of his reverent submission [*godly fear*, NKJV].

Hebrews 5:7

God's Responses in History

Like a spiritual archaeologist I have searched out the overlooked subject of the cry of travail. So let me dust off several accounts from Church history revealing that the power of travail in prayer often precedes the fruit of evangelism: spiritual births.

I found the following entry in the diary of the pioneer evangelist David Brainerd in North America dated July 21, 1744:

> In prayer, I was exceedingly enlarged and my soul was as much drawn out as ever I remember it to have been in my life or near. I was in such anguish and pleaded with so much earnestness and importunity that when I rose from my knees, I felt extremely weak and overcome—I could scarcely walk straight.
>
> My joints were as if it would dissolve . . . in my fervent supplications for the poor Indians. I knew they met together to worship demons and not God. This made me cry earnestly that God would now appear and help me. . . . My soul pleaded long.[3]

Brainerd was a pioneer, leading many Native Americans to the saving knowledge of our glorious Jesus Christ.

Accounts show him kneeling in the snow pleading with the Lord and the Indians for their salvation. (Yes, Lord, give us more of these wrestling intercessors in our day!)

As I continued my search on the subject of the cry of travail, I came across unusual accounts of the life of John Hyde of northern India (1865–1912), who often went into the hills to visit friends and pray. Friends reported that it was evident that "Praying Hyde," as he was known, was bowed down with intense travail of soul. He missed many meals as he holed up in his room, lying on the floor overcome with agony, crying out to the Lord. Often as he walked and prayed, it seemed as if an inward fire were burning in his bones.

It was from this intense burden that Hyde began to petition the Lord to let him win a soul to Jesus every day that year. By year's end four hundred souls had been won to Christ through Hyde's witness. The following year John Hyde cried out before the Lord for two souls daily. Twelve months later it was determined that some eight hundred people had responded to Christ through this prayer warrior's ministry. Even this was not enough for the man known as Praying Hyde! His desperation for souls deepened, and as a result he began to plead, "Give me four souls a day."

Hyde's approach was not to win these souls with typical tent crusades or large rallies. He went for each soul individually in a unique manner. He continued in travailing prayer until he had assurance that he had first won the convert in prayer. Only then, it is said, would Hyde approach someone on the street of an Indian village. Conversation would begin under the Spirit's leadership, and before long both Hyde and the sinner would kneel publicly in prayer. Immediately Hyde would accompany this new convert to water and lead him or her in water baptism.

This pattern repeated itself four times a day as Hyde's burden led him to reach out to lost men and women. Multitudes found Jesus as their Lord as this humble man birthed them into the Kingdom—but first through prevailing prayer.

Most serious students of classic revival have been inspired by the life of young Evan Roberts of Wales, who at age 26 spearheaded a move of the Holy Spirit that touched the entire nation. Gripped by God at the age of thirteen, he attended nightly prayer meetings for the next thirteen years, asking God for revival.

In October 1998 I was pleased to minister in Wales with my dear, modern-day-revivalist friends Wes and Stacey Campbell of British Columbia, Canada. Our tour took us from the north to the south of Wales, speaking in four different cities. We culminated our outreach at a packed house at Moriah Chapel—the very site of Evan's historic outpouring—on October 31, the anniversary date of the orginal breakout of God's presence in 1904.

The Spirit of God hovered as we echoed the same prayer Roberts taught the people in his day to pray: "Send the Spirit now, for Jesus Christ's sake." Then we cried out, "Send the Spirit now more powerfully, for Jesus Christ's sake." Some were bent double in anguish as God gripped their hearts for souls. What a blessing it was to redig the well of revival that had been drawn from so powerfully in the past!

At the close of the meeting, a resident of South Wales came up and showed the Campbells and me newspaper articles he had found that very day in the attic of his house, describing the revival activity of 1904. One lead article was highlighted with a big, bold headline: *Roberts' Soul Travails*. It depicted the awesome sight of the Holy Spirit taking hold of young Evan's being visibly—in public view—as he anguished desperately for souls to be saved.

God heard Roberts' travail. It is staggering to realize that more than one hundred thousand converts came into the Kingdom of God in the great Welsh revival!

Yes, Roberts travailed for souls. Should we not do the same?

A Gripping Experience

In the late 1980s I made more than a dozen trips to the island of Hispañola and the nation of Haiti, the poorest country in the Western Hemisphere. In January 1987 I did some up-front work for Mahesh Chavda for an outdoor crusade to be held in Carfoure, a suburb of the capital, Port-au-Prince (the same crusade in which the grandma was healed of blindness). Laborers cleared the land and work proceeded for our anticipated evangelistic outreach. A lot of blood, sweat and tears went into this venture to proclaim the Gospel of Jesus Christ to these lovely Caribbean people.

We had a tremendous team of about thirty intercessors from across the United States, whom God had amassed as our behind-the-scenes hit squad. This was when I first met Dick Simmons, prayer leader of Men for Nations, based in Washington, D.C., calling men to early morning prayer for revival. Mahesh had met Dick at a campus ministry conference in Richmond, Virginia, a few weeks before, and was so affected by Dick's call to holy, persevering intercession that he invited him to be part of these gatherings. Dick taught the intercessory team in the mornings and we were armed for the day.

Intercession arose constantly before the Lord as we cried out that the powers of witchcraft be overcome by the brilliance of His great light. The country was in turmoil. Political upheaval was in the air. The nation was ripe for change. And by God's grace a season of change came.

In the midst of the crusade—actually, in the middle of the night—the Holy Spirit directed a group of eight of us to a lookout point called Point Boutilleire overlooking a valley, with tens of thousands of inhabitants living below. It was two in the morning. Suddenly, as the Holy Spirit gripped us, we were flung into an intercessory posture that was both intense and unusual. It seemed that the burden of the Lord hit us deep within and we agonized like women giving birth.

We were convulsing on the ground with pains and groans for deliverance for the nation of Haiti, crying out to the Lord for a season of change, deliverance and mercy on the land.

Just as suddenly as the travail came on us, it lifted.

I am sure the other men wondered, as I did, what had hit us. But the Holy Spirit turned on the lights. I saw a vision of a brass bowl covering the sky above us. It was like the picture in Deuteronomy 28:23, which says: "The heaven which is over your head shall be bronze, and the earth which is under you, iron." The bronze and iron symbolize the curse when our prayers do not get through and the seed sown bears no fruit. Then, in my vision, some kind of sharp instrument pierced the brass sky above and light flooded the dark region. It was like a pen hole had now been opened in the heavens and mercy had been obtained for the land. Somehow we also knew that this season of mercy was not permanent but temporary. We praised the Lord anyhow for the window of opportunity.

As it happened, not only did the 77-year-old grandmother get healed of blindness, but a season of new vision and sight came to the nation of Haiti as well. Jean-Claude "Baby Doc" Duvalier, the evil totalitarian leader of Haiti, had been overthrown in 1986 after widespread civil unrest and had to flee for his life. In place of oppression, a spirit of optimism was growing over the impoverished nation as eventually the people were given the right to free democratic elections. Darkness had been exposed; the light of the Lord was coming.

But the pressures of travail had preceded the time of new beginning. An intense spirit of prayer had fallen on us (and probably on many around the globe), an opening appeared in the heavenlies for a time as the light of God shone through.

Eight Barren Women

Since you know the Goll family's true-to-life story of healing from barrenness, you can begin to comprehend how

Michal Ann and I got immersed in this stuff. We had desire. We had received a promise. And even though we had had the sentence of barrenness pronounced loudly over us, we laid hold of the God of the promise.

Before our miracle occurred, I did a study concerning barren women in the Bible that really encouraged us. Guess what I found? Eight barren women specifically healed from barrenness! They had several things in common. They were desperate. They cried out to the Lord. And each brought forth either a prophet or a deliverer of the nation. Let me list these eight women for you:

1. Sarah, who brought forth Isaac (Genesis 11:30; 16:1; 18:1–15; 21:1–8)
2. Rebekah, who brought forth Esau and Jacob (Genesis 25:21–26)
3. Rachel, who brought forth Joseph and Benjamin (Genesis 29:31; 30:1, 22–24; 35:16–18)
4. Manoah's wife, who brought forth Samson (Judges 13:2–24)
5. Ruth, who brought forth Obed (Ruth 4:13)
6. Hannah, who brought forth Samuel (1 Samuel 1:2–20)
7. Elizabeth, who brought forth John the Baptist (Luke 1:7–13, 57)

I have listed only seven barren women, while I told you I found eight examples. Who is the eighth? Isaiah 66:8 portrays her vividly:

"Who has heard such a thing? Who has seen such things? Can a land be born in one day? Can a nation be brought forth all at once? As soon as Zion travailed, she also brought forth her sons."

Zion is the eighth barren woman. She will bring forth her precious fruit in the earth as soon as—when? As soon as

God's chosen people travail, she will bring forth sons. I have often heard it stated that if the Church would cry out like a barren woman longing for children, then we would have revival. I believe this!

What Is Travail?

By now I am sure you are asking, "What is travail?" Let me try to explain it.

As it is in the natural, so it is in the spiritual. Travail is a form of intense intercession given by the Holy Spirit whereby an individual or group is gripped by something that grips God's heart. The individual or group labors with Him for an opening to be created so that the new life can come forth.

The definition of *travail* from *Webster's New World Dictionary* is simple: "very hard work; the pains of childbirth; intense pain; agony." I have found this definition correct in the spiritual realm as well. Travail takes place after you have carried something in your heart for a period of time. It comes on you suddenly. Travail can be associated with the prayer of tears. It is preceded by nurturing the promise; later the strategic time comes to push that promise forth through the prayer canal. Finally you realize that the promise has been born, and you are greatly relieved when the delivery is over!

How have I learned these concepts? By my personal journey, by looking to Scripture and by learning from those the Lord has graciously brought into my life. Like you, I take jewels of truth from others and bring them to my own place of prayer before God.

One of these dear consultants is the prayer leader of Word of Love Ministries in Roswell, Georgia, Pat Gastineau. Let me summarize her teaching on the subject of travail and labor.

The prayer of travail is God desiring to create an "opening" to bring forth a measure of life or growth. If the "opening" was already in place, there would not be the need for travail. Just as the "opening" of the natural womb is enlarged to bring forth the baby, so, travail creates an "opening or way," whereas before the opening or way was closed. With travail, there is always a way opened for life, newness, change or growth.

As stated in the Scriptures, travail comes suddenly and leaves suddenly. 1 Thessalonians 5:3 tells us, "For when they shall say, Peace and safety; then sudden destruction cometh upon them, as travail upon a woman with child." God declares, by the Spirit, that He wants a way opened for someone or something. Then as we yield and comply, God can give the travail that births—for as surely as travail comes, so will the corresponding change.

Accounts of Agonizing and Wrestling in Prayer

Different people, groups, ministries and denominations in the Body of Christ use different terminology to describe similar or overlapping experiences. Associated with the prayer of travail have often been accounts of "agonizing and wrestling" in prayer. Where are these ways today? Where are these holy wrestlers for our generation?

Perhaps one reason that few wrestle in prayer is that few are prepared for its strenuous demands. This kind of prayer can be physically demanding and spiritually exhausting. You recognize what is at stake: the eternal destiny of an unsaved one, perhaps; the success of an urgent endeavor; the life of a sick one; the honor of the name of God; the welfare of the Kingdom of God.

Once again, Wesley Duewel:

Wrestling in prayer enlists all the powers of your soul, marshals your deepest holy desire, and uses all the perseverance of your holy determination. You push through a host of difficulties. You push back the heavy, threatening clouds of darkness. You reach beyond the visible and natural to the very throne of God. With all your strength and tenacity, you lay hold of God's grace and power as it becomes a passion of your soul.[4]

Remember Jacob wrestling with the angel until he received the blessing? Let's look at that passage again:

Jacob was left alone, and a man wrestled with him until daybreak. And when he saw that he had not prevailed against him, he touched the socket of his thigh; so the socket of Jacob's thigh was dislocated while he wrestled with him. Then he said, "Let me go, for the dawn is breaking." But he said, "I will not let you go unless you bless me."

Genesis 32:24–26

As Jacob found out, tenacious, persevering prayer eventually pays off.

"Pin Me Down!"

Michael Sullivant, one of the pastors at Metro Christian Fellowship in Kansas City, Missouri, often tells of a dream the Lord gave him depicting this issue of wrestling prayer. He was shown a scene in which a father and son were wrestling on the ground together. The father could have pinned the child at any moment, but in the delight of play, he let his son pin him down instead.

The Lord revealed to Michael that this is much the way it is with us and our relationship with our heavenly Father. Many of us are practicing pinning God, our Father, down through our prayer relationship. We are building a history before Him. As we grow in our endurance, our prayer muscles are developing. But a day will come—so the Holy Spirit promised Michael—that will please the Father's heart when we grow up as sons and daughters and really have the strength to pin Him down. Not physically, of course, and not that we want our own wills to prevail over His. But we will have wrestled with the God of the promise—what the Almighty wanted to do in the first place!—and won.

May we truly grow in the strength of the Lord to wrestle as Jacob did and win.

Scriptural Accounts of Wrestling

We do not know for certain what Paul meant, but ponder the following passage from Colossians:

> Epaphras, who is one of your number, a bondslave of Jesus Christ, sends you his greetings, *always laboring earnestly for you in his prayers*, that you may stand perfect and fully assured in all the will of God. For I bear him witness that *he has a deep concern for you* and for those who are in Laodicea and Hierapolis.
>
> Colossians 4:12–13, italics added

The NIV says Epaphras was "always wrestling in prayer." Wow! I wonder what his "deep concern," which was expressed through laboring prayer, looked like? One thing we are assured of: It was intense!

When Paul wrote that our struggle, or wrestling match, is against the forces of darkness, he had in mind the backdrop of the Olympic-style games in ancient Greece. Each wrestler sought to throw his opponent onto the ground and put his own foot on his opponent's neck. The Amplified Version renders the passage like this:

> Put on God's whole armor—the armor of a heavy-armed soldier, which God supplies—that you may be able successfully to stand up against [all] the strategies and the deceits of the devil. For we are not wrestling with flesh and blood—contending only with physical opponents—

but against the despotisms, against [the master spirits who are] the world rulers of this present darkness, against the spirit forces of wickedness in the heavenly (supernatural) sphere.

Ephesians 6:11–12

Clearly, when we combine the lessons of Genesis 32, concerning Jacob, and the Pauline epistles cited above, we are given pictures of pinning or wrestling with the enemy, as well as with our heavenly Father, in the divine interplay of prayer. One common thread is for certain in both accounts: Don't give up! Continue in your wrestling match. It's not over till it's over, and it ain't over yet! Continue in persevering, prevailing intercession.

Caring and Bearing in Prayer

Not only are people today learning to kneel on the promises through intercession, but the Lord has been calling many into deeper union and greater intimacy with Christ. A spiritual conception has occurred within the womb of the Church. Desire for a great awakening is growing and stirring within our inner beings, similar to the revival that took place in the English colonies in America in the 1720s and '30s that revitalized the Church. But the Lord wants to release this awakening today not just in one or two areas or regions of the earth. The awakening this time is global in nature. God is looking for a large womb of the entire Body of Christ. No wonder many are feeling stretched beyond their comfort zones!

Let me mention another form of this kind of prayer in which one carries something or someone over an extended period of time (like a baby) and then labors to bring it forth by the Spirit. It is as if this burden is there all the time, and occasionally the Spirit causes it to surface, in order to give it priority in prayer. This is "bearing young in prayer." Usually the intensity of sudden travail is absent in this long-term burden-bearing.

God seems to hand out assignments, which you carry for long periods. Michal Ann and I carry different nations, for example, before Him. In the 1980s it was Haiti; in the '90s it has been the Czech Republic. Another of the "babies" we carry is the Jewish people and the purposes of God for Israel. This caring and bearing kind of prayer has led me into many on-site prayer gatherings around the globe for the Jewish people and for the nations of Israel. (I will share more on this in chapter 9, "Israel: God's Prophetic Calendar.")

As that child grows within you, you can, like a pregnant woman, feel it move an arm or leg within you. The baby is growing and you get to bear the marks. Eventually, after months of formation, the "prayer child" wants to come out!

Let's consider three Greek definitions and examples of bearing young in prayer. (The Scripture quotations are from the KJV, italics added.)

1. *Sustenazo:* to *moan* together jointly. Romans 8:22: "We know that the whole creation *groaneth* and travaileth in pain together until now."
2. *Sun-odino:* to have parturition (or bring forth young). Romans 8:22: "We know that the whole creation groaneth and *travaileth* in pain together until now." To *travail* in pain together or in company.
3. *Odin:* a pang or throe of childbirth. Galatians 4:19: "My little children, of whom I *travail* in birth again until Christ be formed in you. . . ."

Isn't this what we need? We need not only the evangelists but those who nurture and care for the young and call them forth into maturity. I am not suggesting that this form of prayer replaces pastoral care or the importance of teaching ministries. But don't you think it is time for intercessors to arise who will carry the young ones for extended periods of time in their hearts and labor for their spiritual maturity? Let's not just call these spiritual youngsters forth; let's nurture them as well through the power of intercession.

Now let's consider two Hebrew definitions and examples of bearing young in prayer. (Again, the Scripture quotations are from the KJV, italics added.)

1. *Yalad:* to bear young, to beget, act as a midwife, labor, to be delivered of a child.
   - Isaiah 21:3: "Therefore are my loins filled with pain [meaning "the writhing of childbirth"]: pangs have taken hold upon me, as the pangs of a woman that *travaileth:* I was bowed down at the hearing of it; I was dismayed at the seeing of it." Notice that this entire chapter is about the labor of the watchmen.
   - Jeremiah 30:6–7: "Ask ye now, and see whether a man doth travail with child? wherefore do I see every man with his hands on his loins, as a woman in *travail,* and all faces are turned into paleness? Alas! for that day is great, so that none is like it: it is even the time of Jacob's trouble; but he shall be saved out of it."
   - Micah 4:10: "Be in *pain* [the word for *travail*] and labor to bring forth, O daughter of Zion, like a woman in travail: for now shalt thou go forth out of the city, and thou shalt dwell in the field, and thou shalt go even to Babylon; there shalt thou be delivered; there the LORD shall redeem thee from the hand of thine enemies."
   - Micah 5:3: "Therefore will [God] give them up, until the time that she which *travaileth* hath brought

forth: then the remnant of his brethren shall return
unto the children of Israel."

?uwl: to twist or whirl, to writhe in pain, especially
?arturition (travail in birth).

- Psalm 55:4: "My heart is sore *pained* within me: and
  the terrors of death are fallen upon me."
- Isaiah 13:8: "They shall be afraid: pangs and sorrows shall take hold of them; they shall be in
  pain as a woman that travaileth: they shall be
  amazed one at another; their faces shall be as
  flames."
- Isaiah 26:17: "Like as a woman with child, that
  draweth near the time of her delivery, is in *pain*,
  and crieth out in her pangs; so have we been in thy
  sight, O LORD."
- Isaiah 54:1–3: "Sing, O barren, thou that didst not
  bear; break forth into singing, and cry aloud, thou
  that didst not *travail* with child: for more are the
  children of the desolate than the children of the
  married wife, saith the LORD. Enlarge the place of
  thy tent, and let them stretch forth the curtains of
  thy habitations: spare not, lengthen thy cords, and
  strengthen thy stakes; for thou shalt break forth on
  the right hand and on the left; and thy seed shall
  inherit the Gentiles, and make the desolate cities
  to be inhabited."

Wow! Have you ever felt that you carried a burden for
months? Many would call this the burden of the Lord.
Some of these burdens seem to come on us suddenly and
leave suddenly. But there are other graces of intercession that grow within us over time; they twist and turn
till eventually we feel like either the one giving birth or
the midwife assisting in the delivery. Either way life
comes forth.

May the Lord restore to us Spirit-born travail, agonizing and wrestling in prayer, and bearing and caring in prayer as tools to birth and nurture life.

"Elijah, What Are You Doing?"

Over the last decade one of my favorite passages in Scripture has been that of Elijah's prayer encounter in 1 Kings 18. I have preached the revelation of this message in churches, cities and countries around the globe, always with the same result. The gripping burden of the Lord comes on God's people and a new level of travail—at times dramatic!—is released on, in and through them. This understanding came to me as a result of the trials and blessings Michal Ann and I went through as a couple in our attempts to have children.

The following, therefore, is a synopsis of our life message based on the tenacious example of Elijah. It is the bread of our lives.

Elijah said to Ahab, "Go up, eat and drink; for there is the sound of the roar of a heavy shower." So Ahab went up to eat and drink. But Elijah went up to the top of Carmel; and he crouched down on the earth, and put his face between his knees. And he said to his servant, "Go up now, look toward the sea." So he went up and looked and said, "There is nothing." And he said, "Go back" seven times. And it came about at the seventh time, that he said, "Behold, a cloud as small as a man's hand is coming up from the sea." And he said, "Go up, say to Ahab, 'Prepare your chariot and go down, so that the heavy shower does not stop you.'" So it came about in a little while, that the sky grew black with clouds and wind, and there was a heavy shower. And Ahab rode and went to Jezreel. Then the hand of the LORD was on Elijah, and he girded up his loins and outran Ahab to Jezreel.

1 Kings 18:41–46

Let me share that story with you with additions from my own sanctified imagination.

It had not rained for three and a half years (verses 1–2). The land was dry and parched. Conditions in the natural realm were at a point of desperation; and the natural only mirrored the spiritual condition of the people. There was no cloud cover and everyone was being beaten down by the scorching sun.

In the midst of desert-like circumstances, the burden of the Lord was coming on one of God's choice servants. Faith was percolating within Elijah, and he "went to show himself to Ahab" (verse 2) just days before winning a great victory over the prophets of Baal. After calling a witness from heaven to be released, sure enough, fire fell from heaven and all the false prophets bowed low to the ground, declaring that the Lord was the one true God. Elijah was ecstatic!

On the heels of this dramatic intervention, the man of God heard something in his spirit that could not be heard audibly—a sound in the distance not known for more than three years. As he listened, the sound picked up volume. It was a thunderstorm of magnanimous proportions.

Elijah ran from the presence of the Lord into the court of evil King Ahab and proclaimed boldly, "There is the sound of the roar of a heavy shower" (verse 41). Ahab went about his regular routine of eating and drinking. He did not know what to make of this strange, ethereal man who said he heard voices.

Meanwhile Elijah went to one of his favorite places of solitude. He headed off to Mount Carmel—the place where God had showed Himself strong just days before. Positioned on top of the mount, Elijah knew that either God would show up and change the circumstances, or else he himself was about to be stoned as a false prophet.

So what did he do? He took on the posture of humility and desperation. By the leading of the Holy Spirit, he squatted to the ground in awe of his majestic God. The burden of the Lord increased on Elijah for a day of new beginnings to emerge. As the hand of the Lord settled on him, a pressure seemed to build inside this warrior. While unusual stirrings were being stimulated internally, a weight of the glory of God came on him externally. Something was happening.

The next thing we know, Elijah was overwhelmed with the transcendent majesty of God. He hid his face in his hands and pressed his head down between his knees. Then Elijah issued a word to his servant: "Go up now, look toward the sea" (verse 43).

The servant departed and searched the heavens over the Mediterranean Sea. He saw nothing. Climbing back to the top of Mount Carmel, I imagine that he gasped to see Elijah under the burden of God. Cautiously he told his master that things had not changed. The prophet exhorted him to go look again—in fact, to go and look seven times, if need be. Off went the servant, hoping to see something rising on the horizon. Each time he darted back to the top of the mountain to bring his news, only to see Elijah with his face between his knees.

The servant must have wondered, *Master, what are you doing?* But each time the helper went forth again, looking for some sign of rain—to see only the scorching glare of the sun reflecting on the sea. Back and forth this venture went, until the servant, with feelings of despair, reported to his master, "There is only the glaring sun."

By this time the grip of God had its squeeze on Elijah's heart. He appeared to be in the midst of wrestling or agonizing. What *was* he doing? A cry convulsed out of the prophet: "Go look yet another time."

On the seventh time—the number of completion—the servant rushed out, hoping to see a change. As he scanned the sky, something small caught his eye. He peered into the heavens. Sure enough, a cloud had emerged—but only the size of a man's hand. With fire in his being he ran back to declare the good report to the man of God.

There was Elijah in full travail, a desperate labor of love. The young man reported, "I saw it. I saw it! A cloud the size of a man's hand."

I imagine that perspiration spotted Elijah's brow and fire burned in his bones as the intercessory burden began to lift off the prophet of God. Then, in a prophetic unction, he declared, "Go tell that Ahab he had better hurry, because if he doesn't, his chariot wheels are going to get stuck in the mud! For I have heard the sound of a heavy rain."

So it came about that the sky turned black with clouds and wind and there was a downpour.

The Epitome of Travail

Is anyone listening?

This is a fair question to ask. Does anyone hear the sound of another drummer? The God of the universe is speaking, declaring that rain is coming to end the drought. Is anyone listening?

Before a development ever appears in the natural, it must exist first in the heart of God. Before the rain came to end the drought, Elijah heard the rain with his spiritual ears. Even today God speaks first. This creates a spark of faith within a man or woman. Remember, faith comes by "hearing . . . the word of Christ" (Romans 10:17).

But Elijah did not only go out and declare all he had heard. He prayed the promise into being. He literally knelt on the promise.

There are many lessons to grasp here—but let's keep it simple. God speaks. Man hears. Faith is created. Man responds to the spark of faith and prays the promise into being. Tenacity and endurance are required when the desired result seems to be delayed. Even when breakthrough starts to come, it takes eyes of discernment to recognize the day of visitation. We are not to "[despise] the day of small things" (Zechariah 4:10), as a cloud the size of a man's hand grows and consumes the sky in a downpour of mercy, and the drought comes to an end.

Yes, as we see in the encounter with Elijah, travail brings birth. Travail is the posture of desperation. It expresses the urgent prayer of the heart. Could this be the missing key to worldwide revival?

Before we round out the last chapter in this section on "Cultivating a Heart for Prayer" and turn to our middle section, "Cultivating a Heart for the Prophetic," let's make sure our focus and vision are clear.

If we must be born again to enter the Kingdom of God, there must be One who has gone before us. Yes, this is Christ Jesus, the One who travailed of soul for us so that we could be born into His Kingdom. The greatest act of travail was undoubtedly when Jesus on the cross secured an entrance for us into the Kingdom of heaven. Perhaps the blood and water that spilled, when the spear pierced His side, revealed a heart and soul in labor. The waters broke and the Church was born.

If travail was the major ingredient necessary for the Church to be born, surely it becomes a principal application for you and me. May we add travail to our priestly prayers of the heart so that a way can be opened for others to enter the realm of the Kingdom. Even so, let the pains of labor come upon the bride of Christ, that Jesus may receive the rewards for His suffering, as was the goal for the Moravian believers in the 1700s.

May we truly go forth kneeling on the promises—birthing God's purposes through the power of prophetic intercession.

PRACTICAL APPLICATIONS—MAKING IT REAL!

- What are you so desperate for that you cannot live without?

- Discuss in your small group the meaning of travail, laying a scriptural foundation from which to launch.
- Create an atmosphere where you as a group are open and vulnerable to the Lord, and ask the Holy Spirit to come and release the spirit of travail in your midst.
- Ask an older Christian about the secrets he or she has learned concerning cultivating a heart for prayer.
- Listen to my two-tape album called "The Spirit of Travail" (see page 315).

RECOMMENDED READING

Mighty, Prevailing Prayer by Wesley Duewel (Francis Asbury/Zondervan, 1990)

Modes of Prayer by Pat Gastineau (Word of Love, 1997)

TWO

CULTIVATING A HEART
FOR THE PROPHETIC

WANTED

A Generation of Prophetic People

Congratulations! You have now made it a third of the way on our journey together of learning to kneel on the promises. In this second section, "Cultivating a Heart for the Prophetic," I will tear off another portion of my life, like freshly gathered manna, and pray that your heart will be filled with the spirit of revelation as you partake.

What Is New Testament Prophecy?

Anglican bishop David Pytches states, "The gift of prophecy is the special ability that God gives to members of the body of Christ to receive and communicate an immediate message of God to His gathered people, a group among them or any one of His people individually, through a divinely anointed utterance."[1]

In his book *The Holy Spirit Today* Dick Iverson, former senior pastor of Bible Temple in Portland, remarks:

103

> The gift of prophecy is speaking under the direct supernatural influence of the Holy Spirit. It is becoming God's mouthpiece, to verbalize His words as the Spirit directs. The Greek word *prophetia* means "speaking forth the mind and counsel of God." It is inseparable in its New Testament usage with the concept of direct inspiration of the Spirit. Prophecy is the very voice of Christ speaking in the church.[2]

Prophecy, we could say, is the expressed thought of God delivered in a language that no human being in his or her natural gift of speech or knowledge could ever articulate. The substance and nature of prophecy exceeds what the human mind is capable of thinking or imagining. Prophecy comes through the heart and soul of a man or woman, but it issues from the mind of God.

This wonderful gracelet is primarily for the purpose of edifying, exhorting and comforting those whom it addresses (see 1 Corinthians 14:3). It can be expressed as either premeditated or spontaneous utterances by speaking, singing or even writing; through the language of dreams and visions; as a word of counsel; enacted or released through instrumentation and other art forms; or by any other manner of delivery. It brings the voice of God into relevance for our time.

But a message is authentically prophetic only if it comes from the heart of God, magnifies the Lord Jesus Christ and challenges the hearer into greater obedience to God's commands.

Stages of Prophetic Development

As with any gift, there are various levels of operation within the sphere of prophecy. There can be the *occasional gift* that comes on an individual for a specific situation. There is another stage of development, as in any gift or ministry, into which there is a more consistent flow of *prophetic operation* as the believer's faith, gift and experience mature. Some are blessed to step into more of a "residential gifting" that finds regular release in their lives. This could be called a *prophetic ministry*. But this does not necessarily mean the individual has an Ephesians 4:11 *office of prophet*. Only God can bring someone to this level of consistent grace that blooms over time. You can be called, but then comes the training.

At some point, if fruit is borne and as leaders recognize the abundance of fruit that has already come forth, there will be a commissioning into the calling. Normally there is a step-by-step approach of the reception and delivery of this grace, but at times prophecy seems to be a sovereign gift that just comes in full-blown operation early on.

In whatever manner the gift unfolds, one truth is always the same: Gifts are given but fruit is borne. Giftings may appear overnight, but the character necessary to carry the gifts over the long haul comes only by way of the cross in the life of each individual. Good, ripe fruit takes time being exposed to the Son!

Being a Prophetic People

Revelatory giftings of God, I am convinced, are for the many, not just the few. The Lord is looking for an entire generation of passionate people (called the Church!) who will walk in the spirit of wisdom and revelation in the knowledge of the Lord Jesus Christ.

What does it mean to be prophetic or part of a company of prophetic people? God wants each of us to stay so close to His heart that we can speak a relevant word from Him in a contemporary manner into different echelons of society. We are called not only to stand up in a church meeting and speak out a prophetic word, but to be world-changers, history-makers and Kingdom-builders by taking revelatory gifts—the prophetic presence of the Holy Spirit—out into the spheres of influence the Lord has appointed for us.

Don't just get a word; *become* a word for Jesus' sake! Be a contemporary sign from God that will make people wonder what is going on. Let them watch your life and remark, "God must be alive and well on planet earth!"

Michal Ann and I use a simple mission statement for our ministry, Ministry to the Nations: "Equipping the Church and Expanding the Kingdom." This is because there are three major spheres into which we are to release the revelatory life that the Holy Spirit gives us. One is the area of church gatherings (large and small), home meetings and congregational celebrations, on both a corporate and a personal level. This is equipping the Church. The second sphere is the secular community that our lives touch and influence, the marketplace: the arts, government, economics, athletics, every area of life. This is expanding the Kingdom. The third sphere into which we release revelatory gifts is back into the heart of God. This is turning a promise into prayer. (More on the subject of prophetic intercession in the next chapter.)

This, in part, is what it means to be a prophetic people: building a community in love, walking under the Lordship of Jesus Christ and releasing the revelatory presence of the Holy Spirit into every arena of life. Always remember, the prophetic giftings of God are for the many, not just the few.

May a royal priesthood, a holy nation, of passionate people come forth for the honor and glory of Jesus' name. The time has come. Rise up, prophetic army of God, and demonstrate through the acts of the Spirit that King Jesus is the same yesterday, today and forever!

The Prophetic Cry of Moses

The pressures on Moses were tremendous as this anointed man of God tried to lead his complaining people into the Promised Land. His cry to the Lord is found in Numbers 11:14: "I alone am not able to carry all this people, because it is too burdensome for me."

But God had a solution to Moses' dilemma:

> "Gather for Me seventy men from the elders of Israel, whom you know to be the elders of the people and their officers and bring them to the tent of meeting, and let them take their stand there with you. Then I will come down and speak with you there, and I will take of the Spirit who is upon you, and will put Him upon them; and they shall bear the burden of the people with you, so that you shall not bear it all alone."
>
> Numbers 11:16–17

So Moses went out and told the people the words of the Lord. He gathered the seventy elders and stationed them around the tent. Then the Lord came down in the cloud, took of the Spirit who was on Moses and placed Him on the seventy elders.

> It came about that when the Spirit rested upon them, they prophesied. But they did not do it again.
>
> verse 25

What a beautiful depiction, yet what an unfulfilling outcome! With a stroke of the Master's hand, the prophetic presence that rested on Moses was distributed among the seventy and they prophesied—"but they did not do it again."

Thank God this was not the final word on the matter!

For some reason two desperate, hungry men named Medad and Eldad were left in the camp (see verse 26). Apparently they did not show up at the right place at the right time. Nonetheless the Spirit of God came upon them as He had upon the elders, and Eldad and Medad released the prophetic presence out in the camp of the Israelites, where the ordinary, rank-and-file people were busy with their everyday activities.

As I envision this scene, I see two wide-eyed warriors, so hungry for the Lord's anointing that their hearts' cry to a compassionate God was "Give us all you've got! More, Lord!" God saw their hunger and jumped at the chance to smear His presence all over those two no-names.

There is no indication that Medad and Eldad ever quit "doing the stuff"—walking in the supernatural gifts of the Spirit and prophetic revelation. I see them like the Energizer bunny; they just kept going and going. Perhaps they roamed wildly and freely through the camp laying hands on people, getting impressions from the Holy Spirit and expressing God's mighty word to the people. Holy chaos was taking place.

But apparently it was a little unusual. The Israelites had not seen the Holy Spirit operate this way before. Some were probably excited. In fact, they were ecstatic! They had been praying secretly for something like this to happen. Some were uncertain about this unusual phenomenon but were trying patiently to observe what fruit would come of it.

Then there were the others. You know the ones who seldom have anything good to say and who have the ministry of the "wet blanket syndrome"? Well, one young member of this particular religious tribe ran and told Moses, "Eldad and Medad are prophesying in the camp" (verse 27). He said it as though that were something terrible. In reality it represented something tremendous. All the Israelites should have been rejoicing!

Even Joshua got in on the wet blanket act, adding, "Moses, my lord, restrain them" (verse 28). This is like people today who say, "Hey, where's the order? Don't you know all things are to be done decently and in order?" They are appealing to 1 Corinthians 14:40. But whose order is it supposed to be anyway—man's or God's? Jesus never told us we were to control Him and His acts. We are told that the fruit of the Spirit is to control the deeds of the flesh like lust, immorality and greed (see Galatians 5:19–25). Too often we recite 1 Corinthians 14:40 as though it says, "Let nothing be done so that things can be in decent order!" But it actually says, "Let everything be done!"

I am not trying to promote anarchy, doing your own thing or distrusting leadership. But the dove of God needs to be set free from His ceremonial cage. I have heard it said that if the Holy Spirit had been removed from the early Church, ninety percent of what they did would have ceased and only ten percent would have remained. But if the Holy Spirit were taken from today's Church, ninety percent of what we do would remain and only ten percent would cease. Get the picture?

Besides, isn't the reaction of "Hey, where's the order?" similar to churchmen who, through the ages, have wanted to control the activity of the Spirit? In one dimension that is exactly what the Reformation was all about. The separation between clergy and laity was to cease. We are each priests to the Lord (see Isaiah 61:6; 66:21; 1 Peter 2:5, 9; Revelation 1:6). But not only that. Notice what Moses said to Joshua: "Are you jealous for my sake? Would that all the LORD's people were prophets, that the LORD would put His Spirit upon them!" (Numbers 11:29).

Moses' answer revealed God's heart. Let me reiterate that the prophetic spirit is for the many, not the few. The seventy leaders at the tent prophesied only once, but God yearns for a generation of people like Medad and Eldad to arise with a continuous abiding of His prophetic presence. We are each to be priests to the Lord. But it does not end there. Each of us is also to be God's prophetic mouthpiece. A sign for all to read should be hanging on the reader board of every church facility: *Wanted: A Generation of Prophetic People. Sign Up Here!*

For Our Day and Time

Centuries after Moses, the prophet Joel picked up the trumpet of God and declared that in the last days God would pour out His Spirit on all flesh (see Joel 2:28). On the Day of Pentecost Peter grabbed the baton from Joel and proclaimed, "Your sons and your daughters shall prophesy, and your young men shall see visions, and your old men shall dream dreams" (Acts 2:17).

The promise of God's presence being poured out, Peter exclaimed, was to the present generation of his time and to all those who would believe throughout the generations (verse 39). In fact, we are given clear indication, here and in other places, that the more the biblical time period called the "last days" unfolds, the more of God's prophetic anointing will be released.

This promise will be fulfilled, I believe, in our day and time. Let a prophetic generation of desperate warriors for the sake of His holy name arise! Yes, dreams, visions and prophecy will flow among the rank-and-file members of the Body of Christ. We will see "wonders in the sky above, and signs on the earth beneath" (Acts 2:19–20).

Can you see that the prophetic spirit is for the many, not the few? Let the hunger of your own heart be stirred up as you lift your desperate cry to Him for "More, Lord!"

I am firmly convinced that the explosion of power evangelism occurring in many nations today—the demonstration of God's power causing people to come to Jesus Christ—is meant to flow in North America and in all the nations. In the 1990s there has been a resurgence of prophetic empowering. This is intended for the many—for the rank-and-file, "ordinary" members of the Body of Christ—and not just the few prophetic or evangelistic superstars who have so arrested our attention. The Lord will preserve for Himself a praising and praying people passionately in love with Him. Psalm 110:3 describes them: "Thy people will volunteer freely in the day of Thy power." Psalm 102:18 declares prophetically that "this will be written for the generation to come; that a people yet to be created may praise the LORD."

I am convinced that consecutive waves of God's Spirit will continue to unfold until Christ's Church has been saturated with "a spirit of wisdom and of revelation in the knowledge of Him" (Ephesians 1:17). Our Father God will not let up until His people are filled with the revelation of the loveliness of His dear Son. Does this sound inviting? It is! And it is for *you*. Join the cries of thousands upon thousands of others across the globe today who are crying, "More, Lord!"

The wonderful revelatory presence of the Holy Spirit is not something that can be earned. Rather, it is something that can be cultivated through intimacy with Christ and by walking in the normal spiritual disciplines of the Christian life. Let's look at some of these.

Keys to Cultivating God's Revelatory Presence

Recently I saw a church reader board near our home in Antioch, Tennessee, that stated: *God's Presence with Us Is His Best Present to Us.* Is that ever right! We must learn to be a people of His presence. I have found the old adage true: "Some things are better caught than taught."

You can catch a precious revelatory anointing by being around people of the anointing. Whom you hang out with, you become like. So hang out with Jesus, His Word and, whenever you can, people of the anointing.

I think I just heard another one of those questions: "What *is* the anointing?" I use the following phrase to try to describe it: *The anointing is the grace of God that supernaturally enables an individual or group to do the works of Jesus by the manifest presence of the Holy Spirit operating in, on or through them.*

Love the anointing! Get around it, rub up to it and ask God for more of it. Ultimately this "it" is not an "it." It is the living presence of the Person of Jesus in the power of the Holy Spirit.

A prominent evangelist of our day has stated prophetically as a message from the Lord: "The great men and women of God that I am using in the earth today are not because they are something special. I am using them for one reason and one reason alone. It's because they've touched Me and I have touched them."[3] Remember, as you reach your hand upward, there is a hand already stretched out downward ready to touch you. God is ready to distribute His grace freely to whomever is hungry. So love the anointing!

And again, realize that a message is prophetic only if it comes from the heart of God, magnifies the Lord Jesus Christ and brings a generation into the knowledge and obedience of God. One thing is for sure: If a word does not testify about our glorious Lord Jesus Christ (see Revelation 19:10), it is not prophetic, it is pathetic! The message is not about us or me or mine, you see; it is all about Him.

Often people think that if they just hang around others who "do the stuff," they, too, will consistently do the stuff. While you *can* receive from others and be jump-started by what they have, ultimately you will go only as far as your personal relationship with the Lord takes you. Some things God will purposefully withhold from you, so that you will not be able to get them from others but will press in and get them from Him. God as your Father is more interested in a relationship with you than in helping you have a "successful" ministry.

I think I hear a question coming: "So if this prophetic thing is about a vibrant relationship with Jesus, are there keys to entering in? What are some of the revelatory keys that the Holy Spirit has given to you?"

I am glad you asked that. There are several.

Opening Our Spiritual Eyes

One of my favorite passages in the New Testament is Ephesians 1:15–19:

I too, having heard of the faith in the Lord Jesus which exists among you, and your love for all the saints, do not cease giving thanks for you, while making mention of you in my prayers; that the God of our Lord Jesus Christ, the Father of glory, may give to you a spirit of wisdom and of revelation in the knowledge of Him. I pray that the eyes of your heart may be enlightened, so that you may know what is the hope of His calling, what are the riches of the glory of His inheritance in the saints, and what is the surpassing greatness of His power toward us who believe.

There was a ten-year period of my life in which I prayed these verses devotionally every day. I still pray them regularly—at least weekly. I am not one who by sovereign gifting one day suddenly began to see visions and have spiritual dreams. These have unfolded gradually over a period of time, partially as a result of praying these verses.

Out of this history, then, let me share some thoughts and reasonings with you.

In this passage we find Paul, a father and apostle, writing a letter to the church at Ephesus. If he needed to pray this prayer for the model New Testament church of that day, how much more do we need to pray it in our day? Paul prayed for these followers in the faith "that the eyes of your heart may be enlightened" (Ephesians 1:18). Other translations render this *that the eyes of your understanding* [or *the eyes of your faith*] *may be flooded with light.* Wonderful!

Now let me give it to you the way I have prayed this prayer devotionally over the years. At times I lay my hands over my heart and launch forth as follows:

Father, my desire is that You give me the Spirit of wisdom, the precious fear of the Lord. I call forth the spirit of revelation on my life. I welcome the fullness of Your Holy Spirit. Grant this to me that I might be enabled supernaturally to know Jesus intimately. Grace me with Your presence so that I may know You beyond informational knowledge. I want to know You, Lord, just as I am known by You.

Now I ask that you open the lens of my heart as You thrust forth shafts of revelatory light into my inner being. Fill my heart with Your glorious presence so that I can know the hope—the positive expectation of good—of Your calling, purposes and destiny in my life. Grace me so that I may be in touch with the rich deposit of Your glorious inheritance placed within me, as I am now a temple of the Holy Spirit. I declare that there will be many deposits and withdrawals out of this treasure chest.

I also pray that Your light, O God, will flood my being so that I may know and experience the surpassing greatness of Your power toward me. Make me into a believing believer. I call this forth for the honor and glory of Your great name in the earth. Amen!

We need to be like youngsters when it comes to believing in the eyes of our faith. I have taught our children over the years that we all have two sets of eyes: our physical set of eyes and those of the spirit. I have also told them that mothers have *three* sets of eyes, including an extra set located in the back of their heads. (That, of course, is how mothers know what is going on behind their backs!)

One evening our family was sitting at the supper table while I was explaining this concept. Tyler was only about four at the time and believed what Daddy was saying. He promptly got up from the table, walked around the other side to where Mom was sitting and parted her hair inquisitively, looking for her extra set of eyes.

"Oh, Tyler, you can't see them now," I said. "They only open up when they have to."

But we believers need the eyes of our hearts opened up at *all* times! Let's pray, then, in the name of the Lord that they be opened up. Call forth the spirit of revelation of the glorious Lord Jesus Christ into your own life, as I have over these many years. Let's each of us be a child and simply believe that we have an extra set of eyes.

Listening, Watching, Waiting

In order to cultivate a spirit of revelation—the prophetic presence of God in our lives—there is another key for us to use.

The fast-paced, instant society of our day is in diametrical opposition to the gentle, quiet spirits we need to be people of revelation. The Holy Spirit is searching eagerly for those on whose hearts He can write, as on tablets, the revelatory words of God.

Listen with me to Proverbs 8:32–36, as wisdom speaks:

"Now, therefore, O sons, listen to me, for blessed are they who keep my ways. Heed instruction and be wise, and do not neglect it. Blessed is the man who listens to me, watching daily at my gates, waiting at my doorposts. For he who finds me finds life, and obtains favor from the LORD. But he who sins against me injures himself; all those who hate me love death."

These words are filled with life! Look at the three key verbs used here: *listen, watch, wait.* To contemporary Christians these words represent art forms almost lost since the early Church. But look at the promises granted to those who will engage in these seemingly passive activities. These actions are, it appears, some of the ways of God that direct us into the life of God.

The resulting promises:

1. You will be supernaturally blessed.
2. You will find life.
3. You will obtain favor from the Lord.

Great promises! Amen?

But the writer of Proverbs also includes a warning: "He who sins against me injures himself." This sounds to me like a self-inflicted wound. To sin is to miss God. If this is the case, it behooves us all the more to learn these less traveled ways of contemplative Christianity: listening, watching and waiting.

These are not hard ways. But they require a simple application of one of the words tossed out in the midst of the Psalms: *selah*.

Yes, just pause for a while. (That is probably what that Hebrew word means.) We must learn to quiet our souls before God in order to commune with Him. Remember, prayer is not just our talking our heads off to God and telling Him all the things we think He has not done! Prayer is not so much something we do as Someone we are with. This requires a rare commodity—actually pushing the pause button!

True prayer involves *selah*. We must pause long enough to quiet ourselves and bend our ears in His direction in order to listen. You cannot hear what another is saying if you are talking all the time. It is impossible! So pause. Wait. Rest. *Slow down.* You will be amazed how this alone will revolutionize your life.

And you will find that these ancient keys open the door so that the light of revelation can come in.

Anticipating That God Is Moving

Joshua had to learn the ways of listening, watching and waiting just as you and I do. He was the choice prophetic vessel of the Lord to lead the next generation into receiving the fulfillment of God's promises. He, too, had to learn the way of kneeling on the promises.

It came about, whenever Moses went out to the tent, that all the people would arise and stand, each at the entrance of his tent, and gaze after Moses until he entered the tent. And it came about, whenever Moses entered the tent, the pillar of cloud would descend and stand at the entrance of the tent; and the LORD would speak with Moses. When all the people saw the pillar of cloud standing at the entrance of the tent, all the people would arise and worship, each at the entrance of his tent. Thus the LORD used to speak to Moses face to face, just as a man speaks to his friend. When Moses returned to the camp, his servant Joshua, the son of Nun, a young man, would not depart from the tent.

Exodus 33:8–11

Young Joshua was getting the best training anyone can ever receive. He was being a doorkeeper in the house of the Lord. When Moses, the man of God, was no longer visible, the rest of the people apparently vacated the scene and went back to their tents and normal activities. The masses went in for the big stuff—the bells and whistles, so to speak. They were content to worship from afar and were not into the passive game of waiting around. After all, wasn't that just wasting time?

But to Joshua another path had been revealed. He learned the lessons of listening, watching and waiting. How was that? Waiting, he would not leave the tent of meeting until Moses came out from having been in the presence of the Lord. Then, watching, Joshua was the first to see the glow on his master's face. Finally, listening, he was the first to hear the report of what had happened beyond the mystical veil. Joshua's view of waiting was different from the view of most of us. He waited in eager anticipation that the Lord was on the move: He was going to speak, to show His form.

So expectation is the final key that changes the waiting game into an opportunity for the Spirit of revelation to be activated.

An Opportunity Awaits You!

How badly do you want to see a prophetic Church arise? How much do you want the Church to take her rightful position in the context of secular society? Are you willing to do the little things necessary to capture God's presence and be a person of revelation?

A test awaits us all—and an unprecedented opportunity. The world is looking for answers. But will we get off the fast production line of frantic living long enough to receive something that can be heard? God's voice rings with another sound. It is the sound of holiness. The sound of consecration. The sound of revolution. The sound of revelation.

What would it be like for people to have Holy Spirit–inspired prayers resting in their hearts waiting to be echoed back into the throne room of God? How much change would happen if the Spirit of revelation were wedded with holy, persistent, believing petitions shot like arrows heavenward?

There is a call going out, sound and sure. The Holy Spirit is searching for new recruits in the army of God. The Lord has put out a big sign for us each to read: *Wanted: A Generation of Prophetic People.* Yes, such people are desired by God—searched for and desperately needed. A great hunting expedition is underway. The Hound of Heaven is on the loose, sniffing out His prey. We are His targets and He is seeking us with overpowering love and sending out His clarion call. Wanted: a prophetic people filled with the spirit of wisdom and revelation in the knowledge of the glorious Lord Jesus Christ.

Why is this so important? It is not only important; it is necessary if we are to kneel on the promises effectively. How else will we know which of the chocolates from the Russell Stover box we are to pick? Do we select just any of the promises from God's Word to hang on our refrigerators or mirrors and pray back to Him? We will look at this and other concepts in the very next chapter.

First, though, will you sign up right now to be a Medad or Eldad for your generation? Will you dare to take God's revelatory presence into the marketplace and affect the world as no generation ever has before?

The velvet warriors are arising and moving forward on their knees. I think I can hear them travailing as they cry for God's prophetic presence to be flung on them as it was on the elders of Moses' day: "More, Lord! Don't forget me!"

PRACTICAL APPLICATIONS—MAKING IT REAL!

- As directed by 1 Corinthians 14:1, seek after the prophetic gift in Jesus' name.
- Research the Scriptures on visions. Ask the Lord to release them to you.
- Go to a prophetic conference to receive further impartation by the Holy Spirit.
- Meditate on Ephesians 1:15–19, praying this back to the Father every day for the next 21 days.
- Cultivate a spirit of revelation by inviting the presence of the Holy Spirit. Then listen, watch and wait to see what the Lord will do.

RECOMMENDED READING

User-Friendly Prophecy by Larry Randolph (Destiny Image, 1998)

Developing Your Prophetic Gifting by Graham Cooke (Sovereign World, 1994)

THE PROPHETIC
INTERCESSORY
TASK

"The great serpent has coiled himself
around the globe, and who shall set the world free from
him?"[1] This was the message from the "prince of preachers," Charles Spurgeon.

If the serpent had a strong grip in Spurgeon's day, what
can be said about our own? Is the grip of the enemy the
reason a new breed of radical, fierce, yet humble and broken intercessors is emerging on the scene? Remember
Psalm 24:1: "The earth is the LORD's, and all it contains."
We are seeing a joining together of the offices of priest and
prophet. After years of observing the ravages of the serpent's hold, it is time for a company of anointed prophetic
intercessors to come forth and lay hold of God's promises
for our generation.

A Widow Called Anna

One of the most significant yet hidden vessels of the New Testament is the prophetess Anna. After seven years of married life, she was suddenly widowed. We do not know how she lost her husband, if she had children or whether she was left all alone. All we are told is that this sacrificial woman, now age 84, extravagantly devoted the rest of her years to the ministry of prayer and fasting, waiting in the Temple for the coming of the Messiah.

> There was a prophetess, Anna the daughter of Phanuel, of the tribe of Asher. She was advanced in years, having lived with a husband seven years after her marriage, and then as a widow to the age of eighty-four. And she never left the temple, serving night and day with fastings and prayers.
>
> Luke 2:36–37

We do not know the age at which Anna married. In all likelihood she was young, possibly seventeen or even younger. If so, she was widowed by age 24 and then devoted the next sixty years of her life to priestly intercession. In the event that she married a little later in life than was normal for her culture, let's say at 37, then she was widowed at 44 and had spent forty years waiting on God. Or say she got married late in life, at 67. By the time her husband departed, she was the ripe old age of 74. That would mean she had spent ten years in the Temple.

Whew! Whether it was ten years or forty or sixty, she had been at the Temple for a long time, never leaving but crying out to the Lord day and night with prayer and fasting. Anna must have been consumed with a burning passion sustained those many long years in what some would consider a state of inactivity.

Like you, I have seen numerous prayer ministries start but few continue. It takes a prophetic vision to continue such a ministry long term. You need a clear revelation of your target, purpose and goal. Prayer ministries that endure over a period of years, I have found, are those that operate from a context of inspiration. But what inspires them? Burdens and crises come and go. What motivates intercessors or intercessory groups over the long haul?

Only one thing. Like the praying prophetess Anna—and like David, the shepherd-king—we must have a consuming vision of the One we serve. First and foremost we need a vision of our Lord Himself. After all, He is the goal and prize of life.

What Was Her Prophetic Ministry?

In what way can Anna be considered a prophetess? The Scripture does not tell us that she wore a coat of camel's hair or ate locusts and wild honey. I doubt that she pointed a long, snarling finger at people and said brazenly, "Thus saith the Lord!" revealing the secret sins of their hearts. We have no clue that she ever confronted the prophets of Baal like Elijah of old or called down fire from heaven. In fact, we find not even one recorded prophecy from this devout woman.

If she did not give personal prophetic words, then what was her prophetic ministry? She was a woman of the secret place, not with a public ministry at all but interceding in keeping with the purposes of God for her generation. The expression of her prophetic ministry was her enduring intercession. She was a prophetic, intercessory Jesus fanatic!

When Joseph and Mary brought eight-day-old Jesus to the Temple to present Him to the Lord,

> At that very moment [Anna] came up and began giving thanks to God, and continued to speak of Him to all those who were looking for the redemption of Jerusalem.
>
> Luke 2:38

123

Undoubtedly Anna's intercessory burden had included searching through the prophetic promises that had not yet been fulfilled. This verse in Luke tells us that she "continued to speak of [Jesus] to all those who were looking for the redemption of Jerusalem." You see, Anna was looking for a Deliverer, the Messiah, the hope of Israel. She was one of a special task force of prophetic intercessors whom God had ordained for that generation. They were the ones who were listening and watching for the Lord's appearing. Like Joshua they were waiting at the doorway of the tent of meeting in hopes that they would be the first to see the shining forth of the Lord's great presence. Anna was doubtless praying through those beloved prophetic promises of a coming Messiah.

Wanted: A Bunch of Holy Ghost P.U.S.H.ers!

The Lord is searching for an "Anna Company" in our day, intercessors who will pray through the promises of the Second Coming of our lovely Lord and Messiah. Who will pave the way for the coming of the Lord? New recruits are wanted and the Holy Spirit is sending out invitations today. Have you signed and returned yours?

Many of the greatest intercessors of our time have been women. Their sensitivity of spirit, their passion for the things of God, the readiness with which they yield their hearts to Him to plead His cause—all position women for this great calling. It was a woman who anointed Christ prophetically beforehand for burial. Women remained at the cross when the rest of the disciples fled. Women were the first to proclaim, "He is risen!"

The real issue, of course, is not whether you are male or female. To be part of this prophetic, intercessory "Anna Company," all you need is an ever-growing conviction of the purposes of God and a desire to pray through God's prom-

124

ises until you see them fulfilled. These revelatory warriors know how to P.U.S.H.—*Pray Until Something Happens!*

In our day and time the Holy Spirit is drawing together a people who will stand united in a congregation, city or region. God is wooing ones and twos to find one another as covenant prayer partners. He is summoning the leaders in an area to stand together and fight. He is calling all of us in His Body to join hands and collectively take our places until the promises of a great, end-time visitation for our generation have come to pass.

Let us arise, O Church, put off our slumber and cry out until our eyes, like Anna's two thousand years ago, behold Christ. It is time for a congregation of Holy Ghost P.U.S.H.ers to show up on the scene.

Defining Our Terms

Let's summarize a few thoughts on the *priest*, the *prophet* and the task of *prophetic intercession* before we dive off the board into the deep end of the pool.

The job of the *priest* is to plead the needs of the people before the Lord. In the intercessory task he does not represent only himself, but he carries the stones of the twelve tribes of Israel on his heart. In the same way, when we fulfill our priestly duty of standing before the Lord, we represent not only ourselves, but we carry the burdens, needs and cares of others as living stones before our majestic God. Our hearts pulsate with the needs of our cities, congregations and nations. As New Testament priests, we represent others to God.

What is the job of the *prophet?* He represents the interests of God to the people. Having stood in the council of the Almighty, the prophet releases a clarion call to the people of what is in God's heart at the moment. The prophetic person releases words, thoughts, messages and inspirations of that which is beating in the heart of God for right now.

What is *prophetic intercession?* It is the place where the ministry of the priest and prophet unite. A passage in Jeremiah wonderfully portrays this: "If they are prophets, and if the word of the LORD is with them, let them now entreat the LORD of hosts . . ." (Jeremiah 27:18). Prophetic persons do not simply pronounce the word of the Lord only; they pray the promise back to Him! In so doing they actually give birth to it and bring it into being.

Prophetic intercession, therefore, paves the way for the fulfillment of the prophetic promise.

How Does Prophetic Intercession Work?

Every unfulfilled promise of God made to His people is to be pleaded by the Holy Spirit through clay vessels like you and me before God's throne. In prophetic intercession the Spirit of God pleads the covenant promises made throughout history and requires that they be enacted in our day. This inspired form of intercession is the urge to pray, given by the Holy Spirit, for a situation or circumstance about which you may have little knowledge in the natural. But you are praying the prayer request that is on the heart of God. He nudges you to pray so that He can intervene. The Holy Spirit Himself, our personal Guide, directs you to pray in a divine manner so as to bring forth His will on earth as it already is in heaven.

"Now say that again?" you are asking.

Prophetic intercession is the ability to receive a prayer request from God and pray it back to Him in a divinely anointed manner. God's hand comes on you and He imparts His burden to you. This revelatory praying combines the spiritual disciplines we talked about in the last chapter—listening, watching, waiting, praying for God to open our spiritual eyes, anticipating that He is already at work—with the grace gifts of the Holy Spirit. We walk it out by waiting on the Lord in order to hear His voice and receive His burden—whether it is His Word, a concern, warning, condition, vision or promise—that we then pray back to Him in God-inspired, God-directed intercession.

Do you remember my asking at the end of the last chapter how we know which of the chocolates we get to pick out of the Russell Stover box? We let God do the selecting! We do not take one of those plastic loaves of bread with Bible verses inside and randomly select a verse to pray through. No, we combine waiting, listening and reading the Scriptures, letting the Holy Spirit bring to our awareness the promise that is on His heart at that moment. We let God's heartbeat pulsate in our own beings. Isn't that exciting?

Any message—whether it is preached truth, prayed burden or spontaneous utterance—is prophetic only if it comes from God and brings a generation into the knowledge of the heart of God for our time. Prophetic intercession asks not only that men and women make decisions for Christ; it assumes the larger boundary of the great purposes of God. We plead for the maturity of Christ in those who respond—that the new society of redeemed mankind expand to the ends of the earth. This place where priest and prophet unite calls "for the earth [to] be filled with the knowledge of the glory of the LORD, as the waters cover the sea" (Habakkuk 2:14).

Prophetic intercession does not always take place in a prayer room. As a believer receives a burden from the Lord, which can happen anyplace at all, he or she responds by expressing this desire for change back to Him. Sometimes this is accompanied by, or followed by, distinct prophetic actions demonstrated before God, others and the world, as well as before the accuser of the brethren and the hosts of darkness. And some of these activities include on-site location praying.

Let me share an inspiring example of this kind of activity.

A Costly Example

A friend of mine, Norm Stone, was an Assembly of God pastor in Appleton City, Wisconsin. On November 7, 1983, he was attending a conference in which a call was issued for those who had cold hearts and needed more of the Lord. Norm found himself at the front asking God for mercy and to change his heart.

Then it happened. In his heart he heard the voice of the Holy Spirit. It had a ripping effect. The words challenged and changed Norm's heart and, as a result, his life and ministry underwent a major change of direction.

Here is a portion of what Norm heard that life-changing day:

The Lord said to me: "They're killing My children. Will you help Me stop them? Every day their shed blood cries unto Me from the earth . . . as their broken and lifeless bodies are being aborted from the sanctuaries . . . those whom I have desired to bring forth, by whose faith My kingdom would have been exalted. The greatest attack ever waged against My kingdom and My creation is now being fought against the innocent and defenseless. The most insidious scheme ever conceived in the pits of hell has come upon you. This could only have happened because of the hardness of your hearts and the callousness of your spirits. Turn your hearts back again towards Me, and I will give you a heart of flesh. . . . Then your heart will weep as Mine does and your soul will break with pain—as you do, you, too, will start to hear the cries.

"You thought this was a civil rights issue to be decided in the courts of the land, but you are wrong! It is not an issue of rights and liberties; *it is a spiritual battle.* The strongholds of Satan must be broken. He has deceived the people. . . . He has deceived you. He told you lies and you believed them . . . but now it is time to change.

"Take up your sling, gird yourself about and come against this giant . . . and I will give you victory. Say to it, 'You have come this day with your wisdom and strength, but I come against you *in the name of the Lord Jesus Christ, the Son of the living God,* whom you have defied. This day will the Lord deliver you into our hands. You will be smitten and destroyed—so all may know who is the Lord God.'"[2]

As a result of this prophetic word, Norm and his wife, Judy, resigned their pastoral post and launched on a brave adventure. The Lord commissioned Norm to start a ministry called Walk Across America for Life. He was instructed to conduct seven prayer walks across the continental United States, carrying "Baby Choice," a maturely formed aborted child. From my last recollection, Norm was finishing his fifth walk across America.

This faith ministry is one of the highest forms of prophetic intercession I know of in this generation. Based out of Spokane, Washington, with no backing of any denomination or group, this brave family walks in heat, wind and storms to pray, repent and call forth a pricking of the hardened conscience of the Church in America and of the nation as a whole.

Would that we, too, would hear what Norm heard on that pivotal day! O God, smite our hearts with what smites Yours.

"To Breathe Together"

Ours is the privilege of entering into the intercession of Christ, yielding ourselves to Him so that He can function in His priestly ministry before the Father. In prayer we become laborers with Christ and enter into partnership with the Creator of the universe!

The burden of prophetic intercession begins as a flame and grows into a consuming fire as the revelation concerning the purposes of God for our generation increases. It might start as an inner conviction of His will, a sudden awareness of His nearness or hearing the condition of a situation that triggers a response in the prophetic spirit.

All prophetic intercession carries the feeling of something struggling to be born. The heart of the intercessor becomes the womb in which God's prophetic purposes fight to come forth. In this place the struggle between old traditions and new beliefs takes place. As we engage in the revelatory activity of hearing God's voice, we become convinced that a radical revolution of the Christian faith is near. The prophetic intercessor conspires with God for the release of His glory in the earth.

The word *conspire* means literally "to breathe together." It expresses the most intimate joining of life. When God created man from the dust of the earth, He "breathed into his nostrils the breath of life; and man became a living being" (Genesis 2:7). The Hebrew word here translated *breathed* can mean "to breathe violently." This suggests the intensity of cost and effort involved in giving birth. Such was the occasion when there was the sound of a violent wind filling the Upper Room as God sent His Spirit upon and into His newborn Church.

Prophetic intercession is our conspiring together with God, "breathing violently" into situations through prayer to bring forth life. When God's people in community have the spirit of grace and supplication poured out on them (see Zechariah 12:10), they share a joint sense of divine possibility and become excited that circumstances are about to change. The old limits and expectations of what God wants to accomplish are radically overturned.

Prayer embraces new horizons, challenges and possibilities. Suddenly intercessors are liberated from considering conditions from a merely human perspective. As Ephesians 2:6 tells us, we have been "raised . . . up with [Christ], and seated . . . with Him in the heavenly places." These focused warriors now begin to peer intently from a heavenly vantage point. They see with the discerning eyes of the

Holy Spirit. Their intercession assumes a revelatory dimension. As they gather up the promises God has willed for their day and age, they stake claim to them tenaciously in the judicial courts of heaven.

"This all sounds great, Jim," you are saying. "But can you help to drive the point home?"

I would be glad to. Let me share another treasure from my war chest.

Waging Prophetic Warfare

Here we were, spending hours together interceding in the Ukrainian Pentecostal Church in lower Manhattan where my new friend and fellow prophetic intercessor Richard Glickstein pastored a Sunday evening congregation called One Accord. Under the mandate of our senior statesman, Dick Simmons, this group of prophetic intercessors was calling on God early one morning in the fall of 1987 for mercy on our nation.

We had come together from different parts of the United States—Richard from New York City; Dick from Bellingham, Washington; Richard's friend of many years, David Fitzpatrick, a passionate, focused pastor from Michigan; a dear prophetic friend I had brought with me, Kevin Nolker, from the church I formerly pastored in Warrensburg, Missouri; and, of course, myself.

Our nation was embroiled in a hair-raising conflict in the Persian Gulf. Iran and Iraq had been at war for a decade, and it was spilling over into the entire Persian Gulf region. Oil was the precious commodity that the U.S. needed, but the Gulf, which American ships traversed, had been laid with explosive mines. It was an intense time, with President Ronald Reagan squaring off with the Iranian Shiite head of state, Ayatollah Ruholla Khomeini. This was the setting and part of the reason the Lord had led us to intercede.

Under Dick's leadership we met at 5 A.M. on September 23, 1987, to call on the name of the Lord. Different groups of people came and went that early morning until around ten o'clock, as we sought the face of God.

A Map of the Middle East

I was sprawled out on the floor under the front pew of the sanctuary for those five hours, somewhat hidden away. I prayed quietly the entire time using the gift of tongues (see 1 Corinthians 12:10; 14:1–4, 15–16; Jude 20). While praying in the Spirit, I kept seeing in my mind's eye a picture of a map of the Middle East. I would pray and watch, watch and pray, trying to get a clearer view of what this map was and an understanding of what to do with what I was seeing.

As I lay on the floor, praying in tongues and seeing the map, "knowings" were coming to me. I had the conviction that, humanly speaking, circumstances were critical. As I kept peering at the map, I saw something that looked like a tiny island nation. I could see letters spelling out *B–a–h–r–a–i* and then a final letter. I could not tell if it was an *n* or an *m*. But it would not go away! I sensed in the Holy Spirit that there was a U.S. military presence in this tiny nation, which in those pre–Gulf War days I had never heard of. I also knew that Iran, under the influence of the prince of Persia (mentioned in Daniel 10:13), was about to release a preemptive attack against the U.S. on this island that could catapult the world into World War III before God's appointed time.

A heavy thought! But it would not go away.

So I prayed, I watched and I listened to the others intercede. Still the picture and impressions would not leave.

As our time of intercession was winding to a close, I stood to my feet and said sheepishly, "Hey, guys, I have something to share." I went ahead and told them just what I have presented to you. Then I asked for their counsel and suggested that we pray.

They responded, to my great comfort, "First of all, we don't even know if such a place exists. Secondly, if it does, we don't know if the U.S. even has a military presence there. But we do have a history with you and we trust you. So let's pray and see what happens."

And we did.

Clothed with Supernatural Authority

There we were, on a Holy Ghost hunt-and-search party! But it was no party; it was serious business. I was pacing the floor and ended up on the platform standing behind the podium. The brothers followed me there and laid their hands on me.

At once it seemed as though I was clothed with supernatural authority, and a missile of declaration shot out of my mouth. I was as astonished as anyone at what came forth! For about fifteen seconds I was clothed with power—long enough for the Holy Spirit to launch from our midst a weapon of prophetic warfare.

I shouted, "I command the prince of Persia, which is coming against the U.S. military presence on the tiny nation of *B–a–h–r–a–i–something*, to be bound, in Jesus' name!"

That was it. But something happened. We all knew it.

Then, just as quickly as that supernatural authority came, it also lifted. We all looked at one another and decided to do something really spiritual—go get something to eat!

But as we exited the church about ten o'clock and headed to our favorite Russian restaurant in lower Manhattan for a late breakfast, I could not stand it.

"I have to find a library or something," I told my buddies, "and see if such a place exists."

New York University was right across the street, but I kept walking with my friends. Then, to my great delight, we happened on a newsstand. There, sitting on the rack, was a strange-looking newspaper, peach in color. The front-page headline read, *Tehran Threatens to Retaliate against U.S. for Ship Attack.* In the middle of the page the sub-headline stated, *American Navy in Second Confrontation.* Then it showed a map of the Middle East and spoke of the U.S. Naval Command in a place called Bahrain, an archipelago of islands in the Persian Gulf.

There it was, right in front of my eyes! Captivated, I bought a copy of the paper, called *The Financial Times*, a European business newspaper. (I still have it to this day.) Although no American newspaper that I ever saw carried this report, the lead story of *The Financial Times*, dated September 23, 1987, reads:

> In a lengthy address to the U.N. General Assembly on the seventh anniversary of the start of the Gulf war, [Iranian head of state] Khomeini repeatedly denounced the U.N. and the U.N. Security Council in the bitterest of terms. Departing from his prepared text he said, "I want to draw urgent attention to the very grave and immediate danger provoked by the U.S. Administration's latest action which is very dangerous to the whole world. . . . This is a beginning for a series of events, the bitter consequences of which shall not be confined to the Persian Gulf, and the U.S. as the initiator shall bear responsibility for all ensuing events. I declare here that the U.S. shall receive a proper response for this evil act."[3]

Needless to say, I heaved a sigh of relief when I saw this report. Bahrain indeed existed, and God had been directing our praying to avert an escalation of the crisis. The good news is, nothing happened! No retaliation ever occurred. In fact, after this point the conflict began to unravel.

Coincidence? Maybe. We will never know for sure this side of heaven. But I think when the history books of heaven are opened up, we will see that the Holy Spirit was landing on many priestly, prophetic intercessors that day across the global Body of Christ, urging them to pray what was on the heart of God.

Dramatic? You bet! God is waiting on us to take our places before Him—to get in His face!—and then to pray back through intercession the promise of divine intervention.

A Prophetic Appeal for Intercession

In closing this chapter, I would like to present to you a portion of a pertinent prophetic word given by one of the Church statesmen of our day, Jack Hayford, senior pastor of Church On The Way in Van Nuys, California. Although the word was delivered August 1, 1980, it is one of the clearest trumpet sounds I have ever heard.

Read and listen with your heart and see if you do not agree. This word needs to be sounded once again, I believe, in this decade:

> The Lord God would call all of His redeemed in this land to lift up their eyes and look! Over your nation there are leaden skies, clouds of impending judgment which hang heavy with a rain of fury and indignation which this people have brought upon themselves. As sin has risen as a vapor of evil, now clouds of judgment have formed and shall shortly be precipitated in wrath and destruction, except an intercessor rise to hold back the storm.
>
> And so the Lord calls: O Church, cause your words to rise in prayers of intercession unto deliverance. The skies are dropping lower, skies of lead weighted with judgment, but your entry with prayer can save the day. For the Lord would have you see that your intercession, O Church, rises like pillars, extending through prayer and pressing back the impending judgment, pushing the leaden skies upward and backward. Take your place as pillars of prayer, for I would that there be mercy upon this nation rather than judgment; I would there be healing rather than death!
>
> Cause the word to go forth with understanding that My people need not surrender to the storm which threatens. Did I not deliver Nineveh when repentance came? If you

pray ceaselessly until the leaden skies of judgment be lifted by pillars of prayer, then will the light, the glory and the blessing of the Lord flood your land and healing come again. Lift up your voices with praise, raising pillars of intercession, and you shall see the deliverance of God, if you will pray as He directs.[4]

A few years ago I took a train from Heidelberg to Rosenheim, Germany—a six-hour excursion in the middle of the night. While attempting to rest on the train, I kept hearing the gentle voice of the Holy Spirit within. I know He was talking to me as an individual, but He was also imparting a burden for a many-membered band of people to come forth.

Here is what I heard that dear Dove convictingly speak:

Where are My Daniels? Where are My Esthers? Where are My Deborahs? And where are My Josephs?

Repeatedly I heard His piercing, relentless plea:

Where are My Daniels? Where are My Esthers? Where are My Deborahs? And where are My Josephs?

I close out this strategic, pivotal chapter, then, with this plea. I state with conviction that you, reading this book right now, were created "for such a time as this" (Esther 4:14). For such a prophetic intercessory task God brought *you* forth. Will you arise and be one of His radical revolutionaries? Will you be one of the answers to His persistent plea?

You remember the vision I saw, described in the opening chapter, of the velvet warriors moving forward on their knees. Many vacancies exist; you can still sign up. It is not too late to answer the call, volunteer for on-the-job training and be commissioned as one of God's servant-warriors. I think I can hear drumbeats in the background. The march is beginning. Yes, we are kneeling on the promises of God. Humble, persistent warriors are aligning themselves under God's command in order to hear His next orders. In fact, I think I can hear another sound coming forth: "Calling all watchmen! Calling all watchmen! The time has come for you to mount your walls."

Who will answer the call? Will you join me in making history?

PRACTICAL APPLICATIONS—MAKING IT REAL!

- The Lord is searching for an "Anna Company" that will pray through prophetic promises of the coming Messiah until He comes. What are some promises of His coming that you could pray?
- Ask the Holy Spirit to direct you to a covenant prayer partner.
- Pastors, join together across the Body for the task of intercession for your city.
- As an act of prophetic intercession, wait before God in order to hear or receive His burden (His Word, concern, warning, condition, vision or promise), and then respond back to the Lord and to the people with appropriate actions.

RECOMMENDED READING

Intercessory Prayer by Dutch Sheets (Regal, 1996)
Possessing the Gates of the Enemy by Cindy Jacobs (Chosen, 1991)

7

CALLING ALL
WATCHMEN

      One weekend in June 1991 I found myself leading a small prayer retreat in a beautiful, hidden-away spot in the state of Kansas. Our schedule was simple. We had no planned times of teaching, just times of waiting on God. All those precious hours were set apart for worship, intercession and reflection. I was determined in that every hour we would have two or three people "keeping the watch." The Lord wonderfully blessed our simple attempts by releasing the sweetness of His presence as we gathered in His name.

      Since the Lord has often awakened me at two in the morning to watch with Him for an hour or so, I took my normal 2:00–3:00 A.M. hour during the retreat setting.

      During my brief watch, the Holy Spirit gave me a short but clear vision of a plow sitting among other old farm implements.

      I asked the Lord, "What is this?"

The internal voice of the Holy Spirit replied, *These are the ancient tools.*

My next question, obviously, was, "What are the ancient tools?"

Another phrase came to me immediately: *The watch of the Lord. I will restore the ancient tools of the "watch of the Lord." It has been used and will be used again to change the expression of Christianity across the face of the earth.*

These words resonated within my being and left a deposit of faith within me. I knew God would restore the ancient "watch of the Lord" to the Church in our day. *It has been used and will be used again.* These words have rumbled around within me.

Yes, the watch of the Lord has been basically a forgotten model of prayer. It is a lost tool that needs the rust of inactivity scoured off and its edge sharpened. We need this great tool (as well as every tool we can get!) in the utility chest of every congregation and city.

Due to the glaring lack of teaching of this subject, I set out to learn all I could on this overlooked pattern of prayer. My fascinating search led me to a tremendous treasure chest of knowledge in Scripture and Church history. Eventually the adventure led me to the Moravian Christians of the 1700s who founded a village in Saxony (today, an eastern portion of Germany) called Herrnhut, which means "the Lord's watch." In February 1993 my wife and I led a prayer expedition to the community of Herrnhut, where we had a dramatic encounter calling forth the spirit of prayer that had rested on those dedicated Christians many years before.

Those evangelical Czech brothers and sisters were dedicated to "win for the Lamb the rewards of His suffering," and wedded the truths of missions and prayer. Those persecuted believers stewarded an around-the-clock prayer watch that lasted more than one hundred years. While visiting a museum in Herrnhut, I read the following in a letter from John Wesley to Nicolaus Ludwig, Count of Zinzendorf, the young nobleman who provided land for these Protestant refugees from persecution: "When will this Christianity cover the earth as the waters cover the seas?"

Few English-speaking people today use the term *the watch of the Lord*. It is as though there has been a moratorium on the subject over the generations. Books seldom discuss this way of prayer. Yet the importance of the watch of the Lord, even the spiritual discipline of watching in prayer, is very important to the plans and order of God. In several gospel accounts Jesus commanded us to "watch" with Him (see Matthew 24:42; Mark 13:33–37; Luke 21:36; all KJV), particularly in the time called the last days.

But what does the word *watch* mean?

Be Vigilant! Be Awake!

In New Testament Greek the word for *watch* is *gregoreo*. It means "to be awake or vigilant." This is where we get the term *prayer vigil*. Webster's defines this meaning of *watch* as "keeping awake in order to guard; to give a close observation; to be on the alert; or to be alert."

Matthew 26:41 gives Jesus admonition to His slumbering disciples in the Garden of Gethsemane: "Keep watching and praying, that you may not enter into temptation; the spirit is willing, but the flesh is weak." (Similar words are recorded in Mark 14:38.) Paul's counsel is: "Continue in prayer, and watch in the same with thanksgiving" (Colossians 4:2, KJV). Luke 21:36 admonishes us, "Watch ye therefore, and pray always, that ye may be accounted worthy to escape" (KJV). The NASB renders this: "Keep on the alert at all times, praying in order that you may have strength to escape all these things that are about to take place."

Perhaps the Holy Spirit is trying to get a point across! Watching is related to having strength to overcome.

Two Main Uses

We find quickly that the term *watch* is used in two primary ways. One describes an inner spiritual attitude of alertness or being awake in one's heart. The other refers to a specific form of praying. Thus the term *spiritual awakening* has been used in Church history to describe when the Church in a given generation is awakened from sleep and arises to affect every sphere of life.

We must join these two meanings together and become vigilant in our prayer watching. We must join our works with our faith, go into the world and wake it up with the powerful truth of the Gospel of the Kingdom.

Perhaps intercessory watchmen can be compared to the night watchmen or guards of our day. They patrol our cities and guard important places of business while others sleep. They keep awake so that thieves or intruders cannot gain entrance. If a thief does attempt to break in and enter, he will be caught if someone is on the alert. You see, someone is awake on behalf of another.

Watching in the spirit is a powerful tool to bring us into deeper personal communion with our Lord. I love listening, watching and waiting for my Beloved. Watching can also be a laser beam of the Holy Spirit in spiritual warfare, and a form of intercession. Watching is to sleeping as fasting is to eating—a sacrifice we make on behalf of another.

Continuous Movement

There is another reason we must be awake or vigilant. In the kingdom of darkness and in the Kingdom of light, there is continuous movement. The very first mention of the Holy Spirit in the Bible reveals His nature: "The Spirit of God was moving over the surface of the waters" (Genesis 1:2). God the Holy Spirit has been moving from the beginning and has never stopped.

But the devil and his demons are also in constant motion. Remember, Jesus told us that once a spirit has been cast out of its abode, it seeks rest but cannot find it. If the demonic forces do not locate another habitation, they try to come back with more of their buddies (see Matthew 12:43–45).

We find an Old Testament development of this understanding in the book of Daniel. The prophet was told by his heavenly emissary: "I shall now return to fight against the prince of Persia; so I am going forth, and behold, the prince of Greece is about to come" (Daniel 10:20). The prince of Persia, a demonic power, had already opposed this angelic messenger (see verse 13), and now the prince of Greece was about to enter the scene as a major world power. As the book of Daniel parts the curtains of history for us, we are given a larger view of the truth of this movement among the supernatural forces. Spirits, you see, are constantly on the move.

Neither God and His army nor Satan and his league are stagnant. We must open up our spiritual eyes in order to watch and see what activity is occurring. While the enemy comes "to steal, and kill, and destroy" (John 10:10), he does not always use the same tactic to accomplish his will. Paul said, "We are not ignorant of [Satan's] schemes" (2 Corinthians 2:11). Let's keep awake, then, in order to guard. Peter understood this concept and warned the saints of the enemies prowling about in the spirit realm:

> Be self controlled and alert. Your enemy the devil prowls around like a roaring lion looking for someone to devour. Resist him, standing firm in the faith, because you know that your brothers throughout the world are undergoing the same kind of sufferings.
>
> 1 Peter 5:8–9, NIV

Here we are exhorted, in the words of the NASB, to have "a sober spirit," "to be on the alert," to "resist" the devil and to stand firm. The devil does not stand still. Don't be caught off guard by expecting the same stuff each time from the same ol' enemy. He is smarter than that!

A Military Perspective

Historically and biblically, *the watch* is a military term used to define segments of time during which sentries guarded their cities from harm, alerted the citizens of approaching enemies or even welcomed ambassadors of goodwill. These guards remained in their places until their watches were complete and other watchmen took their places.

Isaiah gives us a historic glance of the task of these sentries:

> Thus the Lord says to me, "Go, station the lookout, let him report what he sees. When he sees riders, horsemen in pairs, a train of donkeys, a train of camels, let him pay close attention, very close attention." Then the lookout called, "O Lord, I stand continually by day on the watchtower, and I am stationed every night at my guard post. Now behold, here comes a troop of riders, horsemen in pairs." . . . The oracle concerning Edom. One keeps calling to me from Seir, "Watchman, how far gone is the night? Watchman, how far gone is the night?" The watchman says, "Morning comes but also night. If you would inquire, inquire; come back again."
>
> Isaiah 21:6–9, 11–12

In these Scriptures we see clearly depicted the task of the sentries. They are called to report what they see. They take their stations, guard the city and watch to see who or what is coming near. For example, a declaration of approaching horsemen is given.

Likewise, we need guards on the walls of our cities and regions who will take their places. These watchmen will protect the community of believers from oncoming attacks of the enemy. Oh, how we need this ministry restored in our day!

Specific Watches Listed in Scripture

In the Hebrew culture, the beginning of a new day occurred at sunset. The watch was divided into three-hour sections, with the first watch from 6:00 to 9:00 P.M. Since the Church has Jewish-Hebrew roots, this understanding was carried over into New Testament times.

Watching While Fishing

We observe the Hebrew concept of the watch in Mark 6:48: "At about the fourth watch of the night, [Jesus] came to them, walking on the sea." This early morning watch—between 3:00 and 6:00 A.M.—was the time much of the disciples' fishing took place. Could there be a hint given here to successful spiritual fishing as well? Possibly one of the missing parts of our fishing techniques for the souls of men and women is "watching." We just might catch something!

The Moravians had a pattern: No one worked unless someone prayed. If we joined this concept to our spiritual service, let alone to our natural acts of service, I believe we would see far greater results. Let's add watching to our fishing and pull in nets loaded and overflowing!

Breaking the Powers of Darkness

Numerous examples are given to us in Scripture of those who maintained some kind of hourly prayer vigil. Various distinctions can also be found in the different purposes fulfilled by these various watches.

Exodus 14:24 describes this scene: "It came about at the morning watch, that the LORD looked down on the army of the Egyptians through the pillar of fire and cloud and brought the army of the Egyptians into confusion." Many intercessors comment that the early morning watch, right before the sun rises, is a time of contention. In the realm of spiritual warfare, this is often the time that witchcraft practitioners release their curses.

On God's side of things, the early morning watch is a time to break the power of darkness and call forth the light of Jesus to overpower it. Early morning is a time to enthrone the one true God and declare His wonders through the power of praise. Psalm 101:8 spells this out plainly: "Every morning I will destroy all the wicked of the land, so as to cut off from the city of the LORD all those who do iniquity." Let the morning watchmen take their places!

Waiting for the Light

Psalm 130:5–6 beautifully depicts another aspect of these various watches: "I wait for the LORD, my soul does wait, and in His word do I hope. My soul waits for the LORD more than the watchmen for the morning; indeed, more than the watchmen for the morning." My heart aches within me every time I read this verse. A cry arises within me saying, "Yes, I will wait for the Lord."

Here we are called to a higher task than simply looking into the enemy's camp. We are given a divine motivation that goes far beyond just clicking off the passage of hours. Get a higher picture of this thing; we get to look into God's camp and see what He intends to do. Isn't it awesome? We get to wait for the appearing of the Lord and call forth His manifest presence. Oh, the glory of His brilliant presence!

The Corporate Hour of Prayer

Acts 3:1 tells us there were set hours of corporate prayer in the early Church: "Peter and John were going up to the temple at the ninth hour, the hour of prayer." When 3:00 P.M. rolled around, Peter and John knew they could get in on a prayer meeting, so they joined the other believers in this corporate hour of prayer. It was common knowledge and the practice of the first-century Church.

Imagine how tremendous it would be if you went to visit another city and knew that at a certain hour there would be a public time of intercession. No matter what part of the country you were visiting, you could locate the believers in that city and know you could get in on a prayer meeting.

May this, too, be restored in our churches and cities.

Three Times a Day

Late in the summer or early in the fall, you can hear some serious grunting and groaning going on all across the United States. What is this strange sound? I hear it coming from young people—teenage guys, in fact, at football practice mornings, afternoons and sometimes even evenings. No pain, no gain, they say. The team that sweats together stays together—something like that.

Others have released the sounds of agony more than once a day, too—God's velvet army throughout the generations. King David depicts this model for us in Psalm 55:16–17, an inspiration for many modern-day churches and ministries: "As for me, I shall call upon God, and the LORD will save me. Evening and morning and at noon, I will complain and murmur, and He will hear my voice."

This is the model Mike Bickle and the leadership team at Metro Christian Fellowship in Kansas City have followed for more than fifteen years now. Morning, noon and evening, the sacrifices of prayer and praise and the sounds of deliverance ascend to the Lord. What a blessing! May our Captain hear the sounds of many more "practices" as the velvet army grows in strength and numbers from shore to shore. Remember, the team that sweats together. . . .

The prophet Daniel was one who helped pioneer this model when he, too, lifted his voice three times daily:

[Daniel] entered his house (now in his roof chamber he had windows open toward Jerusalem); and *he continued kneel-*

ing on his knees three times a day, praying and giving thanks before his God, as he had been doing previously.

Daniel 6:10 (emphasis added)

Sounds as if this tune of kneeling on the promises is not a new one after all! It has been sung for a long time. Not only do we get to kneel occasionally, but we can join others who have gone before us.

The Three Stations of the Watchmen

By this time it is obvious that God wants to clue us in on His plans and tip us off concerning the enemy's schemes. But we can have a different vantage point according to what position we hold on the wall.

I have walked the wall surrounding the Old City of Jerusalem. Each section stands at a different height with a specific lookout point and overlooks a different sector of the city. In this complex maze of religious and architectural wonders, you can see entirely different views of the city. It all depends on your position on the wall.

It is the same for us, getting our read in the Holy Spirit. There are many different angles from which we gain our view. Or, to change the metaphor, each of us brings a piece of the jigsaw puzzle of God, and when the pieces are brought together, we can see the whole. Rick Joyner wonderfully pens this in his book *The Prophetic Ministry:*

> The biblical positions of the watchmen were (1) on the walls of the city (Isaiah 62:6–7), (2) walking about in the city (Song of Solomon 3:3), and (3) on the hills or in the countryside (Jeremiah 31:6). Together these can give us a good picture of the operation of this ministry.
>
> The Lord has called spiritual watchmen today who are to serve in each of these three positions. He has some whose only purpose is to be watching within the church for the movement of the King, and to make a way for Him. These

are also called to recognize and report to the elders any disorderly or unlawful behavior. There are also some who have been given a place of vision that enables them to see both inside and outside of the church. And some watchmen are called mainly to roam around as scouts in the world, able to spot such things as the rise of a new cult or a major persecution against the church.[1]

Praying On-Site with Insight

Among the old implements that have been used in the past to help bring God's people into their promised land is on-site locational prayer. Recall the children of Israel, for instance, circling the city of Jericho.

Across the globe these days God is stirring ordinary believers to pray persistently while walking their cities street by street. Some of these velvet warriors use prearranged strategies. Others tend to be more spontaneous. Some of these prophetic intercessors make wide-ranging appeals, while others pinpoint their petitions like smart bombs for accurate delivery.

Prayer targets vary in distance just as targets of the military do. Some prayer weapons focus on far-reaching points way beyond the intercessors' own homes and neighborhoods. It is hard to stop at your street, so most of these marching prayer commandos eventually burst into prayers for their entire campus, city or nation. No quick fix is envisioned among these street warriors. Most of these prophetic and priestly intercessors do not imagine themselves to be holding flickering candles against an overwhelming darkness. Rather, they light long fuses in anticipation of major explosions of God's love being set off around the globe. Expectancy seems to expand with every mile.

Some Pointers about On-Site Praying

This is not a new approach to an old concept. It is an ancient approach with fresh application for our day. Let me clarify the concept of on-site locational prayer with the following simple points:

1. It is directed intercession: A target is painted and research done on the purposes for which the city was founded, major wars or battles fought, any destiny declared by the founding fathers, offenses and sins committed, etc.
2. It is intentional prayer for a preset period of time.
3. It is on-site intercession in the very places those prayers are expected to be answered.
4. It is prayer with insight. Research and geographical identification are combined with dependence on the Holy Spirit's guidance. The gifts of the Spirit are employed and revelatory insight with wisdom is sought.
5. It is a refreshment, not a replacement, for normal prayer meetings.

Today, in many of our neighborhoods, you can find signs posted stating, *This is a Neighborhood Watch area.* They mean that this residential area is watched at night by its citizens. They are looking out for one another. Wouldn't it be great to have a whole city under the watch of the Holy Spirit? As this form of praying on site with insight grows, maybe we will have entire cities canvassed by prayer walkers. Signs could then be put up that say, *This city is under spiritual surveillance.* Awesome!

May the watchmen come forth, taking their positions on the walls.

The Importance of Journaling

Just as it takes more than a good hammer to build something, so we need to learn about other tools that make the watch of the Lord more effective. Journaling is one of those simple, practical, biblical tools you need to add to your intercessory tool chest. It is a great aid to help you grow in your discernment of the activity of the Holy Spirit in your life. It has been most helpful to Michal Ann and me.

Journaling is simply keeping notes of your prayers, noting God's answers and recording what the Holy Spirit seems to be saying through various channels, including the revelatory gifts. Keeping a spiritual record is a common biblical experience. 1 Chronicles 28:11–19 offers an example of journaling that did *not* become Scripture, thus setting the pattern for our experience today.

God speaks to His children much of the time. Often we do not differentiate His voice from our own thoughts, however, and we are timid about stepping out in faith. If we learn to discern His voice speaking within us, we will be more confident in our walk in the Spirit. Journaling is a practical way of sorting out God's thoughts from our own.

For many the simple discipline of recording what you believe you hear from God is one of the missing steps in the Christian walk of hearing God's voice and seeing His form. Over time you will learn the continuity of the language the Holy Spirit speaks. Proper interpretation will jump many strides forward as you simply add the tool of journaling in your listening, watching and waiting prayer experience.

Lessons from Habakkuk

I will stand on my guard post and station myself on the rampart; and I will keep watch to see what He will speak to me, and how I may reply when I am reproved. Then the LORD answered me and said, "Record the vision and inscribe it on tablets, that the one who reads it may run. For the vision is yet for the appointed time; it hastens toward the goal, and it will not fail. Though it tarries, wait for it; for it will certainly come, it will not delay."

Habakkuk 2:1–3

First, the watchman goes to a quiet place where he can be alone and become still. Second, he quiets himself within by watching to see what the Lord will speak. Last of all, when God does begin to speak, the first thing He says is, "Record the vision." Then Habakkuk writes down what he is sensing in his heart.

Practical Suggestions for Journaling

The following very ordinary guidelines may make your journaling more successful:

1. Find your own quality time and, if possible, use it. Avoid times when you are sleepy, fatigued or anxious.
2. A simple spiral notebook is fine. Even a tape recorder can be good.
3. This is a personal journal. Grammar, neatness and even spelling are not critical issues.
4. Date all entries. State where you were and whom you were with when you had the experience.
5. Include dreams, visions, possible interpretations, personal feelings and emotions in your report.
6. Develop your knowledge of the Bible. *Rhema*, God's immediate word, is tested against the *logos*, the written Word. Include any Scriptures that come to mind.
7. Do not get bogged down with details. This is a summation, not an encyclopedia!
8. Realize that understanding will unfold over time.

Enjoy the journey. This is not intended to be an ordeal. It is just a simple tool to be added to your utility chest.

Walking with Others

As watchmen on the wall, we must remain connected with the others in the Body of Christ. We must not be lone rangers with smoking pistols or shoot at any old thing that shows its head. We must get confirmation on any leadings and sightings and pass them on, if possible, to those in authority. Although, as you have surmised, I highly value the role of the watchman, I also realize the Holy Spirit does speak to more than just you and me. Let's walk with the leaders of our cities, then, and submit our impressions to others. Only then, when confirmation has come and the green light has been given, can we pray for the aversion of the enemy's schemes. "For if the bugle produces an indistinct sound, who will prepare himself for battle?" (1 Corinthians 14:8). We must hear a clear call before jumping into battle.

We need each other. Watchmen need caring pastors. Prophets need the balance of teachers. Pastors need the exhortation of prophets. Elders need watchmen. When each part does its part, then all the parts will work together. But when each part is doing another's part, nothing gets accomplished.

There are overlaps yet distinct differences between the watchmen on the walls of a city and the elders who sit at the gates of that city—those in positions of spiritual authority. Prophetic, intercessory watchmen tune in to what is about to occur and then give a report to the elders at the gate. The elders are then given the authority either to open or close the gates of a city or region to the force that is about to appear (and has already appeared on the revelatory screen). The watchmen communicate what they see and hear. The elders and pastors discern and act in response.

This might sound a bit visionary and lofty. But "where there is no vision, the people perish" (Proverbs 29:18). Don't you think it is about time we implement cooperative flowing together in a city or region? For too long the various ministries in our churches have walked in isolation from and competition with one another. As we have not esteemed and honored the different leadership parts, the Body of Christ has suffered.

153

Trust is the main ingredient needed. But trust comes only by relationships and relationships take time. Each of us has to get out of our own little world and into someone else's. Until the pastors and elders learn to value the intercessory watchmen God has placed in their cities, the enemy will continue to wage successful attacks. But these prophetic watchmen also have to rid themselves of feelings of neglect and rejection and be cleansed from the spirit of offense so their ministries can be received.

One of the blessings that eventually emerged in my former home of Kansas City was the well-orchestrated, citywide prayer effort initiated by Ministries of New Life, an evangelical organization devoted to intercession for the heart of America. There was an understanding and valuing of the different servant giftings functioning together. At times the citywide prayer gatherings would recognize and divide into four groups: pastors, itinerant ministries, praise and worship leaders and intercessors. All four categories were brought together to seek the Lord, to communicate and to fellowship together. What a blessing it was to see each gift valued and received!

How I long to see the divine cooperation of gatekeepers and watchmen flowing together in the purposes of God in every city and nation!

Promises for Those Who Watch

As we conclude this chapter, let's get inspired for the watchman's task by peeking into some of the promises that await those who watch.

Avoiding Temptation

Jesus came back to His sleeping disciples and chided Peter and the others:

"So, you men could not keep watch with Me for one hour? Keep watching and praying, that you may not enter into temptation; the spirit is willing, but the flesh is weak."

Matthew 26:40–41

What a blessed promise we are given! Each of us has weaknesses, but here we are shown the way of escape. Jesus exhorted His disciples to join *watching* with their *praying* so that the spirit man would rise up stronger than the weakness of the flesh. If we, too, do what Jesus counseled His disciples to do, we will succeed. God's Word actually says we will not only overcome temptation but we will avoid being tempted!

"That you may not enter into temptation" is quite a promise to consider. May the way of escape be made evident to each of us as we do what Jesus said to do: "Keep watching and praying."

Consider, too, the value of lifting up a prayer shield on behalf of our spiritual and secular leaders. Watchmen of old could detect beforehand the wiles of the enemy and cut off the attack before it even came into effect. "Keep watching and praying" goes hand in hand with Jesus' direction for us to pray that the Father would "lead us not into temptation, but deliver us from evil" (Matthew 6:13). In private devotions we do this for our own lives, but in intercession we do it on behalf of others.

Clean Garments

Another promise comes from Revelation 16:15: "Behold, I am coming like a thief. Blessed is the one who stays awake and keeps his garments, lest he walk about naked and men see his shame." What a graphic picture is painted here— standing naked in shame before your peers! On the other hand, give close attention to the positive promises listed: deliverance from shame, embarrassment and guilty emotions, and standing before the Lord and others in clean garments. Wonderful!

Do you see the correlation? Watching with prayer can be used as the laundry soap of heaven to get and keep your garments clean. It also ties in with the promise of avoiding temptation. Remember that Jesus is coming for a bride "having no spot or wrinkle or any such thing" (Ephesians 5:27). The intercessory form of watching is an ancient agent used to cleanse the Body of Christ from defilement.

Prepared for His Coming

Do you want to be ready for the Second Coming of Jesus? Do you want to be able to resist and avoid the enemy's attempts to plunder your house? None of us knows when our hour to stand before the Judge of all will come. Whether it be through the Second Coming of our Lord Jesus or through our homegoing by the graduation of death into His presence, let's be prepared.

Matthew 24:42–44 (KJV) gives us a key:

"Watch therefore: for ye know not what hour your Lord doth come. But know this, that if the goodman of the house had known in what watch the thief would come, he would have watched, and would not have suffered his house to be broken up. Therefore be ye also ready: for in such an hour as ye think not the Son of man cometh."

Now that is a promise I want desperately to receive. I want to be ready by virtue of watching.

In fact, the Holy Spirit is awakening the slumbering bride to be prepared for His Second Coming. The Master will truly have an empowered, passionate bride waiting eagerly for Him with her lamps burning brightly with fresh oil (see Matthew 25:1–13).

The Goal

I yearn for the day the devil will be bound and no longer free to roam the earth. Revelation 20:1–3 portrays this glorious event:

> I saw an angel coming down from heaven, having the key of the abyss and a great chain in his hand. And he laid hold of the dragon, the serpent of old, who is the devil and Satan, and bound him for a thousand years.

I have a question for you: What is the chain the angel uses to bind up the serpent, and where did the angel get it? I think this mighty chain is a weapon of spiritual warfare.

Could it be that as our intercessions and watchings arise to the Lord Most High, He in turn commissions one of His angels to go forth? The angel then takes the great chain of prayer from all of Church history and constrains the devil with it. I like to think that the chain in the angel's hand is the great chain of prayer!

As Rick Joyner has stated, "The Lord wants His people to know when He is going to move, when judgment is coming, and when the enemy will come."[2] Oh, may the baton be passed from one watch to another. May true, simple and powerful forms of intercession and guarding take place. May the watchmen come forth and take their places on the walls, crying out to God day and night. May the ancient tool of the watch of the Lord, which has been used in generations past, be restored in our day to help change the expression of Christianity.

With a loud, blaring trumpet placed to my lips, therefore, I am releasing a blast calling forth these guardian watchmen. Let's listen, wait and watch to see what the Lord is saying. Let's walk with others and rebuild the walls of salvation around our cities. Let's kneel vigilantly on the promises.

And let's remember that all guards need ammunition. Now that we are learning to take aim by watching to see what the enemy is doing, it is time to discharge our weapons. We will discover the bullets of the Word of God that must be loaded into our prayer guns in the next chapter, "Reminding God of His Word." So if you are ready, aim, turn to the next chapter, load and be prepared to pull the trigger!

PRACTICAL APPLICATIONS—MAKING IT REAL!

- Take a weekend prayer retreat.
- Pray in the Spirit and ask Him to show you what the Father is doing right now.
- Pastors and leaders, I encourage you and your intercessors to establish a watch of the Lord in your church or city.
- Establish hours of corporate prayer in your church.
- Pray on site with insight with others in strategic locations to break open a way for the King of glory. Use the guidelines given on page 150.
- As a watchman, journal what you hear, feel, see, dream and experience. Refer to the practical suggestions given on page 152.

RECOMMENDED READING

The Lost Art of Intercession by Jim W. Goll (Destiny Image, 1997)

The Watchmen by Tom Hess (MorningStar, 1998)

REMINDING GOD
OF HIS WORD

If you are ready for some ammunition for your gun, then this chapter is loaded with bullets that will knock out the enemy's artillery. But before we load and shoot, I want to take a moment to clean out the barrel—to make sure we know and believe in what we are doing.

Throughout the generations a people have arisen who believe God's Word, the Scriptures, to be true. This is as it should be. They have declared, "God said it. I believe it. That settles it."

The holy Scriptures are indeed the infallible, inspired Word of God. I will fight for that just as much as the next guy. The Bible is our standard for doctrine, salvation and moral conduct. But a couple of problems exist in this overly simplified assertion.

First, it seems to me that some who thump the Bible the hardest are also—at least part of the time—those who experience the life of God the least. I think this is because at least one ingredient has been left out of their recipe. I am convinced that there is more to it than "God said it. I believe it. That settles it."

Sincere people may believe in the inerrancy of Scripture yet deny that God's power and gifts are active today. For many reasons they believe that acts of divine power and the release of the gifts of the Holy Spirit are not necessary or valid for our time. This theological belief system, termed cessationism, affirms belief in God and says that His Word is true. Yet for many reasons it often engenders sterile Christianity.

Sincere statements may be brought forth out of an unbelieving mind that expects nothing, while faith is from the heart. Today, as in all times, the Holy Spirit is looking for believing believers.

I have a word for the cessationist: Cessationism is going to cease! God is on the move. He is baring His holy right arm and demonstrating acts of strength and power that are confounding the wise. Just as Jack Deere, a former associate professor of Old Testament at Dallas Theological Seminary, along with many other evangelicals, has gone through a paradigm shift and been changed by encounters with a supernatural God, so many others also will be surprised by the voice and power of the Holy Spirit in the days ahead.[1]

There is a second problem with this typical three-phase statement. (I am not saying it is wrong; it is incomplete. So please bear with me as I attempt to unfold this principle. We are now cleaning out the barrel of the gun!) It has to do with the overriding theme of this book. A more complete summary statement goes something like this: "God said it. I believe it. We'll pray it and then we'll see it." Many people stop short of the call to pray the Scriptures through—actually to remind God of His Word.

A major missing element in the equation of experiencing the Word of God, then, is praying the Word back to God. Prayer is the force, you see, that revitalizes and energizes

God's Word, with the result that the pray-er receives answers—sometimes dramatic ones—and actually helps to bring about God's purposes on earth. Awesome!

And that brings us back to kneeling on the promises. We must believe God's Word is true, of course. But then we must act on it. So one of the first steps of taking action is asking God to do what He wants to do for us. It is the ancient art of reminding God of His Word.

A Prerequisite: Knowledge of the Book of Promises

In order to remind God of His Word, we must first be intimately acquainted with His precious Book of promises. Get to know your weapon before you use it! The Word of God is as essential to prayer as oxygen is to breathing and nourishment is to health. We must be assured absolutely, therefore, if we are to claim His promises, that the Bible is the Word of God.

This might sound as though I am vacillating. I am not at all. My revised statement also starts with, "God said it. I believe it." First we must believe God's Word is true and remember that it will "not return to [Him] empty" but will accomplish the purpose for which He sent it (Isaiah 55:11).

Why the Bible Is God's Word

Take the time to get to know your weapon well. Let it become comfortable in your hands.

With this train of thought in mind, let's look at the following ten foundational reasons we can know the Bible is the Word of God:

1. Because of its amazing unity.
2. Because of its indestructibility.
3. Because of its historical accuracy.

4. Because of its scientific accuracy.
5. Because of its prophetic accuracy.
6. Because of the reliability of the copying process.
7. Because of its universal appeal.
8. Because of its amazing circulation.
9. Because of its absolute honesty.
10. Because of its power to save.

Joining Prayer and the Word

When I get to heaven, one of the people I want to meet is Andrew Murray—the Dutch Reformed preacher who made a dramatic impact on the nation of South Africa in the nineteenth and early twentieth centuries. The simplicity and piercing quality of his writings have been a guiding light to my own Christian experience.

Let me quote to you from his famous work *With Christ in the School of Prayer* on the subject of joining the Word and prayer:

> "If ye abide in me, and my words abide in you, ask whatsoever ye will, and it shall be done unto you" (John 15:7, KJV). The vital connection between the Word and prayer is one of the simplest and earliest lessons of the Christian life. "I pray—I speak to my Father; I read—my Father speaks to me." Before prayer, God's Word strengthens me by giving my faith its justification and petition. In prayer, God's Word prepares me by revealing what the Father wants me to ask. After prayer, God's Word brings me the answer, for in it the Spirit allows me to hear the Father's voice.
>
> When God reveals Himself in His words, He does indeed give Himself—His love and His life, His will and His power—to those who receive these words, in a reality that surpasses our comprehension. In every promise, He gives us the power to grasp and possess Him. God's Word gives us God Himself.[2]

Is this not what we are all after? As we become intimately acquainted with the Word of God, we become intimately acquainted with the God of the Word. Then, as we meditate and pray God's Word back to Him, the God of the Word takes on wings in the form of the power of the Holy Spirit to enact the Word we have just prayed.

Isn't God's plan awesome? Just think, He lets us ask Him to do what He wants to do for us. What a mystery—and a privilege!

Needed: A Wedding to Occur

Christians who believe in the current-day operation of the gifts of the Spirit need to make sure their arsenal includes one of the foundational evangelical truths: the integrity of the Scriptures as the inspired, infallible Word of God and the final authority in salvation, doctrine, conduct, reproof and correction. Many evangelicals, on the other hand, need to add the fervor, faith and power of the present-day ministry of the Holy Spirit. We need a wedding between the school of the Word and the school of the Spirit. Then and only then can we proceed with assurance into the fullness of what God has in mind for this generation.

Years ago I heard revivalist statesman Leonard Ravenhill declare, "If you have the Word without the Spirit, you will dry up. If you have the Spirit without the Word, you will blow up. But if you have the Spirit with the Word, you will grow up." I say amen to this simple declaration.

The Task of Reminding

We saw in the previous chapter that watchmen on the walls are desperately needed in the Church today. But what is their task after they have mounted the walls? Yes, they are called to hear what the Lord is saying, but then what? Are there other tasks these intercessory watchmen are to engage in?

Of course! We are called to the glorious, laborious—even mundane, at times—task of reminding.

Asking God to Do What He Wants

Our primary Scripture is Isaiah 62:6–7:

> On your walls, O Jerusalem, I have appointed watchmen; all day and all night they will never keep silent. *You who remind the Lord,* take no rest for yourselves; and give Him no rest until He establishes and makes Jerusalem a praise in the earth.
>
> emphasis added

In chapter 1 we looked briefly at four definitions of the task of the intercessor, and discovered from this passage in Isaiah that one of the jobs to which intercessors are called is reminding the Lord of promises and appointments not yet met and fulfilled.

What does it mean to "remind the Lord"? Does He have a case of spiritual amnesia and forgets what He said He would do? No, of course not. He has simply determined not to do this task alone. It is the blessed mystery of being a co-laborer with Christ in His vineyard that God is looking for a people on earth who will come into agreement with His plans in heaven.

Remember, "If two of you agree on earth about anything that they may ask, it shall be done for them by My Father who is in heaven" (Matthew 18:19). This is not just human agreement about what we want God to do. It is an invitation for us to come into agreement with God's plans, pursuits and desires. Then, in agreement with one another *and* with God, we ask (or remind) Him to do what He wishes to do.

Ezekiel 36:37 tells it this way: "Thus says the Lord God, 'This also I will let the house of Israel ask Me to do for them: I will increase their men like a flock.'" This passage contains a key, I believe, to the Lord's church growth methodology: What He promises will not come unless we ask Him to do what He wants. I think I can hear the voice of my Master whispering, *I will let you ask Me to do what I want to do for you!* He declares in Jeremiah 1:12: "I am watching over My word to perform it."

This is the holy, awesome privilege of kneeling on the promises. It sounds as though Ezekiel and Isaiah sang our song those many years ago. We are to be humbly yet tenaciously reminding God of His Word.

The "Until" Clause

As we take another look at our foundational Scripture in Isaiah, we might find that we have in our hands a super-speed repeating machine gun! Remember, we are to be God's secretary bringing before our boss the strategic appointments on His prophetic calendar.

"How long are we supposed to do this?" I think you just asked. My answer is simple: I don't know. Isaiah 62 gives us a clue, though. We find a distinctive emphasis in this passage that I call "relentless reminding." Did you notice the word *until?* "Give Him no rest until. . . ." That might be a long time!

Remember Anna, the praying prophetess we spoke about in chapter 7, whose prophetic acts of intercession and fasting probably continued anywhere from ten to sixty years? I do not know how long your "until" clause will be. But I have a word for you: Continue.

The Holy Spirit loves the quality of tenacity. Luke 18:1–8 points this out in the parable of the widow who pleads with the unrighteous judge until she wears him out. Relentless, she just will not take no for an answer! Jesus said of the judge:

"For a while he was unwilling; but afterward he said to himself, 'Even though I do not fear God nor respect man, yet because this widow bothers me, I will give her legal protection, lest by continually coming she wear me out.'"

verses 4–5

165

Indeed, holy, bold, prevailing prayer often includes an element of divine stubbornness. Like the widow, you will not take no for an answer.

But remember the analogy I have suggested about the Russell Stover box of candy. We do not just close our eyes and point at any old chocolate in the box. Nor do we stick our fingers into all of them and see which one we think we will like best. Rather, we meditate on the Word of God and let Him choose which promise we are to remind Him relentlessly about. Tenacity is good, but not when it is nothing more than stubborn selfishness.

Knock on the Wood Table

The "until" clause reminds me of a story I have read and also heard from people behind the scenes about activity that led to a mighty revival in Argentina in the early 1950s, one generation prior to the present-day revival in that same country. The story centers on the prayer life of missionary R. E. Miller. Let me recall part of this true story for you.[3]

Edward Miller, a missionary from the United States in the early 1950s, had spent years of tireless, zealous activity in Argentina, pastoring churches, holding tent meetings and conducting personal evangelism, with little fruit. It seemed to him that he had tried everything. So, after having done all he could, he decided to try prayer.

He began on his new course of action by praying eight hours a day for revival in his own life and in his community of Mar del Plata. He continued leading Sunday services at his little church but spent most of the rest of the week in intercession before his God.

After six months of waiting on God, searching the Scriptures, fasting and praying, the Lord finally spoke to Edward Miller. It was a simple message: *Continue!*

So he did—relentlessly, as though his very life depended on it.

Months passed. Miller kept the eight-hour watch until God spoke again. This time the Lord told him to announce ongoing public prayer meetings that week that would begin the following Monday night at the church from 8 P.M. until midnight.

Miller argued with the Lord, telling Him that if he held such a prayer meeting, the only ones to come would be little old ladies, and all they would do was sit and watch him pray.

This did not seem to startle the Lord. He seemed to reply, *I know.*

So Miller announced the meeting. Sure enough, three little old women were all who came. Miller was right about his next objection, too. The ladies just sat and watched him pray for the next four hours. But pray he did.

At the end of the meeting, he asked if anyone had received anything from God. One of the women, the wife of a backslidden man, raised her hand. She described a strange desire to come up and knock on the wood table at the front of the sanctuary. But she felt that would be foolish, so she declined.

Pastor Miller dismissed the meeting and all went home.

The next night the prayer meeting continued. The same three little women came and sat and watched Edward Miller pray—yes, for another four hours. At the close Miller asked the same question, only to get the same response. The meeting closed and they all went home.

They met for the next two nights, with the same results. The woman with the backslidden husband felt compelled, she said, to come to the front and hit the wood table, and refused to do so.

Frustration began to settle in on Pastor Miller. He had no idea why God would lead her to do that, but how could he get her to comply?

On the last night of the scheduled prayer meeting, the same three women came and sat and watched Brother Miller pray. At the close he asked the same question and received the same response from the same woman.

But this time Miller said, "Sister, we're all going to walk around the table and hit it."

He hoped she would follow them, gather enough courage and knock on the table herself.

Miller passed by and hit the wood table, followed by two of the women. Then the third woman stepped up to the table and knocked on it. When she did, the Holy Spirit swept though the little church and overwhelmed them with glory and a sense of His presence. All three women were baptized in the Spirit and began worshiping God in a language they had not learned.

The news spread and people began to come nightly. Eventually the fire of revival spread to the capital city of Buenos Aires, where tens of thousands gathered in an outdoor sports stadium in 1954 and the Lord saved and healed many under the powerful ministry of Tommy Hicks. It was the beginning of the great Argentine revival of the early 1950s.

Now what was that word Edward Miller heard? *Continue!* As intercessory watchmen on the walls, we need to continue reminding God relentlessly of His Word.

Praying the Written Promises of Scriptures

The basic question must still be asked: What are we to remind God of?

Let's look at two of the most common bullets we are to load into our gun: the written promises of Scripture and the present-day revelatory promises that have been spoken by the Holy Spirit.

1. Scriptural Pleas before His Throne

First we are to bring before God's throne the written promises of Scripture. This first category (which I have addressed in this chapter thus far) includes all the promises of God—whether for individuals, families, the Body of Christ, Israel or the nations—and any of the magnificent themes stated in Scripture. This alone is an immense subject. Praying the Scriptures is a beautiful art that magnifies God and enriches the soul of the student involved. It is worth the time and investment for your own personal edification, let alone gaining the skill of learning a prayer vocabulary and receiving answers to such requests.

In the gracious privilege of praying the Scriptures, we are exhorted to come boldly to the throne of God. We are instructed, even commanded to bring strong pleas before our righteous Judge. Glance with me at Isaiah 43:26 from three different translations:

> "Put Me in remembrance; let us argue our case together, state your cause, that you may be proved right."
>
> NASB

> Put me in remembrance: let us plead together: declare thou, that thou mayest be justified.
>
> KJV

> Oh, remind me of this promise of forgiveness, for we must talk about your sins. Plead your case for my forgiving you.
>
> LB

Reminding God of His Word includes presenting your case and detailing your holy arguments before Him. This not only pleases God but helps you to understand your need more completely, releases compassion within you, strengthens your holy boldness and arms you with great hunger and holy desperation.

Pleading Your Case before God

The following are seven ways you can plead your case before God, with a few scriptural examples after each one:

1. *Plead the honor and glory of God's name* (2 Samuel 7:26; Psalm 23:3; 31:3; 79:9; 106:8; 109:21; 143:11).
2. *Plead God's relationship to you* (Job 10:3, 8–9; 14:15; Psalm 19:14; 33:20; 40:17; 46:1; 63:7; Isaiah 41:14; 54:5, 8; 63:16; 64:8; Malachi 3:17; Romans 8:15).
3. *Plead God's attributes* (Deuteronomy 9:18; Nehemiah 9:33; Psalm 4:1; 27:7; 30:10; 86:6, 15–16; 89:1–2; Isaiah 16:5; Daniel 2:18).
4. *Plead the sorrows and needs of the people in desperate circumstances* (Psalm 137:1–4; Lamentations 2:20; 5:1).
5. *Plead the past answers to prayer* (Psalm 27:9; 71:17–18; 78; 85:1–7; 105; 106; 136).
6. *Plead the Word and promises of God* (1 Chronicles 17:23–26; 2 Chronicles 6:14–17).
7. *Plead the blood of Jesus* (Exodus 12:5–23; Romans 5:9; Ephesians 1:7; Colossians 1:20; Hebrews 9:22; 10:19–23; 13:12; 1 John 1:7; Revelation 12:11).

An Example of Praying the Scriptures

As an example of praying the Scriptures, let's take the prophetic promise from Joel 2:28–29 and turn it into conversation with God. I, like many others, have often taken this wonderful promise into the hearing of our magnificent Messiah:

> Lord, I bring into Your hearing Your great promise of a last days outpouring of Your Holy Spirit. You have said, "I will pour out My Spirit on all mankind; and your sons and daughters will prophesy, your old men will dream dreams, your young men will see visions. And even on the male and female servants I will pour out My Spirit in those days."
>
> Holy God, for Your honor and glory in all the earth, I call out to You to fulfill Your Word. Release the mighty rain of Your grace and power on my city. Release demonstrations of Your great love as You have done in generations past.

Pour out Your Spirit on all flesh in my neighborhood [city, nation]. Send forth revival as You have never done before. Pour out Your Spirit on the old, the young, the male, the female, those in closed countries and those in free. Do this for the glory of Your Son, that He might receive the reward for His suffering.

As I make this holy appeal to Your throne, honor Your great name in all the earth by fulfilling Your Word. In Christ's name and for His sake I pray. Amen!

For your enrichment I have prepared an appendix called "Scripture Promises for Reminding God," located on p. 279, inspired and adopted from the teaching and prayer ministry of Pastor Mike Bickle of Kansas City. This is a great tool to get you started on this glorious journey of reminding God of His Word.

2. Revelatory Promises

The second ammo we are given in presenting our case before our righteous Judge is that of rehearsing before the throne the current-day revelatory promises that have been spoken by the Holy Spirit to us as individuals, families, groups, congregations, cities, regions or nations.

Earlier I mentioned cessationists. These sincere Christians do not believe God has given any new revelation since the canon of Scripture was completed. I appreciate this view but have experienced otherwise. While I agree that no fresh "revelation" is on a par with the holy and inspired Scriptures, I believe God does continue to speak today to those willing to listen and obey.

Such revelatory promises—hearing the voice of the Lord through personal communion; the *logos* (written Word) being breathed on and becoming a *rhema* (spoken word) in our hearts; visitations from God; the language of dreams and visions; and other biblical means—come from the heart

171

of our heavenly Father through the current operation of the gifts of the Holy Spirit.

Valuing the Promise

A passage from Paul to Timothy helps us understand our response as believers to these revelatory promises:

> This command I entrust to you, Timothy, my son, in accordance with the prophecies previously made concerning you, that by them you may fight the good fight, keeping faith and a good conscience, which some have rejected and suffered shipwreck in regard to their faith.
>
> 1 Timothy 1:18–19

First we see that Paul valued the gift of prophecy. He instructed his son in the faith not just to listen to the revelatory words that had previously been given over his life, but to "fight the good fight" with them. He seemed to indicate that these prophetic insights were weapons with which to wage war.

Second, Paul told Timothy that these spoken promises were tools to help him stay his course, keep the faith and remain faithful to the Lord and His calling on Timothy's life.

And finally, Paul contrasted the ways of others who had suffered shipwreck, and gave Timothy insight, in the jealousy of God, on how to avoid this in his own life.

Impressions and revelations must align with the principles of God's Word and be confirmed by brothers and sisters in Christ as authentic, true promises from the Father's heart to us. Otherwise we will be wasting our time chasing some elusive fantasy and end up (as Paul warned) shipwrecked, having attempted to build our lives on shifting sand.

But once you have secured an authentic prophetic promise, load it, take aim and shoot! Fight the fight and wage war with the prophetic.

Fighting with the Revelatory Promise

In Ephesians 6:17 we are told to take "the sword of the Spirit, which is the word of God." The Greek term used here for *word* is *rhema,* a spoken word from God. Revelatory giftings are mighty weapons of warfare. We pray a prophetic promise back to the heart of our Father.

At times, however, after we have done so, we must declare the word to our circumstances and any mountain of opposition standing in the way. We remind ourselves of the promise that lies ahead, and we remind the devil and command any foul spirits—for example, the spirit of discouragement—to back off, declaring what the written and spoken promises of God reveal.

Each of us has purposes, promises and a destiny to find, fight for and fulfill. So take your "Thus saith the Lord" to battle with you and fight!

This is what I did with my dream of *You will have a son and his name will be called Justin.* I spoke that word over Michal Ann's and my bodies, prayed the dream back to God and waged war with it by telling barrenness and the devil to depart. Believe me, that dream came in handy! Michal Ann and I used our revelatory promise as a megaphone with which to declare life where there was no life, and it became a sword of the Spirit in my hand for several years to wield against the onslaught of the enemy.

Let Faith Arise!

You can do the same. Take any promises that have been spoken to you by the Holy Spirit and turn them into persistent prayer, reminding God of His word. I say, "Smoke them pistols!" Use these confirmed, authentic words from heaven to create faith within your heart. Let them pave the way for the entrance of ever-increasing faith in your life: "Faith comes from hearing, and hearing by the word of Christ" (Romans 10:17).

Have you heard any words from Jesus lately? Just read the red print in the grand Book and let those words sink deep, deep, deep into your spirit. You will be giving something for the wind of God, the Holy Spirit, to blow on and become the quickened (spoken) word of the Lord to your heart. Faith will leap up inside of you, and you will have divine "knowings" (probably the gift of faith). When that happens, you know that you know that you know. You might not know *how* you know—but you know everything is going to be all right!

Remember what the Holy Spirit spoke to Michal Ann when she had yielded her right to have children: *I appreciate your attitude, but I am not requiring this of you. I say to you, You must fight for your children.* So fight we did! In fact, one time I came running out of our bedroom after being in prayer and told my wife, "Now Annie, get your gun!"

Recall the words from Isaiah 62:7: "Give [God] no rest until. . . ." So pray *until!* Michal Ann and I prayed until we finally hit the target.

Discovering Your Prophetic Destiny

Has the Lord spoken a "prophetic destiny" to you or to your family, congregation, city or nation? Each of us has a wonderful destiny in God waiting to be discovered and fulfilled. When I was growing up, I heard the statement "If you aim at nothing, you will surely hit it." Sad to say, that is the way most of us direct the energies of our lives—haphazardly. But we need a clear target. Let's discover the purpose of God for our lives and take aim.

Not only does the Lord have special, unique plans for you as an individual, but for your family, city and nation as well. What is the personal prophetic destiny of your life? What is the redemptive gift of God for your city? For your nation? Was there a blessing declared by the pioneers who brought forth your city? What are the foundations on which your city was inaugurated? Has that destiny been fulfilled? Have you researched it? Has it been confirmed?

Please realize that the word you kneel on, pray into and war with might not be a word given directly to you. It could be a promise given to another, or a revelatory insight passed down from generation to generation. We in the Body of Christ, you see, are interdependent. We are to honor the many different members of the Body and receive the grace that has been bestowed on each one. We need one another.

So we do not wage war solely with the personal prophetic words we have received. We can build and battle with the words given to others as well.

Daniel's Example

When Daniel entered into intercession for the restoration of Israel from Babylonian captivity, he did not receive that word directly. He was reading the prophecy of someone from a previous generation—the promise from the Lord through Jeremiah. We find this promise in Daniel 9:2: "In the first year of [Darius'] reign I, Daniel, observed in the books the number of the years which was revealed as the word of the LORD to Jeremiah the prophet for the completion of the desolations of Jerusalem, namely, seventy years."

Apparently Daniel was researching the prophetic destiny for his people, who lived in captivity in a foreign land, and reading the prophetic revelation foretelling what was going to happen. The children of Israel, because of their sin and disobedience, had been taken captive and were dwelling in Babylon. Daniel himself had grown up in that foreign land. But he was a man of the covenant.

What was the promise he was laying hold of? It is found in Jeremiah 29:10:

Thus says the LORD, "When seventy years have been completed for Babylon, I will visit you and fulfill My good word to you, to bring you back to this place."

Some Bible commentators believe it was in the sixty-third year of Babylonian captivity that Daniel meditated on the promise given to Jeremiah. It was not even his own prophecy! How did Daniel respond to it? When he read the promise, the Holy Spirit quickened it and made it alive to him, relevant to his situation.

I do not believe Daniel said simply, "Well, bless the Lord. God said it, I believe it, that settles it!" Nor did he say, "Well, guys, Jeremiah said it. That's gonna be it. Hallelujah! Now everybody just wave your hands!" No, he responded to the prophetic promise with wisdom and action:

So I gave my attention to the LORD God to seek Him by prayer and supplications, with fasting, sackcloth, and ashes.

Daniel 9:3

Daniel meditated on the word and sought the Lord for understanding and for wisdom applications so the promise could be fulfilled. Then he responded to the promise with humility and holy tenacity. He confessed the sins of his people and removed the obstacle—sin—that was standing in the way of the fulfillment of the prophetic destiny for his people in his day:

And I prayed to the LORD my God and confessed and said, "Alas, O LORD, the great and awesome God, who keeps His covenant and lovingkindness for those who love Him and keep His commandments, we have sinned, committed iniquity, acted wickedly, and rebelled, even turning aside from Thy commandments and ordinances."

verses 4–5

This man with "an extraordinary spirit" (Daniel 5:11–12; 6:3; see also 1:4, 8, 17) confessed the sins of his people as if they were his own, though he himself had not bowed the knee to foreign gods (see Daniel 3:15–18; 6:10). Although he had not personally committed sins of wickedness, idolatry and rebellion, he humbled his soul with fasting and confessed those sins as his own:

> "O my God, incline Thine ear and hear! Open Thine eyes and see our desolations and the city which is called by Thy name; for we are not presenting our supplications before Thee on account of any merits of our own, but on account of Thy great compassion. O LORD, hear! O LORD, forgive! O LORD, listen and take action! For Thine own sake, O my God, do not delay, because Thy city and Thy people are called by Thy name."
>
> verses 18–19

This is how Daniel responded in his day. Should we not do the same in ours?

An Amazing Intervention

What came about as a result of Daniel's tenacious, holy pleading? While he was still confessing sin, speaking and praying, the Lord sent the archangel Gabriel to grant Daniel insight and understanding of God's ways (see verses 20–23). The curtain between the temporal and the eternal is parted in the following chapters and we are given a glimpse of true spiritual warfare and how prayer releases heaven's arsenal to war on man's behalf (see Daniel 9:23; 10:12–21).

Eventually the revelatory word to Jeremiah was fulfilled and the children of Israel were released to return to their homeland, just as the prophetic promise had stated. Do you see the steps used to bring the promise into being? Yes, the prophetic destiny of Daniel's generation was fulfilled—but not until an intercessor stood in the gap, met the conditions, knelt on the promise and reminded God of His word.

A Personal Assignment

In July 1977 I attended the Kansas City Conference in Kansas City, Missouri, one of the first ecumenical gatherings of Pentecostals and charismatics from the mainline denominations in North America. Some fifty thousand believers assembled in different locations around the city during the mornings and afternoons, and came together as one in Arrowhead Stadium in the evenings. I well remember how, at the end of the announcements one night, a priest rushed to the microphone and proclaimed, speaking the Spirit-inspired promise of God: "Kansas City, I will give you a new heart!"

The proclamation about the city in which I was living rang true in my spiritual ears, and to many others as well. The problem was, there was dissension and division among the churches in Kansas City (as in many other cities and regions). One stream of Christianity flowed in conflict and competition with another, as another prophecy from the Kansas City Conference declared: "Mourn and weep, for the Body of My Son is broken."

So what do you do, watchmen?

Well, for years I took that simple word, stood on the walls of my city and region and reminded God of His promise to give Kansas City a new heart. Although our city was rocked with division and spiritual contention, I (and undoubtedly many other watchmen on the walls) took that promise and prayed it, sweated it, cried it, agonized over it.

For more than a decade the spirit of division and alienation in the Midwest seemed to have a greater foothold than ever. In 1990 a major spiritual controversy erupted in Kansas City and I found myself smack dab in the middle of it. But the Lord had set me as a watchman for the heart of

America. I had not chosen the assignment; He had. And behind the scenes He was raising up a wonderful prayer and reconciliation movement. Much prayer, fasting and confession of sins was taking place in many denominations and renewal streams of the Body of Christ. Cleansing was beginning. The Lord was at work to wash the wounds and heal the spiritual heart.

Many other hidden intercessors and I stood on the walls for relational unity. I challenged one leader to speak to another. At times I wondered if change would ever come. But since every promise of God is contested by the powers of darkness, we cannot battle on the natural plane (see Ephesians 6:12). We must battle on the spiritual plane by kneeling and then standing on the promises.

After several skirmishes, humility, light, integrity and unity eventually won out in Kansas City. It was not until eighteen years later that I felt the short prophetic promise given in 1977 had been somewhat fulfilled and I was released from carrying that burden before His throne.

Things had changed. Reconciliation had taken place between the "streams." A new heart of unity had come forth as pastors humbled themselves one to another. A new ministerial fellowship came into being, bringing together in relational unity groups that had previously been at odds with one another. Many rivers of pure water flowed from the heart of America to the rest of the Body of Christ across our nation and the world. What joy and relief filled my heart when Kansas City began to receive a new heart!

And me? Oh, I got reassigned by the Holy Spirit to move to a different city. I have received God's burden and prophetic desire for Nashville. Now I find myself with a longing for "Music City, U.S.A." to be cleansed from her idolatry and truly become a "city set on a hill"—perhaps one called "Worship City, U.S.A."

May this word come into being, and may every prophetic promise in your life, church and city come into being, for the honor of Jesus' great name in all the earth.

The Goal

Did you catch the goal of the relentless reminding, which is also stated in Isaiah 62:7? "Give Him no rest until He establishes and makes Jerusalem a praise in the earth" (verse 7). Does this sound intense, strategic, even "end-timey"? You got it. We are invited to labor for the purposes of God to be established in our generation. We are to come into agreement with our Messiah Jesus and echo His prayer: "Your Kingdom come on earth as it is currently being manifested in heaven."

God is not just offering us a place of personal petition. He is calling warrior watchmen to remind Him relentlessly of His predetermined prophetic purpose for a last days outpouring of His Spirit on all flesh, to be fulfilled on both the Church and Israel. He wants to make Jerusalem a glorious representation of His presence in the earth.

There is something so uniquely wonderful in the purposes of God for Israel and the Church that once you catch a glimpse of it, you are undone by God's multifaceted wisdom. As it was in Daniel's time and Isaiah's time, so it is coming about again. Watchmen are showing up on the walls and giving God "no rest until He establishes and makes Jerusalem a praise in the earth." (We will take a closer look at this subject in the next chapter, "Israel: God's Prophetic Calendar.")

There are many different aspects of our high and holy calling of kneeling on the promises. We are kneeling on the promises until God's Kingdom has come, until His will is done on earth as it is in heaven. Do not let go of the hem of His garment. Wrestle until . . . !

Now It's Your Turn!

Now it is time to take the bullets and actually load them into your gun. The Lord might let you have some good practice rounds, but He is delighted when we learn how to take the bullets of Scripture and revelatory gifts and load them into the gun of prayer. Let's proceed, coupling wisdom and faith in this art of reminding God of His Word, and keep loading and shooting until "the knowledge of the glory of the LORD" fills the earth "as the waters cover the sea" (Habakkuk 2:14).

Before we close this chapter and take a look at Israel, God's prophetic road map, let's turn to Andrew Murray once again. Together let's kneel on the promises by declaring a prayer of dependency from his fabled book *With Christ in the School of Prayer:*

> Blessed Lord! I see why my prayer has not been more believing and effective. I was more occupied with my speaking to You than with Your speaking to me. I did not understand that the secret of faith is this: There can be only as much faith as there is of the living Word dwelling in the soul.
>
> Your Word taught me so clearly to be swift to hear and slow to speak. Lord, teach me that it is only when I take Your Word into my life that my words can be taken into Your heart. Teach me that if Your Word is a living power within me, it will be a living power with You, also. Amen.[4]

The principles we have discussed of reminding God of His Word are the same whether you apply them to your personal life, family, congregation, city or nation. Study to show yourself approved. Meditate on the Scriptures and let the Holy Spirit speak a promise into your heart. Then take the two-edged sword—the written *and* the spoken word—and kneel on the promise. Bring it into God's hearing. Pray it back to Him. When necessary, use the promise as a sword of the Spirit and declare to the powers of darkness that they must step back at the word of the Lord. It is time to say, "Ready, aim, fire!" Then, having done all, stand (see Ephesians 6:13).

In the Kingdom of God, little keys open big doors. Daniel used the keys of study, meditation, prayer, humility, confession and perseverance to unlock the destiny of God for Israel in his generation. Can you do the same? It is your turn. In fact, it is our turn. Together let's kneel on the promises of God our Savior. Let us do so until. . . .

Before we know it, we will not simply be singing this old song made new; we will be living it. After all, isn't that what the Christian walk is all about?

PRACTICAL APPLICATIONS—MAKING IT REAL!

- The Holy Spirit is looking for people who will come into agreement with God's Word, then request (remind) Him to do what He wants to do for us. Use Appendix 1 on page 279 to remind God of His prophetic promises not yet fulfilled.
- Pray the promises back to God, bringing them to His hearing. Then, if necessary, use the promises as a sword of the Spirit and declare to the powers of darkness that they must step back at the Word of God. Then take your stand.
- Set aside a season of time and pray the apostolic prayers. Refer to Appendix 1 for this listing.
- Bring any promises given through revelation by the Holy Spirit before the Father as a request to remind Him of the not-yet-fulfilled prophetic destiny.
- Take a promise of Scripture devotionally, memorize it, then pray it over your heart for the next week.

RECOMMENDED READING

Praying the Scriptures by Judson Cornwall (Creation House, 1990)

The Complete Works of E. M. Bounds on Prayer (Baker, 1990)

9

ISRAEL

God's Prophetic Calendar

The playing board has been set and the pieces have been chosen. It seems as if God has been conducting a monumental chess game throughout the ages, waiting for the strategic moment in history to make His move. It is the strategic positioning of His intercessory knights and prophetic bishops, all being brought together for a sweeping move—one that all the world will observe closely. No eye will miss the mysterious and fascinating time on God's prophetic calendar when He steps down from heaven once again into the world of space and time. It is time for the unveiling of the mystery of Israel as the apple of God's eye (see Zechariah 2:8), the centerpiece of attention on God's chessboard.

Although Israel as we know her today is only a little more than fifty years old, the Jewish nation is actually one of the oldest on earth. These people and their land reach back to the time of Abraham's prophetic pilgrimage and the covenant promise of God to him and his descendants (see Genesis 17:4–8). But after what many considered to be a silence of two thousand years, this land has been reborn. Israel is once again the showpiece being displayed before the eyes of the world.

A few years ago, while hosting a gathering in the Atlanta area called "A Cry to the Lord," I was preparing to speak for the first time on the subject of "The Mystery of the Church and Israel." While in worship I saw a vision of an angel standing in the corner of the room. The angel was dressed in a brilliant white wedding gown, and I heard the words, *I have come to release a message on the wedding of the Church and Israel.* With fresh strength and encouragement I began to unfold a message about the exodus of the Jews from the biblical land of the north to their homeland in Israel.

No book combining the themes of intercession and the prophetic realm would be complete without considering this biblical centerpiece, Israel. In this chapter, therefore, I want to unwrap this treasured gem for you from a scriptural and historical point of reference.

Brief Historic Overview

How could a remnant of scattered and persecuted Jewish people, who went through their darkest hour in Hitler's Holocaust, come forth all at once as a sovereign nation within their age-old boundaries? Not without divine intervention, for sure, although many Israelis today believe they did it all on their own. Let's sketch this history briefly.

On November 29, 1947, the General Assembly of the United Nations adopted a resolution requiring the establishment of a Jewish state in Palestine. The following is a portion of the Proclamation of Independence read by David Ben-Gurion on May 14, 1948:

> The land of Israel was the birthplace of the Jewish people. Here their spiritual, religious and national identity was formed. Here they achieved independence and created a cul-

ture of national and universal significance. Here they wrote and gave the Bible to the world. Exiled from the Land of Israel, the Jewish people remained faithful to it in all the countries of their dispersion, never ceasing to pray and hope for their return and the restoration of their national freedom.

Our call goes out to the Jewish people all over the world to rally to our side in the task of immigration and development and to stand by us in the great struggle for the fulfillment of the dream of generations for the redemption of Israel. With trust in Almighty God, we set our hand to this Declaration on the Sabbath eve, the fifth of Iyar, 5708, the fourteenth day of May, 1948.[1]

Just a day later, on May 15, 1948, while this creation had barely come forth, five Arab nations assaulted the newborn Jewish babe. Egypt, Syria, Jordan, Lebanon and Iraq (forty million Arabs, 1.5 million of them armed) attacked Israel in what became known as the Israeli War of Independence. The war continued for eight months with heavy casualties on all sides. The miracle is that Israel, which had just been reborn, could not be destroyed (see Isaiah 54:17).

In 1967 the Six-Day War should also have ended in disaster for Israel, but God's mercy again prevailed. The Sinai, the Gaza Strip, the West Bank and the Golan Heights were occupied by the Israelis in only six days. This conflict also saw the notable capture by the Jews of the Jewish quarter of Jerusalem and the remaining Western (Wailing) Wall of the Temple. All holy Jewish and Christian sites were controlled by the Israelis at that point.

And consider the outcome of the surprise 1973 Yom Kippur assault. The Arabs, backed by one of the world's two nuclear superpowers, the Soviet Union, attacked on two fronts; but Israel, coming close to major defeat, again came out the victor. Taken by surprise on their highest holy day, the Israelis were pushed back as the Arabs made territorial gains. Yet by what I believe was divine intervention, Israel regained all her land. Once again the hand of God, working in part through the agency of human beings, protected the outnumbered and despised Jewish nation.

Prophetic Foretellings

The history of God's divine protection of Israel since it was reborn as a nation in 1948 is a brilliant study in its own right. The promise of God's regathering and protection of Israel is not based on anything good she has accomplished as a nation. Rather it is a declaration of God's greatness. Eventually God and God alone will be glorified through it. If Israel deserved pardon, she would not need God's grace. It is only through receiving His grace that she can restore to Him the glory of which her sins have robbed Him. Paul, the Jewish apostle to the Gentiles, paints this picture for us brilliantly in Romans 11:6: "If it is by grace, it is no longer on the basis of works, otherwise grace is no longer grace."

Let's look at some significant Old Testament prophecies regarding Israel's dispersion and regathering.

Jeremiah's Declaration

Jeremiah, the weeping prophet, glimpsed through the lens of time that Israel's faithful, covenant-keeping God would offer His stretched-out wings as a place of divine protection to His people during their ingathering to the Promised Land:

> Hear the word of the LORD, O nations, and declare in the coastlands afar off, and say, "He who scattered Israel will gather him, and keep him as a shepherd keeps his flock."
>
> Jeremiah 31:10

Jeremiah was declaring prophetically to the Gentile nations what the will of God was for their inhabitants. This was a declaration concerning a sovereign extraction that already has, yet still will, transpire.

We find three truths contained in this one verse from Jeremiah. First, it was God Himself who scattered Israel from her own homeland. Second, the same God who scattered Israel will regather her to her own land. And third, God will not merely regather Israel but keep her and put a divine hedge of protection about her as she is regathered.

Hosea's Pronouncement

Hosea 1:10 reads:

. . . It will come about that, in the place where it is said to them, "You are not My people," it will be said to them, "You are the sons of the living God."

This piercing prophetic statement was given concerning the condition of the house of Israel at a time when she was in a state of rebellion and sin ("You are not My people"). But God's critical word of judgment did not end there. Isn't it amazing? With every word of judgment there is also a ray of hope. God's true word cuts deeply at times—but these cuts are ultimately for the purpose of healing and restoring.

On the heels of His judgment God offered a phenomenal promise (just as He does in our lives). In the very place— the land of Israel—where they were told they were not His people, "It will be said to them, 'You are the sons of the living God.'"

This one verse speaks of physical restoration and relocation and also of the spiritual rebirth or revival that will take place among God's covenant people when they are returned to their covenant-given land. A miracle of major proportions is being declared here. What a reflection of the awesome faithfulness of our Father!

Two Regatherings Predicted

With the needed foundation in place of God's grace and His faithfulness, let's trace a few more steps back in history and glance at the topic of the Diaspora (the dispersion) of the Jewish people in history.

The First Regathering

It is my understanding that Scripture speaks prophetically beforehand that the Jews would suffer two major dispersions, or scatterings, from their own land, followed by two regatherings.

The first was in the years when the prophets Daniel and Ezekiel were exiled in the land of Babylon, that period in which the Jews of the Judean kingdom were displaced from their country after the destruction of the Temple, Jerusalem and commonwealth by Nebuchadnezzar (see Daniel 1:1–6). It was around 605 B.C. when Daniel and his associates were carried away. Their restoration to the land began in 538 B.C. (see 2 Chronicles 36:22–23; Ezra 1:1–4), and the Temple remained unrestored until 515 B.C. (see Ezra 6:15), about seventy years after its destruction in 587 B.C.

In the last chapter we looked at the life of Daniel. Let's take a moment to review.

Daniel, a prophet of the one true God, was in captivity with the children of Israel in Babylon—a foreign land with a foreign culture and gods and ways. It was perhaps in their sixty-third year of captivity, while meditating on the Word of God (see Daniel 9:2), that Daniel received a revelation based on the prophetic promises of Jeremiah:

> "This whole land shall be a desolation and a horror, and these nations shall serve the king of Babylon seventy years. Then it will be when seventy years are completed I will punish the king of Babylon and that nation," declares the LORD. . . .
>
> Jeremiah 25:11–12

> "Thus says the LORD, 'When seventy years have been completed for Babylon, I will visit you and fulfill My good word to you, to bring you back to this place.'"
>
> Jeremiah 29:10

Not only did Daniel believe the word and declare it as revealed to Jeremiah—that at the end of seventy years of Babylonian captivity, the children of Israel would be released from their enslavement and return to their own land—but Daniel sought the Lord for any reasons or blockades that could stand in the way of the prophetic promise being fulfilled (see Daniel 9:3–19). Daniel then responded to the prophetic word by kneeling on it. He entered into confession of the sin of his people as his own. The verse that summarizes his confession is Daniel 9:19:

> "O LORD, hear! O LORD, forgive! O LORD, listen and take action! For Thine own sake, O my God, do not delay, because Thy city and Thy people are called by Thy name."

(It is interesting to note as an aside that it was also in the seventieth year of Communism in the former Soviet Union that this evil power broke up and the Gospel of the Kingdom of Jesus Christ was free once again to be proclaimed. The Iron Curtain was lifted and Communism crumbled right at the seventy-year mark.)

The fact that the word of the Lord happened precisely as had been declared through the lips of Jeremiah, and knelt upon by the prophet Daniel, gives us an example of prophetic intercession at its best. At the end of seventy years the Israelites were released into the beginning fulfillment of the prophecy of their first return to their covenant land. The walls of Jerusalem began to be rebuilt.

Many more cyclic years of faith, sin, repentance, revival and restoration continued, but the word of the Lord had been fulfilled and God had shown Himself true to His promise.

The Second Regathering

That was not the only dispersion and regathering prophesied by God's watchmen. Isaiah 11:11–12 states that the Lord would set His hand a second time to recover a remnant of His people:

> It will happen on that day that the Lord will again recover the second time with His hand the remnant of His people, who will remain, from Assyria, Egypt, Pathros, Cush, Elam, Shinar, Hamath, and from the islands of the sea. And He will lift up a standard for the nations, and will assemble the banished ones of Israel, and will gather the dispersed of Judah *from the four corners of the earth.*
>
> emphasis added

This Scripture clearly depicts a second dispersion and, at some point, a second regathering. The first dispersion did not send these wandering Jews in many directions at once. They remained together as an entity—a persecuted yet identifiable people in a foreign nation. But the second scattering would send them to regions beyond the known existence of Isaiah's day—to the four corners of the earth. It is my understanding (as well as that of many others) that we are seeing this second great regathering beginning to be fulfilled right before our eyes in this generation.

Let's make it simple. The Scriptures explain that there would be a regional dispersion followed by a regional regathering. Then there would come a second worldwide dispersion followed by a second worldwide regathering. When did the second dispersion occur? It began around A.D. 70 under the Roman ruler Titus, when the Jewish people once again fled their homeland and ran for their lives. For many hundreds of years they scattered—not just for five hundred years, or a thousand, or even fifteen hundred years, but for approximately nineteen hundred years they

were banished from their homeland to the four corners of
the earth.

Regarding the regathering from this second dispersion,
Ramon Bennett, in his book *When Day and Night Cease*,
writes:

> The second gathering began with the trickle of Jews into
> Palestine after the turn of the last century. The trickle be-
> came a stream after 1948 and then a river during the 1950's
> and 1960's. The river is now in flood stage and in danger of
> bursting its banks with the masses arriving from the last
> vestiges of the (former) Soviet Union.[2]

I love it when it seems as though the purposes of God
unfold right in front of your eyes! From my vantage point,
that is exactly what I see occurring in the Middle East today.

Bumped into a Divine Appointment

Let me veer off for a few moments on a personal course
and tell you a true-life story that occurred on my first return
trip from Israel in 1987. Though this event took place more
than a decade ago, perhaps as I relay this fascinating
encounter you will pick up a little more of God's heart for
the destiny and purposes of Israel today.

As I was flying home from that first trip to Israel, I got
bumped up mistakenly into first class. What an accidental
blessing—and a divine appointment! I ended up sitting next
to a stately gentleman and my spiritual antennas began
buzzing. (The gifts of the Holy Spirit started operating.)
Under a kind of spiritual mandate, I began talking with this
gentleman and speaking out of the overflow of my heart. I
knew nothing about him but felt a curious desire to share
from the prophetic Scriptures with him.

"Would you like to know what's next on God's prophetic
calendar?" I asked.

Even I wondered what I would say next!

He looked at me intently, curiously. So I began to tell him that, from the perspective of prophecy, Russia and the Eastern European countries would be freed from the grip of Communism and that an exodus of the Jewish people of grand proportions would soon be occurring from the biblical "land of the north." Quoting from Isaiah and the passages I already quoted from Jeremiah, I told him that circumstances in the Middle East would change radically as a result of this great return to the land.

Since my seat partner appeared to be listening intently, I continued talking. What would jump up into my throat next?

Fishermen and Hunters

I took him to Jeremiah 16:14–16, which states:

"Therefore behold, days are coming," declares the Lord, "when it will no longer be said, 'As the Lord lives, who brought up the sons of Israel out of the land of Egypt,' but, 'As the Lord lives, who brought up the sons of Israel from the land of the north and from all the countries where He had banished them.' For I will restore them to their own land which I gave to their fathers. Behold, I am going to send for many fishermen," declares the Lord, "and they will fish for them; and afterwards I shall send for many hunters, and they will hunt them from every mountain and every hill, and from the clefts of the rocks."

Rarely had I had such an attentive audience! The fellow leaned toward me as if to say, "Is there more?" I could hardly believe I was sharing at such lengths with a total stranger! But I plowed ahead, explaining my understanding of these verses as the dove of the Holy Spirit seemed to rest quietly on me.

I began to talk about the terms *fishermen* and *hunters* as stated in Jeremiah, and what they could possibly mean. The Lord always moves first in mercy, I explained, before releasing His judgments. I told him that the fishermen Jeremiah spoke of were sent out first and used to call forth the Jewish people to return to their homeland. In fact, one of the first phases of "fishermen" occurred as early as 1897, more than one hundred years ago, when the secular leader Theodor Herzl released an early prophetic call at the first World Zionist Congress held in Basil, Switzerland, for the establishment of a Jewish state.

Another round of God's master chess board moves happened in 1917 when Jerusalem was liberated by General Allenby and the British forces from four hundred years of Turkish domination. The Balfour Declaration was signed, calling for a national home for the Jews.

I continued to turn a few pages of history as I explained that in 1933 God first sent fisherman Zeb Jabotinsky, one of the early Jewish pioneers in Palestine, who warned the Jews of Germany: "There is no future for you here. Come back to your land while the doors are still open."[3] Then I jumped to July 1938 and rehearsed the League of Nations meeting with leaders from Europe, the United States and other nations to discuss the Jewish dilemma. Hitler had sent spies into this gathering, I told him, to send a report back concerning the nations' stand on this crucial issue. But because the leaders of the nations decided not to take a stand, the spies thus reported to Hitler that he could do whatever he wanted. This gave the Nazi leader the momentum to go ahead with his plans.

The times changed at that point, from the fishermen of mercy to the hunters of judgment being released. What followed eventually led to the slaughter of six million Jews and the horrific judgment of World War II under Hitler's reign of terror. The hunters indeed came as the Scriptures predicted: "They will hunt them from every mountain and every hill, and from the clefts of the rocks."

God's Great Treasure

After hearing about the fishermen and hunters, the gentleman seated next to me pulled out his notebook, took a few notes and appeared to write down some Scripture references. Then he closed his pad and began to probe gently, asking who I was, where I was from, what I was doing on this trip and whether I had talked with any international military leaders.

I realized I had pushed some buttons but had no idea, when the Lord encouraged me to share at such lengths with a stranger, that he was in such a position of responsibility and decision-making. In fact, this man turned out to be the deputy secretary of the Joint Chiefs of Staff in President Reagan's administration and in charge of military strategy over the Middle East.

I must admit, it was kind of exciting! I guess the Lord wanted him to know what was coming next. As I shared from the Scriptures with him, I knew some of God's great treasure was being placed into his heart. And for the following few weeks and months, I found myself praying that God's Word would not return void to this man's heart but accomplish the purposes for which He sent it (see Isaiah 55:10–11). My own appetite was whetted to be bumped into more divine appointments in Jesus' name!

May He lead each of us into opportunities to draw people's attention to Israel, the centerpiece of attention on God's chessboard!

More about the Second Regathering

The side roads can be filled with lots of interesting sights to pause and gaze at. But let's turn back onto the main boulevard with Jeremiah and look in more depth at what the prophetic Scriptures say about the second regathering.

A clarion call of this second regathering can clearly be heard from Jeremiah's trumpet:

> "Behold, I am bringing them from the north country, and I will gather them from the remote parts of the earth, among them the blind and the lame, the woman with child and she who is in labor with child, together; a great company, they shall return here. With weeping they shall come, and by sup-plication I will lead them; I will make them walk by streams of waters, on a straight path in which they shall not stum-ble; for I am a father to Israel, and Ephraim is My first-born."
> Hear the word of the LORD, O nations, and declare in the coastlands afar off, and say, "He who scattered Israel will gather him, and keep him as a shepherd keeps his flock."
>
> Jeremiah 31:8–10

These verses and others graphically paint for us this regathering process, with specific mention of "the north country" as one of the primary places of exodus and re-turning. To understand the regions involved, we must look at the geographical context. It is interesting to note that Moscow is located directly north of the little piece of land in the Middle East that we call Israel.

Yes, the Lord holds the compass of proper understand-ing of His Word. To get the correct reading, however, we must stand in the right place. Israel is the pupil, the center of focus, of God's eye (see Zechariah 2:8), and we must read the prophetic Scriptures with this in mind.

Some of the specific conditions of the returning people are stated in Jeremiah as well: "The blind and the lame, the woman with child and she who is in labor with child" (verse 8). Hold this thought for a moment; I will return to it with a dramatic, contemporary fulfillment.

Jeremiah also explained how God's people will be led out: "With weeping they shall come, and by supplication I will lead them." What is supplication? *Strong's Concordance* renders the meaning of this word simply as "strong prayer." Awesome! Once again we are given the secret of the fulfillment of the prophetic promise: the desperate prayer of the heart (weeping) and praying the promise back to God (supplication).

Here again we find God's purposes birthed through prophetic intercession. May I tell you a vivid testimony that will drive this point home?

A Contemporary Fulfillment

In chapter 4 I mentioned my dear friend from the Czech Republic, Moravian pastor Evald Rucky. In early spring of 1991, you recall, he suffered from a heart condition while ministering in Sweden and was taken to the hospital. His doctors said he had fallen into a coma. But as Evald understands it, the Lord let him escape to heaven for a while to enjoy His presence before being called back by his best friend's tears.

While Evald was caught up in the Lord's presence, he had various experiences and remembers being shown a few events before they actually transpired on earth. At one point he was shown a white bridge that rose up out of Ethiopia, reached through the clouds and came down into Israel. As Evald watched, he saw some fifteen thousand dark Ethiopian people crossing over the bridge into Israel.

"What is this?" Evald asked the Lord.

His guide, the Holy Spirit, answered him, *Oh, these are My ancient Jewish people that I will bring home from Ethiopia to Israel.*

Evald quizzed further: "How does this come to pass?"

Again an answer came: *Why, this, too, happens in answer to the prayers of the saints.*

What a sight and what an explanation! But what was it that Evald actually saw?

In May 1991, just a few weeks later, a historic event occurred called Operation Solomon. The headline of the June 1, 1991, *Jerusalem Post* read, *Operation Solomon Flies 14,400 to Israel in 24 Hours. Ethiopian Jewry Rescued.* The article went on to state:

> Israel made history Saturday completing a massive airlift of some 14,000 beleaguered Ethiopian Jews from the Addis Ababa to their ancestral homeland in a breathtaking 24 hours. Operation Solomon, conducted by the IDF and in coordination with the Jewish Agency, foreign ministry and other bodies, as well as the Ethiopian government, brought tears to many of the thousands of the Israelis who took part in a reunification of the Ethiopian Jews with their 20,000 family members already in Israel.[4]

Now let me quote to you from an Associated Press news release concerning the same historic event. The tone of this newspaper's article sounded a lot like Scripture. The bold headlines declared, *Israel Rescues 15,000,* and the subhead, "Massive Airlift Transports Ethiopian Jews to Safety." Now for the amazing article:

> Israel brought 15,000 Ethiopian Jews to their promised land, plucking them out of the besieged Addis Ababa in a dramatic two-day airlift that ended Saturday. Operation Solomon's 40 flights brought virtually all of the Ethiopian known Jews held to be the descendants of one of the lost ten tribes of Israel to their new lives in the Jewish state. The airlift, the largest such evacuation that Israel has ever mounted, was reminiscent of the Biblical exodus. The newcomers walked, hobbled and were carried down the gangways. Many were clad in flowing robes with only the humble possessions they could carry. One old woman knelt and kissed the tarmac. Four babies were born aboard the

flights. "This is a very moving experience," said one of the pilots. "It's not everyday one gets to play a part of making history."[5]

Old news at this point, you say? Sounds to me like prophecy of Scripture being fulfilled! In the rapidly developing events of our day, let's not forget the exploits God has already done to fulfill His unchanging word.

Remember Jeremiah's prediction: "Among them the blind and the lame, the woman with child and she who is in labor with child" (Jeremiah 31:8). Yes, they came hobbling and some had to be carried. Four women gave birth in the midst of their flight. Amazing—fulfilled to the very detail!

Consider also Ezekiel's prophecy:

> "I will establish for them a renowned planting place, and they will not again be victims of famine in the land, and they will not endure the insults of the nations any more. Then they will know that I, the LORD their God, am with them, and that they, the house of Israel, are My people," declares the LORD God.
>
> Ezekiel 34:29–30

Brought from out of famine, established in their own land. Perhaps now the veil will be lifted from these precious Ethiopian Jews and they will come to know Jesus as their glorious Messiah.

In the meantime, remember the question my friend Evald asked of his heavenly guide: "How does this come to pass?" In the answer, *Why, this, too, happens in answer to the prayers of the saints*, we see prophetic intercession being used once again to give birth to the promises of God. How does it work? God's pure prophetic promise, whether in Scripture or by the authentic release of the gifts of the Spirit today, is knelt upon in humble, persistent prayer by believers in Christ—and answers come tumbling forth!

Needed: Desperate Measures

During a time of special prayer and fasting in 1988, called by Clyde Williamson from Toronto and termed the Esther Mandate Fast, intercessors worldwide consumed no food or liquid for three days to call out to the Lord for the release of the Jews from the "land of the north" and their return to Israel. Participants prayed through the verses in Jeremiah and Isaiah that we have been looking at. A remnant of believers around the globe reminded God of His Word. And guess what happened? The Lord heard this compassionate plea, Communism fell, and these verses continue to be brought to pass.

This time of fasting was similar to what Esther did to avert the judgment of death on the entire Jewish population of her day. Desperate circumstances call for desperate measures. God heard the urgent cries of prayer and fasting in Esther's day and spared the lives of His people.

Today Israel is a nation of nations. People have come from well over 140 different countries to live in Israel. More than one hundred languages are spoken in this melting pot of Jews in search of their destiny. Ancient prophetic promises are being fulfilled in our day as the second regathering continues to take place. The key to accurate prayer is praying in the will of God, and He grants revelation from both His Word and His heart, extending invitations for us to join in the holy act of agreeing with Him.

The act of praying a promise back to God in its various forms is an awesome privilege and a tool used to shape history.

Scriptural Prophetic Promises for Israel

Now that your interest level has been raised a bit, let me give you a few scriptural promises not yet fulfilled that we can kneel on together in order to see God's prophetic destiny for Israel come to pass.

Ready for the adventure? If so, meditate on the following list of promises and appointments on God's prophetic calendar for Israel and let them sink deeply into your heart. Then pause, take a deep breath and plunge into the wonders of prophetic intercession for Israel as the burden of the Lord comes on you for God's chosen people.

Here are a few Scripture promises for you to pray back to our wonderful Lord:

The Regathering

"Do not fear, for I am with you; I will bring your offspring from the east, and gather you from the west. I will say to the north, 'Give them up!' And to the south, 'Do not hold them back.' Bring My sons from afar, and My daughters from the ends of the earth."

Isaiah 43:5–6

"The days are coming," declares the LORD, "when they will no longer say, 'As the LORD lives, who brought up the sons of Israel from the land of Egypt,' but, 'As the LORD lives, who brought up and led back the descendants of the household of Israel from the north land and from all the countries where I had driven them.' Then they will live on their own soil."

Jeremiah 23:7–8

Salvation through Our Messiah Jesus Christ

"I will pour out on the house of David and on the inhabitants of Jerusalem, the Spirit of grace and of supplication, so that they will look on Me whom they have pierced; and they will mourn for Him, as one mourns for an only son, and they will weep bitterly over Him, like the bitter weeping over a first-born."

Zechariah 12:10

I am not ashamed of the gospel, for it is the power of God for salvation to every one who believes, to the Jew first and also to the Greek.

Romans 1:16

Brethren, my heart's desire and my prayer to God for [the Jews] is for their salvation.

Romans 10:1

Prayers for Jerusalem

Pray for the peace of Jerusalem: "May they prosper who love you. May peace be within your walls, and prosperity within your palaces." For the sake of my brothers and my friends, I will now say, "May peace be within you." For the sake of the house of the LORD our God I will seek your good.

Psalm 122:6–9

For Zion's sake I will not keep silent, and for Jerusalem's sake I will not keep quiet, until her righteousness goes forth like brightness, and her salvation like a torch that is burning.

Isaiah 62:1

There are numerous other scriptural prophetic promises for Israel and the Jewish people. Those listed here are but a tiny sampling just to get you started. I have compiled an appendix in the back of this book entitled "Scriptures for Praying for Israel" for your study, meditation and intercession. I trust you will be thrilled to see an outline filled with prophetic promises for you to kneel on and rehearse before the hearing of our great God and King.

Come join me on the walls, watchmen, and let's lift a cry for Israel.

Proclaim, Praise and Pray

Before we close out this last chapter in the second section of the book and start the final section, "Applications for Prophetic Priests," let's look at one more verse from Jeremiah to highlight some scriptural applications each of us can make.

Jeremiah 31:7 perhaps summarizes better than any other verse the believer's practical response to God's prophetic invitation:

> Thus says the LORD, "Sing aloud with gladness for Jacob, and shout among the chiefs of the nations; proclaim, give praise, and say, 'O LORD, save Thy people, the remnant of Israel.'"

Three important and distinct actions are pointed out to us in this verse. They are the words *proclaim, praise* and *say.* The word *say* in this context refers to prayer, since we are exhorted through "saying" to talk to God. In this verse, then, the handmaidens of the Church are given three successive keys to insert into the prison door on behalf of the Jewish people, to help deliver them into God's destiny for them. These keys are *the power of proclamation, the power of praise* and *the power of prayer.*

At this juncture in our travels together, I have an exhortation for you. Much of the time we are waiting to reach perfection before we will launch out. Well, just do it! Take the promises of God's Word and proclaim them. Announce the destiny of God to the heavens. Proclaim the good will of the Lord to the cities and their inhabitants. Ascribe to the Lord the honor and glory due His name, for He is indeed good. And pray from your heart! Stop theorizing and do something, for Jesus' sake. Be one of the Holy Ghost P.U.S.H.ers needed to show up on the scene—those who "Pray Until Something Happens."

My wife and I have a beautiful picture with these words written on it: *Proclaim, Praise, Pray.* It was given to us by Tom Hess, founder of the House of Prayer for All Nations located on the Mount of Olives right outside Jerusalem. The picture acts as a wonderful reminder to us of our privilege and responsibility as watchmen on the walls for Jerusalem.

The burden for Israel is now a large part of who Michal Ann and I are as prophetic intercessors. Everything we do on behalf of Israel is connected to one of these three simple activities: proclaiming God's Word, praising His holy name and praying—confessing our sins, as Daniel did, and reminding God of His Word, as our many forerunners of old did.

Like Elijah I have called for the drought to end and for a time of mercy to begin. I have prayed for the peace of Jerusalem. I have been awakened in the middle of the night just to sit, wait and listen to the voice of God concerning His purposes for the Jewish people. I have been called into the active service of being on the alert in the night watches during times of war.

If you are like me, you want to get beyond theory and into real-life application, letting the rubber meet the road. If so, cry out to the Lord for His prophetic destiny for the Jewish people to be fulfilled. Like my friend Evald in the Czech Republic, you might ask, "How does this come about?" The still, small voice of Jesus responds, *Oh, this also comes about by the prayers of the saints.*

So pause right now. Quiet your soul in order to listen. Let the Holy Spirit tune your heart to hear the song the angels are singing in heaven right now. May *Elohim*, the Creator and supreme Being, give you the Spirit of wisdom and revelation concerning His prophetic calendar for Israel, and may His heart for Jerusalem beat in your own as we help give birth to God's purposes through prophetic intercession.

PRACTICAL APPLICATIONS—MAKING IT REAL!

- Take several of the Scriptures from Isaiah and Jeremiah relating to Israel's future and pray them back to the Father, asking Him to bring forth His Word.

- Wait on the Lord and ask Him to shine His light in your heart to expose any areas of anti-Semitism or false teaching toward Israel and the Jews. In confession and repentance bring these before the Lord.
- Meditate on the list of promises and appointments in God's prophetic calendar for Israel, letting them sink into your heart. Then plunge into prophetic intercession for God's people.
- Save your money and plan to participate in one of many prayer journeys into Israel, praying the promises on site with insight.

RECOMMENDED READING

When Day and Night Cease by Ramon Bennett (Arm of Salvation, 1992)

The Last Word on the Middle East by Derek Prince (Chosen, 1982)

THREE

APPLICATIONS
FOR PROPHETIC PRIESTS

CRISIS INTERVENTION THROUGH INTERCESSION

Where are My Daniels? Where are My Esthers? Where are My Deborahs? And where are My Josephs? These words that echoed in my being as I rode the train from Heidelberg to Rosenheim, Germany, a few years ago have stuck with me. There was a pleading, an urgency, in these almost haunting tones in the middle of the night.

What is the Holy Spirit searching for? For those with "an extraordinary spirit" like Daniel (Daniel 6:3) to whom He can give understanding of the end times. He is scouring the earth to find those prophetic watchmen who arise like Esther "for such a time as this" (Esther 4:14). He searches our churches for Deborahs (see Judges 4:4–5) to emerge from their comfort zones and go forth into the world mak-

209

ing a difference, even in society and government. And He is looking for Josephs, an interpreter of dreams and a wise administrator who saved his people from severe famine (see Genesis 41:56–57). Where are these courageous men and women of God for this generation?

I am convinced in every fiber of my being that to live successfully in the hours ahead, we must have the anointing of crisis intercession like these biblical characters who have gone before us. Where are the Praying Hydes of our day who will win souls in prayer and then proceed to win them one by one through life's daily routine? Perilous times lie ahead as the last days unfold (see 2 Timothy 3:1). We need a new generation of those who will walk in the anointing— like intercessor Rees Howells, whose prayers kept Great Britain from the invasion of the Nazis in World War II.

In October 1998 I was honored to visit the Bible school that Rees Howells founded in Swansea, Wales. I visited with his elderly son, Samuel Howells, still active at age 86 in his priestly role of intercession before the throne. What a joy it was to be in the very room where crisis intercession arose on behalf of the Jewish people!

Doris M. Ruscoe, a student at Mr. Howells' Bible school, tells of some of these anointed prayer gatherings in her book *The Intercession of Rees Howells*.

> As each crisis in the war developed, the Holy Spirit guided our prayers and each time we knew that victory had been gained in the spirit before the news came over the radio or in the newspapers of victory on the field of battle. So great was the burden that there were times when Rees Howells could only wrestle alone with God in his room, while members of the staff carried on with the meetings.
>
> During the Battle of Britain, in the autumn of 1940, when Britain stood alone against the enemy and our airmen were fighting desperately to withstand the enemy attacks, especially on London, Rees Howells said, "Christian England will never be invaded." The enemy offensive, intended as a

preliminary to invasion, came to a climax on September 15, a day we remember again for the assurance of victory. The attack failed and the invasion did not take place.[1]

I am convinced we need another level of supernatural empowerment to do the work of crisis intervention—the holy, bold, intercessory work when "mercy triumphs over judgment" (James 2:13).

At the close of my appointment with Samuel Howells, I asked how his father, Rees Howells, had received revelation from God on what to pray. Did it come by dreams, visions, the burden of God—or just how? Mr. Howells' remark to me was short and piercing: "Oh, you must understand, the Lord's servant was possessed by God."

That answered it all! New levels of authority with God and over the enemy come from new levels of possession by God.

Now let's investigate the life of Amos, who combined the two great emphases of mercy and judgment. His bold cries of crisis intercession released heaven's intervention. To learn the lesson that mercy triumphs over judgment, let's take a look at this tough yet tender warrior of the Lord, in whose life these traits were uniquely woven together.

Visions to Amos: Revealing, Repenting and Relenting

Amos was a shepherd and fruit farmer. He came from Tekoa, a small village six miles south of Bethlehem. Although he was a native of Judah, his mission was to the northern kingdom. And even though he had not been trained in the prophetic schools, the Lord called Amos out from his flock, saying, "Go prophesy unto My people Israel."

This country boy dug beneath the veneer of temporal prosperity and exposed the inherent weakness and decay in Israel that was inviting doom. Righteousness—Amos' dominant note—was necessary for the security of the nation and for the stabilizing of her faith. Where righteousness was lacking, no amount of ritual would ever avert judgment. The same is true today.

The Locust Swarm

> The Lord GOD showed me, and behold, He was forming a locust-swarm when the spring crop began to sprout. And behold, the spring crop was after the king's mowing. And it came about, when it had finished eating the vegetation of the land, that I said, "Lord GOD, please pardon! How can Jacob stand, for he is small?" The LORD changed His mind about this. "It shall not be," said the LORD.
>
> Amos 7:1–3

Through visionary revelation, the Lord warned Amos of coming devastation to the vegetation of the land in the form of a swarm of locusts. Amos responded to this prophetic warning through immediate, bold intercession, appealing to God's mercy: "Lord GOD, please pardon!" (verse 2).

The cry for pardon seems to have been made by Amos and Amos alone. Neither Hosea nor Isaiah nor any of the other God-fearing prophets of the time joined in. To Amos alone the vision appeared, and by him the intercession was made.

Perhaps this was because of the relationship between responsibility and authority. Amos, a farmer by trade, was given the revelation of the destruction of the crops. This judgment would have decimated the people of God and society and hit Amos personally as well. And from his place of responsibility he was granted authority through prayer. Amos cried out to God for pardon for his people. He acknowledged that they were due the judgments shown but pleaded for the relenting of God's wrath.

After his cry of repentance he reminded the Lord of the condition of "Jacob," referring to Israel, the northern kingdom: "How can Jacob stand," asked Amos, "for he is small?" (verse 2). Here Amos was bringing to the Lord's attention that those people bore His covenant name in the earth. Despite their wickedness they carried God's name and reputation, and Amos pleaded on the basis of God's reputation in the earth.

He stood in the gap between God's righteous judgments that were due and the need for mercy on the people's behalf. He boldly put his face into God's face!

The Consuming Fire

Thus the Lord GOD showed me, and behold, the Lord GOD was calling to contend with them by fire, and it consumed the great deep and began to consume the farm land. Then I said, "Lord GOD, please stop! How can Jacob stand, for he is small?" The LORD changed His mind about this. "This too shall not be," said the Lord GOD.

Amos 7:4–6

After his intervention in the locust judgment, Amos continued to look, and saw on the heels of it a second judgment coming. This time a consuming fire was about to be kindled against the farmland. Amos again cried, "Lord GOD, please stop! How can Jacob stand, for he is small?" (verse 5).

We need the same tenacious, watchful, responsive spirit in prayer. Normally when the Church wins a victory, we celebrate and maybe even let up our guard for a while. Amos did not do this. He remained keenly observant and prepared to intervene.

The Lord changed His mind, therefore, about the judgment by fire: "This too shall not be" (verse 6).

The Plumb Line

If you could get a reading of the spiritual atmospheric conditions of Amos' day, one thing you would notice for sure: Change was in the air. Yes, God had averted a couple of judgments, but idolatry was rampant. Report card time had come. To see this, let's pick back up reading from Amos once again:

> Thus He showed me, and behold, the Lord was standing by a vertical wall, with a plumb line in His hand. And the LORD said to me, "What do you see, Amos?" And I said, "A plumb line." Then the LORD said, "Behold I am about to put a plumb line in the midst of My people Israel. I will spare them no longer. The high places of Isaac will be desolated and the sanctuaries of Israel laid waste. Then shall I rise up against the house of Jeroboam with the sword."
>
> Amos 7:7–9

Israel had been constructed, so to speak, with a plumb line. Everything in her original foundations had appeared plumb. God had approved of her. But now she had become a different people and the plumb bob did not hang the way it used to. (Does this sound familiar?)

Very early on Jeroboam, king of Israel, had introduced calf worship (see 1 Kings 12:25–33). Thus the people became wicked and departed from the way of the Lord (see 1 Kings 13:33–34). So God stirred Amos by showing him the plumb line and saying, in effect, "I have noticed how Israel, like a wall that was once upright, has been gradually giving way. In the past I have overlooked it, but now I cannot." This is what God says to every individual, generation, institution, society, kingdom or nation that ceases to be upright.

Amos' warnings to Jeroboam were in vain. Amaziah, the high priest, actually told Amos to leave: "Go, you seer, flee away to the land of Judah, and there eat bread and there do your prophesying!" (Amos 7:12–13). His services were no longer wanted.

Our Own State of Affairs

Reader, open your eyes. Tell me, what do you see? Pastor, what is happening in your midst? Prophetic intercessor, what is going on right now? Both church and secular leaders have been falling. Sin is being uncovered. People's hearts are on trial. The winds of pressure are blowing. Could this be a sign to us?

God has a high, commanding view of all that is built on the earth. He measures, observes and tries us. Just as a mason uses a plumb line to determine the straightness of the wall, so God judges the uprightness of our human actions, and He is dropping a plumb line into the midst of His Church and the nations.

Whatever a man loves most governs him. If he loves pleasure most, his character is sensual. If he loves money most, his character is worldly. If he loves knowledge most, his character is philosophic. But if he loves God most, his character is divine.

What is God's evaluation of the character of the Church in our day? Of you and me? What is the Holy Spirit requiring of us in these days? In order to be vessels that can contain His gifts and power and not be destroyed by them, we must yield to the wonderful—and at times gruesome—work of the cross. We must cultivate the fear of the Lord, run away from evil and be embraced in the arms of our merciful Messiah.

As we cultivate the fear of the Lord, let's remember that when it comes to judging a nation, the Lord has an order that He follows. He evaluates the character of His people *before* He judges the character of the world:

> It is time for judgment to begin with the household of God; and if it begins with us first, what will be the outcome for those who do not obey the gospel of God? AND IF IT IS WITH DIFFICULTY THAT THE RIGHTEOUS IS SAVED, WHAT WILL BECOME OF

THE GODLESS MAN AND THE SINNER? Therefore, let those also who suffer according to the will of God entrust their souls to a faithful Creator in doing what is right.

1 Peter 4:17–19

First God judges His household; only then does He move to phase two: judging a godless society. He will judge the world in the Church, then the world by the Church. As it was in Amos' day, so it is today. The influence of the twentieth-century Church is small in world esteem, personal holiness and true demonstrations of the Holy Spirit's power. We have crippled ourselves through prayerlessness, unbelief, sectarianism, inactivity, selfishness, internal bickering, intimidation and choking out the Spirit's presence and power through ceremonialism. As we turn the millennium corner, we will find that God has stopped winking at the gap between His righteousness and our national morality. His bride is wearing a soiled garment and He has decided it is time to clean her up—to make her pure and holy, without spot or wrinkle.

In the same way that God listened to Amos' plea and relented concerning the locusts and fire, I believe He has been holding off major national judgment against America and many other nations in recent years—not because we have changed but because of the cry of His saints. If these great judgments had been fully released in the early 1990s, the Church would have been crushed. But God wants us to be strong in the hour of national judgment and a place of refuge for those seeking shelter from the storm.

Will we be ready? The time clock of judgment is ticking away. In fact, I believe we are headed into some shaky times, unless intercession once again changes the mind of God.

In the last decade we have seen a shaking of the leadership in the Church worldwide, particularly in North America. Covered sins have been and will be unveiled. I am convinced that this housecleaning will continue as the Holy

Spirit deals severely with the motives of our hearts, especially those of us called to leadership. Many prophetic watchmen see, at the close of this purifying, a convergence of a wave of power evangelism in the midst of national difficulties that could include circumstances such as economic hardship, new strands of epidemic diseases, natural disaster and the ever-looming possibility of regional war.

But the turn of the century could bring an outpouring of the true spirit of conviction of sin, not only in the Church but in society in general. Prayer in that day will not be a charismatic fad. It will be the life source of a militant people going forth in displays of miraculous power that have barely been seen since the New Testament Church era.

What Is God's Plumb Line?

The grand old Book. By it we, too, ought to be trying ourselves. Every thought you cherish, every word you utter and every deed you perform determines the condition of the moral wall of character in your life—to be tested by God's holy Word.

Bricklayers are not foolish enough to think that if they build a wall not perpendicular to the ground, it will stand. Similarly when a man, ministry or nation grows up crooked, dishonest or untruthful, the consequence is the same: The wall will eventually give way. We must build the walls of our own lives with the concrete of moral purity, by the Holy Spirit's enablement, and based on the principles of God's Word.

"Lord God, Please Stop!"

Amos received five visions concerning the destiny of the nation. The first of these was the locust plague; the second, fire sweeping the nation. Both of these plagues were averted by the prayer of the prophet. Amos' third vision was of the plumb line revealing the nation's weakly constructed foundation. Fourth was the basket of summer fruits disclosing the rottenness of the nation that had repudiated God's word. Herein it was proclaimed that a famine would come—not of bread and water, but of "hearing the words of the LORD" (Amos 8:11). The fifth and last vision revealed the hopelessness of escape from the vengeance of God (9:1–4).

These visions were progressive in nature. Each came with an opportunity for repentance. But each progressive judgment seemed harder to avert.

"Help, Lord!" needs to be our serious plea. Numerous people are sounding the trumpet of prayer in our land. But most do not tell you why. Are we headed toward serious trouble? In my eyes we are. What lies ahead? It depends on whether there are any Amoses who will cry, "No, Lord God, please stop! The Church is not ready; we are not yet what You destined us to be." The Holy Spirit is looking for a destitute people, you see, who walk what they talk and obey what they pray. He seeks a people who have power with God in prayer.

"Jacob is small." We must repent, confess our unbelief toward an omnipotent God and cry to the Lord for the healing of the broken Body of His Son. Labor for strength and zeal to overcome passivity. Conquer the power of selfishness by choosing a life devoted to the cross. Repent of internal slander and bickering and speak those things that give grace to the hearers. Cast off the spirit of intimidation and arise in the faith of our God. Break the bonds of religious ceremonialism and let the Spirit of liberty reign.

A Modern-Day Example of Crisis Intercession

What I am about to tell you may blow your mind. It certainly did mine! But all these events are true, and I will tell you the story from my set of lenses just as it happened.

Over the years I have been privileged to participate in various intercessory gatherings in numerous cities and nations, for a wide range of purposes. I was in Yugoslavia in 1990, for example, for special evangelistic crusades with my dear friend Mahesh Chavda, just a few months before the ethnic conflict broke out. I walked the streets of Zagreb, Croatia, and Sarajevo, Bosnia, and prayed over those cities. I was struck by the beauty of where East met West, both architecturally and spiritually.

While I was staying in a hotel room in Sarajevo, I was reading a challenging book on intercession. Looking out the windows of my third-floor room, I lifted a prayer: "Lord, place upon me the imprint of the eternal value of prayer."

I will never forget that prayer because of the immediacy of the answer that came. At the very moment that I launched that prayer out my third-story window, a Muslim cleric stepped out of the doorway of the tall minaret (one of the slender towers) of the mosque directly across the street. We stood eyeball to eyeball. Our eyes met. Then he began to release one of his five calls of prayer a day to the Islamic faithful to cry out to Allah.

I was smitten as my short prayer was answered immediately by the imprint of this stunning sight.

If they who serve a false god can call out to their god five times a day, I thought with a shudder, *surely the Lord will preserve for Himself a generation of Daniels who will bend the knee and cry out to the one true God, and give themselves no rest until He establishes His Kingdom rule on earth.*

The Lord gave me a heart for those people during the evangelistic crusades, as hundreds of them came to faith and received the healing touch of Jesus. Later, when I flew out of Belgrade with Mahesh, something left with me. It seemed like a tiny portion of God's heart had been deposited inside of me for that region of the world and for its people.

Four years later, in February 1994, I found myself in the Czech Republic for the Central European Reconciliation Conference. I was thrilled to be back in the beautiful homeland of rich Church history of the likes of John Huss, the reformer excommunicated for revealing corruption in the clergy; and John Amos Comenius, bishop of the Bohemian Brethren who yearned for the unity of all Christians; and Count Zinzendorf, passionately devoted to Jesus, who longed to bring Christianity to the world.

The war in Sarajevo—the site of the beginning of World War I, where Archduke Francis Ferdinand was murdered—was at its height and threatening to escalate out of sight. This ethnic, regional and religious war was volatile. Catholics from Croatia, Orthodox from Serbia and Muslims from Bosnia Herzegovina were battling fiercely, and horrible crimes against humanity were commonplace.

Before the prayer conference in Prague, I ministered for a few days to church leaders there. An American friend, Jeff Karas, was my traveling intercessory companion.

One night Jeff was given a dream in which he saw three hunters with bows and arrows lined up ready to shoot. The last hunter hit the bull's eye. After this occurred, there was snow on the ground.

Jeff described his dream to me and asked for input.

"It has something to do with the prayer conference we're going to," I told him. "But I don't have time to process it right now. I have to get ready for the meeting. Somehow it will just play out."

I thought little more about it.

A few days later we traveled north of Prague to participate in the reconciliation prayer conference. The purpose of the gathering: to bring delegates from across Europe to seek God's face, through acts of reconciliation and intercession, to intervene in the horrific war in the former Yugoslavia. Pastoral and intercessory delegates assembled from countries as diverse as Hungary and Great Britain, Croatia and Belgium, Germany and Bulgaria, plus many other nations. (Jeff and I were the only delegates from the Western Hemisphere.) The summit was chaired by Johannes Facius, international coordinator for the International Fellowship of Intercessors, and Dan Drapal, team leader of Christian Fellowship of Prague, Czech Republic.

A Pattern of Progressive Prayer

The prayer that came forth was a model that had been worked out through trial and error over the years. It was unlike any prayer gathering I had ever attended—not because it was so intense, or even because it was tangibly anointed, but because of its patience.

The first day of prayer was spent in personal repentance. We broke into small groups and confessed our sins to the Lord and to one another. Teaching was interspersed, but the main agenda was cleansing the land—this time, the land of our own hearts.

We spent the next day confessing the sins of the Church. Once again, in small groups, we named the sins of our own congregations and denominations, both currently and historically. Teachings were brought from Church history to enlighten us as to our spotted past and give us good ammunition for the place of corporate identification of sin. Often we had to turn to someone of a different persuasion, humble ourselves and ask for forgiveness. At times it did not seem that much was transpiring, but patience was the winner.

On the third day we began to confess our national sins. Having covered many of our personal and church sins, we could now delve more deeply into the sins of our ethnic backgrounds and nations.

This is where it got all the more interesting. Struggles began to surface as a person from one nation found prejudice against another rising to the top. But as long as grace was given and light came, we continued to declare, "O Lord, please forgive us, for we have sinned." Again the pace was slow. There were no great spiritual fireworks, just a pattern of progressive confession of sin.

On the fourth and final day, I had been away from home for more than 25 days, since I had been in Albania for three weeks prior to the conference. I had not seen a newspaper that I could read, heard a radio program that I could understand or seen a television program that gave me any understanding of what was going on in the world. I was weary and took the afternoon to rest in my hotel room and seek the face of God.

A Strategic Encounter

Then it happened. In my room I began to hear airplanes circling overhead. They buzzed for some time. I couldn't figure it out. We were quite a distance from any airport. But it almost sounded like war planes. What was happening?

Then I heard a word resound in the hotel room. It was not the still, quiet voice of God in my heart, but the external voice of the Lord speaking in the room: "If you do not pray, the planes will come." Then, in a vision of what looked like physical letters hanging against the wall, I read the name *Klaus*.

My spiritual antennas were pulled out, and "knowings"— divine reasonings—came to me. Somehow—apart from any knowledge of current events, since I was in the dark about them—I knew that the guns of Serbia were poised in the mountains overlooking Sarajevo and ready to strike. Internally I knew that NATO was giving the Serbs 48 hours to remove their weapons from the mountains or they would come and bomb out their sites. I also sensed that the Serbs were planning an attack of their own and that they, too, might send planes within 48 hours to bomb Sarajevo.

It was a crucial hour.

I waited and prayed some more, then left my room to look for the two primary leaders of the conference, Johannes Facius and Dan Drapal. In this setting I was a watchman, not an elder at the gate, and I knew I was to submit the revelatory experience to the ones with delegated authority. Secretly I hoped that submitting the information to them might be all I was to do with it.

First I told Dan of the event.

"Do you know the names of our nation's governmental leaders?" he asked me.

I assured him I did not.

"The last name of the leader of the Czech government is Klaus," he said.

Interesting! Was this to signal the leaders that this experience was from God?

Then I found Johannes and shared the encounter with him. He, too, quizzed me, asking if I had been listening to the radio. Apparently they had just heard an emergency report a few minutes before, while I had been in my room, announcing that NATO had given the Serbs 48 hours to remove their artillery from the mountains surrounding Sarajevo or they would come with planes and bomb their entrenched sites. I was stunned.

The word God had spoken, however, was, "If you do not pray, the planes will come." And now we were headed into the last night's meeting.

The Three Hunters

After worship and teaching, Johannes called me to the front and asked me to share the word I had received. Unemotionally I told of the revelatory activity, then took my seat.

Then prayer time came. We had spent three days kneeling on the promises—through personal repentance, humility and confession of sin. Now it was time to stand and fight. To my surprise Johannes called three men to lead us into aggressive intercession—a prayer leader from England, another from Amsterdam and me.

One after another, the three of us launched the prayers of intervention that the Lord gave us. I was the last in the lineup called on to shoot his ammo.

As I prayed, something came on me, and for a few seconds I was clothed with supernatural confidence and the authority of God. It might have been the gift of faith in operation in an intercessory dimension. In any case, it was as if prophetically I had been given a bow and arrow. It reminded me of my New York City prayer encounter back in 1987 when I prayed with a burst of authority about an Iranian military action against the U.S. presence in Bahrain.

Feeling somewhat unattached to what was going on around me, I pulled back the string of the bow and released a powerful arrow of prayer, commanding the powers of darkness to pull back off of the mountains and for God to intervene.

"In the name of Jesus," I heard myself declaring, "I command the powers of darkness to be bound up over the mountains of Sarajevo, and that the planes will not come!"

Authority came upon me and then it lifted.

The meeting ended, and once again I was left in that familiar position of "Now what was *that* all about?"

As I walked back to my seat, Jeff sounded excited.

"Do you remember the dream I told you about a few days ago?" he asked. "Remember how I saw three hunters and the third one hit the mark? Well, that just happened, and the third hunter was you!"

Then Jeff reminded me that at the end of the dream there had been snow on the ground. We both thought that was interesting. But the temperature now, even though it was February, was unseasonably warm.

We filed the tidbit away, the meeting came to a close and we went to bed.

That night the temperature dropped dramatically, and the next morning we found snow on the ground.

A sign from God? Perhaps. We had confessed our sins—personal, ecclesiastical and national—and interceded on behalf of the ethnic fighting. Isaiah 1:18 gives us this insight:

"Come now, and let us reason together," says the LORD. "Though your sins are as scarlet, they will be as white as snow; though they are red like crimson, they will be like wool."

Maybe the Lord was giving us an indication in the natural realm, through the blanket of new snow, that cleansing had indeed taken place in the spiritual realm.

The Result

While this is all subjective stuff, you cannot deny the accuracy and intricacy of the events back in 1994. What actually transpired? The blessing and problem with prayer is that you cannot measure its effects by weights and measures and scientific proof. But let me share the little bit I think I know.

First, the Serbs pulled their guns out of the mountains. Second, no retaliatory warplanes were sent. And finally, instead of escalating into a major war, this regional conflict began to wind down from that point on. Divine intervention took place through the power of intercession. Mercy triumphed over judgment.

The breakthrough was not the result of one prayer and reconciliation conference, of course. It was the result of God's people throughout the earth lifting up a cry for crisis intervention, and then possibly—just possibly—God's authority being released into a specific setting to be enacted.

I am not saying the conflict in the former Yugoslavia is over. It is far from over. It is like a bubble in wallpaper; it just keeps moving around. Prayer, watching, fasting and intercession must continue to be lifted up for that historic field of battle.

Take encouragement from this encounter, however, and continue in our fight of humble, holy, bold intercession.

Applications for Us Today

You already know that I believe in crisis intervention through the power of prayer. Intercession draws a line in the sand and calls for darkness to end and for light to come. While judgment looms over the nations and perilous times are coming, let's not sit in the valley of despair.

Amos, like all the true prophets, did not leave his hearers in the depths of despair, but revealed the brightness of a new day. In the last word of his address, he declared God's promise to release His people from captivity and "plant them on their own land, and they will not again be rooted out from their land which I have given them" (Amos 9:15).

In Amos' day judgment was partially averted or cut short. But it did eventually come. What will be our outcome today? Yes, the plumb line is dropping in front of our very eyes. How do we measure up? How will we respond? Has the plumb bob been released in the middle of your heart? Rend your heart, and perhaps God will relent of His wrath, leaving a blessing instead.

Get God's Perspective

In the midst of all this intense stuff, look up and get God's perspective. Remember, even judgment is ultimately for the purpose of redemption. Listen to the writer of Hebrews: "My son, do not regard lightly the discipline of the LORD, nor faint when you are reproved by Him; for those whom the LORD loves He disciplines, and He scourges every son whom He receives" (Hebrews 12:5–6). Realize, too, what Isaiah 26:9 aptly depicts: "At night my soul longs for Thee, indeed, my spirit within me seeks Thee diligently; for when the earth experiences Thy judgments the inhabitants of the world learn righteousness."

While I am one who emphasizes crying out to the Lord for intervention, there comes a time when God's judgments are His mercy. In that setting, just move aside and let God be God. He knows what is best and what is needed, and when. But keep on crying out all the while for mercy.

In order to "lift up [our] eyes to the mountains" (Psalm 121:1), we have to lift our chins off our chests, take our eyes off ourselves and look up. In other words, so long as our attention is on ourselves, we will not get His view on a matter. So in the midst of crisis, whether personal, congregational or national, look up and see what your heavenly Father is saying and doing.

Add a Dose of Patience

While we are considering "Applications for Prophetic Priests" in this section of the book, add a word to your arsenal: *patience.*

In today's fast food mentality, the last thing we want to hear is "Wait!" or "Not yet!" And the last thing we want to do is engage in a pattern of progressive praying, as the reconciliation conference followed step by step in Prague. Often we treat prayer as if we can drive up to a reader board, place our order, pull forward to the service window and pick up our food—fresh and hot every time! At times the Lord whets our appetite with fast service. Often we find, however, that He is not simply in the process of giving us an answer but of making us into the solution. This recipe takes time and has that old-fashioned ingredient in it, patience.

Although there was a dramatic breakthrough at the prayer conference in Prague, what I took home with me was a fresh perspective on patience in the pattern of progressive praying.

Be Sure to Forgive

Releasing and walking in forgiveness is one of our most powerful weapons of spiritual warfare. It disarms the enemy and strips him of his right to knock us out. This is true on all levels, whether personal or corporate. If you are to stay in the battle for the long haul, forgiveness is a necessity, not a luxury. (I will address this subject more in the next chapter, "Wisdom Issues for Intercessors.")

Too many of us can tell war stories of people, churches and ministries that entered the conflict to win and instead got all beaten up. Rather than shaking up the camp of the enemy, we got all shook up ourselves. The key of forgiveness unlocks many treasures currently held in darkness.

Seek Wisdom

Do you remember one of the three prayers the Lord gave me while I was growing up? "Lord, give me wisdom beyond my years." Horror stories abound of well-meaning people who ended up like debris along a highway after a hit-and-run accident. There must be protection for those called to the field of crisis intervention.

To be an effective crisis intercessor takes wisdom. So in all our getting, as Proverbs 4:7 reminds us, let's "acquire wisdom [and] get understanding."

Keep on Building

As we round the corner into the next chapter, I trust you are being stirred to action. God is examining His Church and dropping the plumb line of His Word, truth and standards into the midst of the Church and the nations today. Don't hold back. Take your place on His wall, wait, listen, aim and then shoot.

Remember, He is looking for the Daniels, Esthers, Deborahs and Josephs of our generation—for such a time as this. He is looking for you. It is time for the grace of crisis intercession to be poured out once again. Come join me for the adventure of your life! Together let's join those who have gone before us on the walls in crisis intercession, where mercy triumphs over judgment.

PRACTICAL APPLICATIONS—MAKING IT REAL!

- Ask the Lord to help you envision your heart for crisis intervention through intercession. Seek the Lord for revelation for this kind of authority in prayer.
- Pick a tragedy in the earth today and begin to lift up a cry for mercy for those severely affected.
- Next, take the Scripture promise of Jeremiah 29:11 and meditate on it. Now remind the Lord of His Word in this current situation by praying the promise back to Him.
- Ask the Lord for a spirit of faith and rebuke the enemy and his devouring work in Jesus' name concerning this crisis situation.

RECOMMENDED READING

Rees Howells, Intercessor by Norman Grubb (Christian Literature Crusade, 1987)

Shaping History through Prayer and Fasting by Derek Prince (Spire, 1973)

11

WISDOM ISSUES
FOR INTERCESSORS

Not long ago, while sitting at the supper table with Michal Ann and our four young arrows, I asked them a serious question: "If the Lord let you ask Him for one thing, and you knew He would grant it, what would that one thing be?"

That certainly got their attention! The children lit up like Christmas trees, all glowing bright.

"You mean it, Daddy?" asked Rachel, our youngest, eyes gleaming.

"Yes, I want to know from the deepest place in your heart. If God gave you one request, what would you ask for?"

GraceAnn, our second child, was the first to declare her answer: "A horse, of course!"

Rachel followed suit. "Yes, Daddy, a horse!"

Tyler perked up and said he wanted a racecar. I think he said he wanted it to be fast, too.

Justin, the oldest, with a philosophical and studious bent, pondered the question. "Now just one thing, right, Dad?"

"Yes, what one thing would you ask for?"

Justin responded by saying he would ask for a million dollars.

The rest of them all chimed in at that point and decided they wanted to change their requests and ask for a million dollars, too.

Then it was my dear wife's turn to answer.

"I know what I would choose," Michal Ann said. "I would tell God, 'I choose Your choice. You choose for me!'"

Well, the kids got the idea. They sighed as if to say, "There go Dad and Mom again!" But maybe they really did get the picture.

Yes, let's choose God's choice. What would it be? What one thing would He want us to ask for?

At various times in my life I have asked for the power of God to set the captives free. (I still am asking for more of His Holy Spirit's power in my ministry.) At other times I have cried out for finances to be able to extend His Kingdom. (I still need this, too.) On other occasions I have cried out in the night for deliverance from besetting sin and for an imparting of the holiness of God. (I am still desperate for and seeking this, too.) Many times I have sought the Lord for a compassionate and merciful heart. (I really continue after this one.)

But I need to hang in for the long haul and not just flare like a Roman candle display, shooting up into the night with a quick, brilliant flash and people "oohing" and "ahhing," only to fizzle out as quickly as I shot up. If I were given only one thing to ask for, I would take after the example of King Solomon and ask for wisdom for life's journey. It is the ingredient necessary for each of us to make it for the long haul.

One of the three Holy Spirit-inspired prayers from my youth—"Give me wisdom beyond my years"—is a prayer I will continue to lift up till I go to my grave. I need wisdom more today than yesterday, and I will surely need more tomorrow than I do today.

Let's look for a moment at this well-known request from the heart of Solomon.

Solomon's Wise Choice

After the death of his father, David, Solomon established himself over the kingdom. We read in 2 Chronicles 1:1 that "the Lord his God was with him and exalted him greatly." One of Solomon's first acts as king was restoring the bronze altar used in the ceremonial offerings of worship. After the altar had been returned to its proper place of function, a thousand burnt offerings were presented to the Lord.

That night God appeared to Solomon and said to him, "Ask what I shall give you" (2 Chronicles 1:7).

Solomon responded to this awesome request, "Give me now wisdom and knowledge, that I may go out and come in before this people; for who can rule this great people of Thine?" (verse 10).

God granted Solomon's request. How could He refuse? When we ask God for more of Himself, He always responds. Thus Solomon became one of the wisest rulers on earth.

How did Solomon know to ask for wisdom? Did the idea just pounce on him when he reached a certain age? I don't think so. Proverbs 4 gives us a clue. Here Solomon tells his own sons how David had instructed him, while he was still young and tender in heart, in the value of wisdom. Shouldn't we follow his example and pass on to the next generation the things that are really important in order to live this life meaningfully?

> Hear, O sons, the instruction of a father, and give attention that you may gain understanding, for I give you sound teaching; do not abandon my instruction. When I was a son to my father, tender and the only son in the sight of my mother, then he taught me and said to me, "Let your heart hold fast my words; keep my commandments and live; acquire wis-

dom! Acquire understanding! . . . Do not forsake her, and she will guard you; love her, and she will watch over you. The beginning of wisdom is: Acquire wisdom; and with all your acquiring, get understanding. Prize her, and she will exalt you; she will honor you if you embrace her. She will place on your head a garland of grace; she will present you with a crown of beauty."

Proverbs 4:1–9

Consider the action verbs stated here—the things Solomon was instructed to do to gain this thing called wisdom: *Hear, give attention, do not abandon, hold fast, keep and live, acquire, do not forsake, love, acquire, get, prize, embrace.* No passivity here! I love the last two words the most: *prize* and *embrace.*

When you prize something, you appraise its value highly. You protect it, realizing it is rare, extremely precious or even priceless. You may even be willing to sell all you have to obtain it.

When you embrace something, you hold it closely to your heart and cherish its essence. You realize you must give your whole self to it in order to be embraced by it in return.

When we prize and embrace wisdom, we actually become an expression of it.

Lessons from the Trenches

But where do we as intercessors, soldiers in God's battle, start in our quest for wisdom? We may love and desire wisdom, but how do we actually learn it? Far too often we ask God for wisdom only to find the highways of intercession and spiritual warfare littered with casualties piled on top of casualties. Our spiritual Jeeps and tanks push along, ignoring warning signals that a curve lies ahead, and end up in the pile of "vehicles for God." Or we may find ourselves in the ditch or stalled along the roadside, burned out for Jesus simply through overheating or sheer exhaustion.

At the other extreme, many inspiring preachers, teachers and authors seem not to live on the same planet that you and I inhabit. They come across as super-spiritual gurus whom nothing ever daunts or hinders. Nothing seems to hit them between the eyes. Nothing ever sideswipes them or even dazes them temporarily. I have a hint for you: Behind many of their pasty smiles are families left in their dust, disillusioned and ready to throw in the towel.

There must be another way!

Having been around this mountain a few times myself, and having seen many people treading like hamsters on the never-ending wheel of misfortune, let me share some lessons I have learned (and am learning!) in the trenches regarding the pitfalls and perils of intercessory warfare. This, in fact, is how we learn wisdom—in the trenches doing the stuff. We shoot, get shot at, then learn to position ourselves differently. It is called wisdom.

Do you see the connection to our theme of kneeling on the promises? Wisdom is a vital application for those called into birthing God's purposes through prophetic intercession. God will give us wisdom if we ask Him (see James 1:5), but like good soldiers in training, we have to learn how to use it.

Copy-ism versus Relationship

In the beginning someone may seek the Lord with all his heart, and God touches him with special grace for a distinct calling. Through trial and error the Lord perfects His plan through this person as He perfects His work *in* him. Relationship. Then someone else comes along, sees his apparent success and asks, "How are you doing such a great work for God?" The one learning the lessons explains the blueprint God is giving him. But others turn the process of becoming into a machine of doing. Someone else sees the principle and writes a book about it. Another comes along, reads the book and tries to implement the vision. Copy-ism. Years later we encounter the vehicle wiped out on the side of the road: "Been there, done that. It didn't work."

Too often, out of haste, we take a principle of the Spirit and try to make an assembly-line production out of it. The preaching of the cross is nowhere to be found in this type of cookie-cutter entrepreneurism. Somewhere along the way we have lost the vitality of "relationship" and replaced it with the cheap substitute of "copy-ism." In our haste to succeed, we just mimic what someone else has received.

Intimacy versus Warfare

Although I have never served in active military duty, I have fought in many "air" wars. I have spent many sleepless nights watching for the enemy's next move, waiting for orders from my Commander-in-Chief, on the alert for whatever was needed next. I have crouched in the trenches of warfare, thinking the man next to me was my comrade, only to be stabbed in the back by the enemy camouflaged in sheep's clothing. I have spent days fasting, not just because my heart was overwhelmed with Jesus' loveliness but because I was desperate for help or because my heart was breaking for someone.

This part of the Christian life is not about wine and roses, intimate times and hangin' with Jesus. I love and actually prefer the romance of being the bride of Christ. But that is not all there is. In fact, one time I had an interesting vision of the bride of Christ in her beautiful attire. The Holy Spirit instructed me to look closely at how she was dressed. Guess what I saw? The bride wore army boots!

We need to be the fighting bride (see Ephesians 5:25–27; 6:13–18). We must hold tightly to God's hand (intimacy) while moving out with His authority (warfare). It is not one or the other; it is intimacy in order to war effectively.

It takes guts to be in the army. Courage is needed in today's soft Christian society. Why? Because serving in the military is tough. When you hit the enemy, he likes to hit back. One of the tricks for surviving in the battle is to be like a rhinoceros with a thick skin and a big heart. I don't have that one down yet. Many of us, in fact, tend to be hard-hearted or thin-skinned. But somehow, as we grow in wisdom, we must learn to be both tough and tender.

Honoring the Vets

While I was growing up, children were taught to honor our veterans of war. Every Memorial and Armistice Day my dad, along with the other men and women who fought for our nation, were honored in our little rural Methodist church. A special seating section was set aside just for them. They were proud to have helped their nation in a time of need. They wore their uniforms or VFW blazers and Legion hats and came marching in together. No matter what branch of the service they served, they were now all one unit—veterans of conflicts and world wars.

I love and respect the veterans of God's army, too. They attempted something for Christ's sake. They might not have won every battle but they made sure the enemy did not get the final blow. I like to find these vets, snuggle up to them and rub in some oil of the Holy Spirit's honor and comfort. Sometimes I befriend these unsung heroes in the Body of Christ and tell them their journeys have been important. When the Holy Spirit permits, I see if they will open up the treasure chests of their lives.

Some of the vets I have learned to value the most are the ones with the most scars. Scars do not come by sitting on the sidelines but by fighting in battles. Note that I did not say wounds. Wounds continue to fester because of unresolved infection. But a scar is present only when the infection has been removed and healing has come. The stripes we receive while serving in God's army are the battle wounds that we have let Him heal. Cleansed wounds become healed, and once healed they become battle scars, and battle scars are translated into medals of honor awarded for valiant fighting during times of war.

One older couple my wife and I dearly love are Bob and Nina Lyons. You have probably never heard of them, but they are veterans of wars gone by and, in my book, two of God's generals. Well into their eighties now, with more than fifty years of full-time humble, Pentecostal heritage behind them, they could tell you stories that would curl the hair on the back of your neck! Stories of God's presence in the meetings years ago with Aimee Semple McPherson, A. A. Allen, Jack Cole, William Branham, Martha Wing Robinson, Brother Waldvogel and many other names, big and little.

There are three main things I love about these two guiding lights. First, Bob and Nina speak constantly of Jesus; they never lift up an individual minister or ministry. Second, they love prayer and God's presence more than life itself. And third, although they have seen and experienced much, they have never pitched their tent. They know there must be "More, Lord!"

Yes, Lord, when it is all said and done, let there be more done than said. Let me be like my elderly friends Bob and Nina, and be a bright, steady guiding light pointing the direction to the one Man, Christ Jesus. Amen.

Principles to Guide Us As We Grow in Wisdom

After saying all I have just said, I want to move cautiously in the realm of offering principles on obtaining wisdom. I am not interested in giving "ten easy steps to success" or a quick way through. But there are some principles I have learned in the battle. If you realize these are merely signposts along the path, lessons I am learning in the process of becoming, then we are safe.

Let's proceed, then, with ten distinct wisdom applications for intercessors.

1. Get a Life!

Often it seems that people involved in prophetic, intercessory and spiritual warfare are so engaged in the seriousness of their task that they miss the joy of common, everyday living. Some of us try so hard to discern every breeze that passes by, to interpret the meaning of every bird that flies by the window, every snake in the grass, that we become granola Christians—nutty, flaky and fruity!

My basic counsel is, get a life. Go for a walk; it will help your soul. Find a hobby; it will do you good. Go work out at the health club. Exercise and release the tension. Your natural body will thank you and others around you might like you better. And who knows? You might even make a new friend. Do not forget the basic issues of taking care of yourself—rest, exercise, eating well—and don't neglect friendships and fun. As one of my friends has said, "Learn to laugh at life, yourself and the enemy. Kick up your heels and enjoy the ride!"

There is more to life than conferences, summits and grand conventions. Take a break. Eat a banana split. Go out on a date with your spouse. Jump on the trampoline with your kids. Go to a movie, play, concert or ballgame. Do not just watch life; live it! For Jesus' sake, yours and your family's, get a life.

Wow, point number one was really heavy, wasn't it?

2. Avoid Criticizing at All Costs

Do you know what undoes intercessory groups more than anything else? It is not lack of vision, leadership or even overt spiritual warfare counterattack. It is immature application of discernment of another's problem that gets expressed through criticism. The next thing you know, backstabbing settles in, and without a major cleansing, the group splinters and the devil wins again. How? Through subtle, simple, old-time criticism. It is impossible to pray together if criticism is in your midst.

Once I attended an Intercessors for America Conference in Washington, D.C. At one of the sessions the jealousy of the Holy Spirit came on me and I began to prophesy. I remember the word clearly: "We are now living in the time of the coexistence of the house of David and the house of Saul. You who have been waiting, yearning, believing, longing and praying for the house of David to come forth can disqualify yourselves from being part of what you've been waiting, yearning, praying and believing for, if you sow accusation and critical speech toward the house of Saul while it yet stands. For remember, you, too, have come forth from Saul's loins."

We must not allow our discernment of problems and needs to turn into criticism through impatience and frustration. We will give vocal expression to this discernment in some manner. We will either turn the discernment into intercession or else it will eventually leak out the other side of our mouths as gossip and slander. Criticism does not just affect the person hearing the word; when passed around, it holds up the whole camp from going forward.

When you discern the enemy, one way to respond is to pray to the Father for the release of the opposite spirit. If you discern a spirit of division, for example, then pray for unity and love for the brethren to come forth. Love covers a multitude of sins. Avoid criticism at all costs.

3. Forgiveness Is a Necessity

Second Corinthians 2:10–11 brings us a great wisdom application for all areas of the Christian life—all the more important for intercessors and leaders: "Whom you forgive anything, I forgive also; for indeed what I have forgiven, if I have forgiven anything, I did it for your sakes in the presence of Christ, in order that no advantage be taken of us by Satan; for we are not ignorant of his schemes."

If criticism remains, it becomes an incubator for bitterness and unforgiveness. One of the highest weapons of spiritual warfare is the giving and receiving of forgiveness. So forgive. When you forgive, you are releasing grace to someone else. In fact, one of the best ways you can release grace to yourself, a friend, your family, your church, and leadership, both secular and spiritual, is to forgive.

Peter wrote: "God is opposed to the proud, but gives grace to the humble" (1 Peter 5:5). When you confess your sins to another, you become a candidate to receive grace. Confession is an act of humility. The proud never confess they are wrong. They cannot see their own faults. But the humble confess their sins and thus receive grace. Healing begins to flow in and through vessels of grace. This is why James 5:16 says to "confess your sins to one another, and pray for one another, so that you may be healed."

How does healing come? Confession of individual and corporate sin is an attitude and action of humility that draws God's grace onto the scene. And where there is an atmosphere of grace, there Holy Spirit gifting will flow.

The opposite is true as well. Lack of forgiveness is an act of pride. God opposes the person who refuses to forgive as an act of love, to bring him or her back into alignment through holy resistance. The lack of forgiveness is like leaving the back door wide open, giving Satan license to carry out his strategies against us.

I have already said that forgiveness is not an option; it is a necessity. I, for one, believe it is one of the highest weapons of spiritual warfare. The apostle Paul was saying in 2 Corinthians 2:10–11 that when we forgive, we take the advantage away from Satan. Like Paul, then, let's not be ignorant of Satan's schemes. Forgive and turn the tables on the devil. Shut the door on his access point and give grace to others by walking in forgiveness.

4. Stay with Your Highest Weapons

The Holy Spirit had tipped me off several months ahead to clear my schedule for February 1992. I sensed Him saying to me, *I want you to be a man of prayer during a time of war in the month of February 1992.*

Sure enough, that was the exact time, after Iraq invaded Kuwait, that the coalition of troops led by the United States was engaged in conflict in what became known as the Gulf War. Once again, though I was not suited up in military uniform, I, along with many others, was in the trenches of prayer.

During one of those weeks I went to Atlanta to pray with my friends Pat and Gene Gastineau and their prayer ministry. While I was there, Pat and I were discussing spiritual warfare tactics and she gave me some wise counsel.

"The Lord has given you and Michal Ann an anointing in worship and praise warfare," she said. "Don't try to put on *our* shoes. Wear what God has given you. You need to stay with your highest weapons."

Now that was wisdom! It was as though I could hear My Master's voice in those words.

As in natural war, so in spiritual warfare. Before you send in the hand-to-hand ground troops, you send in the air patrol. Let's be wise! Bomb out the enemy's bunkers first through the weapons of high praise. Stay with it long enough to get the Holy Spirit's witness—peace, knowing, certainty; then send in the ground troops, shooting the artillery at specifically determined targets.

I would like to add a few words about praise, since that is my highest weapon. Yet praise, like prayer, is a weapon we all can wield. Remember, God uses our praise to bind up or chain up the enemy. Psalm 149:5–9 powerfully depicts this:

Let the godly ones exult in glory; let them sing for joy on their beds. Let the high praises of God be in their mouth, and a two-edged sword in their hand, to execute vengeance on the nations, and punishment on the peoples; to bind their kings with chains, and their nobles with fetters of iron; to execute on them the judgment written; this is an honor for all His godly ones. Praise the LORD!

Like most Christians, I love this passage. Notice that it does *not* say that the task of lifting up passionate praise, which is used to bind up kings and nobles, is a task for the special elite. It "is an honor for all His godly ones." Well, beloved, guess who "all" is? We get to tie up the enemy's works by declaring what the Word of God, the two-edged sword, says has already been accomplished through the blood of the cross and by lavishly praising the Lord.

Let me list a few scriptural qualities concerning the power of praise and thanksgiving:

1. Praise is the place of God's residence (Psalm 22:3).
2. Praise is the way into God's presence (Psalm 100:4; Isaiah 60:18).
3. Praise is a garment of the Spirit (Isaiah 61:1–3).
4. Praise is a powerful weapon of deliverance (Psalm 50:23; Acts 16:25–26).
5. Praise is a means of silencing the devil (Psalm 8:2; Matthew 21:16).
6. Praise is the way into Christ's victory (Psalm 106:47; 2 Corinthians 2:14).
7. Praise is a sacrifice (Jeremiah 33:11; Hebrews 13:15).

Yes, praise is one of our highest weapons. Like Fifle in the kids' movie *An American Tale*, we have been given the privilege of declaring, "Release the secret weapon!" Know *your* highest weapon and use it mightily.

5. Stick Close to the Blood

There is a principle that runs throughout the Scriptures: "The life of the flesh is in the blood" (Leviticus 17:11). Not only is there life in the blood, but innocent blood, when shed, has a particular attribute: It cries out. The blood of Abel spilled on the ground could be heard by the Lord. He came running to find out what was going on. Perhaps Abel's blood was releasing a screech: "Vengeance! I want vengeance!"

Before the presence of our Judge in heaven, there is blood that speaks more fervently than the blood of Abel. What does this blood declare? The blood of Jesus reminds the Father continuously of the sacrifice of His sinless Son. The blood of Jesus ever cries out, "Mercy! Mercy! Mercy be!"

Scripture recounts many benefits concerning what the blood of Jesus has done for us. According to Revelation 12:11 the believers "overcame [the accuser of the brethren] because of the blood of the Lamb and because of the word of their testimony, and they did not love their life even to death." Let's look at a few of these biblical benefits:

1. By the blood of Jesus I have been forgiven (Hebrews 9:22–28).
2. The blood of Jesus cleanses me from all sin (1 John 1:7).
3. I have been redeemed by the blood of the Lamb (Ephesians 1:7).
4. By His blood I am justified—"just-as-if-I'd" never sinned (Romans 5:9).
5. By His blood I have been set apart (sanctified) for a holy calling (Hebrews 13:12).
6. Peace has been made for me through the blood of the cross (Colossians 1:20).
7. I have confidence to enter the holy place by the blood of Jesus (Hebrews 10:19).

Do you know the safest place to be? Close to the blood. Stay with the main and the plain of Scripture. Stick close to the blood. We overcome by testifying what the blood of Jesus has accomplished. His triumph over the powers of darkness is enforced as we agree with and declare the benefits of His precious blood. Yes, stick close to, be adhered to and testify what the blood of Jesus Christ has accomplished.

6. Err on the Side of Compassion

If you must err, do it on the side of compassion and mercy. I know we can go too far with anything, but prophetic intercessors need to stay out of casting judgment, as much as possible, and err on the side of compassion. When possible leave the pronouncing of God's judgment on a matter to the mature and tested.

What is compassion? The necessary ingredient needed to move in the works of Christ. *Webster's* says it is the sympathetic consciousness of another's distress together with a desire to alleviate it. Ken Blue, in his sensitively written book *The Authority to Heal*, states: "The kind of compassion Jesus was said to have for people was not merely an expression of His will but rather an eruption from deep within His being. Out of this compassion of Jesus sprang forth His mighty works of rescue, healing, and deliverance."[1]

Everything Jesus did and does relates to who He is. Everything we do is connected with who Jesus is in and through us. In order to be effective—whether for street-level evangelism, pastoral missions involvement or whatever ministry we engage in—we must have a current revelation of God's nature in and toward us. We must know the Father's love for us to be enabled to move in His love through us. Otherwise we engage in nothing more than a bunch of obligatory, religious, dry works.

Consider the following verses, given in various translations, to fuel your fire of compassion.

Psalm 78:38-39, NKJV: "[God], being full of compassion, forgave their iniquity, and did not destroy them. Yes, many a time He turned His anger away, and did not stir up all His wrath; for He remembered that they were but flesh, a breath that passes away and does not come again."

Psalm 78:38-39, Amplified: "[God], full of (merciful) compassion, forgave their iniquity, and destroyed them not; yes, many a time He turned His anger away, and did not stir up all His wrath and indignation. For He [earnestly] remembered that they were but flesh, a wind that goes and does not return."

Psalm 86:15, KJV: "Thou, O Lord, art a God full of compassion, and gracious, longsuffering, and plenteous in mercy and truth."

Psalm 86:15, NIV: "You, O Lord, are a compassionate and gracious God, slow to anger, abounding in love and faithfulness."

Lamentations 3:21–23, KJV: "This I recall to my mind, therefore have I hope. It is of the LORD's mercies that we are not consumed, because his compassions fail not. They are new every morning: great is thy faithfulness."

Lamentations 3:21–23, Amplified: "This I recall, therefore have I hope and expectation: It is of the Lord's mercies and loving-kindnesses that we are not consumed, because His (tender) compassions fail not. They are new every morning; great and abundant is Your stability and faithfulness."

Do you get the picture? Our Father's nature is one of love, patience, lovingkindness and mercy. Learn compassion. Release compassion. Lift up the cry for mercy! God's heart is poised with grace and mercy toward us, but we must experience His heart of compassion, whatever the ministry endeavor, before we can extend His heart of compassion to others.

7. Allow No Common Ground

This point is worthy of a whole chapter or even a whole book. In John 14:30, an eye-opening verse, Jesus is talking about His authority over the devil: "I will not speak much more with you, for the ruler of the world is coming, and he has nothing in Me." The Amplified Bible gives us some insight into this passage in the way it translates this last phrase: "He has no claim on Me—he has nothing in common with Me, there is nothing in Me that belongs to him, he has no power over Me."

Do you see the correlation? Terry Crist in his book *Interceding against the Powers of Darkness*, casts light for us on this subject:

> The reason Jesus was so effective in spiritual warfare . . . why He was able to confront the devil so effectively . . . in the wilderness encounter [was that] Jesus recognized the law of purification. The reason Jesus could stand in such power and authority and deal so effectively with the wicked oppressor of the nations was because no common ground existed between Him and His adversary. When the devil struck at Jesus, there was nothing whatsoever in Him to receive the "hit." When Satan examined Him, there was nothing for him to find. Jesus and Satan had no relationship one to another, no common ground. There was nothing in Jesus that bore witness with the works of darkness! One reason so many ministers and intercessors have been spiritually "hit" by the fiery darts of the enemy is because they have not responded to the law of purification.[2]

Let me try to explain my present understanding on this vital matter.

When God gives you true, authentic discernment or releases the gift of discerning of spirits to you, what are you to do with it? Before you go chasing after external dragons and territorial spirits, first make sure there is nothing you hold in common with the enemy. Let the finger of God probe inward into your heart, mind and actions. Let conviction settle in concerning your life, family, church or ministry. Repent when necessary. Bring cleansing to your own life through the power of the blood of Jesus and yield to the work of the cross. Tear up the legal basis—the right of the enemy—to attack you first. Then you can take authority over the external enemies without receiving horrendous repercussions from the backlash of spiritual warfare.

Sometimes sincere, gifted believers have common ground with the enemy and proceed, foolishly and prematurely, to wage war against a principality or power of darkness that has active access into their own lives. The back door, as I said earlier, is open. We first must close this door of access and only then go forth to set other captives free.

This does not diminish the completed work of the cross. Jesus defeated the devil on Calvary and we are called to enforce His victory. But when we go after an enemy with whom we have ground in common, we are inviting trouble. This is one of the major reasons many intercessors and their families get beaten up. A back door is open and the devil hits back! Remember Paul's statement in 2 Corinthians 2:11: "We are not ignorant of [Satan's] schemes."

I am convinced that this issue of cooperating first with the laws of purification through repentance, sanctification and the ministry of deliverance is vitally important. Let the finger of God go internal and conquer your personal enemies. Then you will have assurance that you can stand up against the spirits of wickedness in the heavenly places and win!

8. Avoid Lures

Have you ever gone fishing? A smart fish does not bite at everything that floats by. Personally I love to fish for trout. They have keen eyesight and do not go after every lure.

Trout have to be convinced that the bait is right before they make a commitment.

Perhaps we should "go to the trout" to learn a lesson on wisdom applications. Do not chase after every lure that comes along. Lures can be distractions. When the devil shows his head, keep your focus on Jesus. Sometimes the enemy purposefully paints a target of himself to sidetrack us from the target toward which the Lord has directed us. At times the enemy intentionally manifests his presence just to derail our attempts at pure devotion to Jesus and into chasing any old demon. He is trying to capture and keep our attention.

Remember, when the devil knocks, send Jesus to answer! That might sound trite but I don't mean it like that. One of the ways we can send Jesus to answer is by simply not giving the devil the time of day. Do not follow him! We are called to follow Jesus. Too many prayer meetings turn into following the devil. We must "[fix] our eyes on Jesus, the author and perfecter of faith" (Hebrews 12:2).

This is a simple but powerful wisdom issue. As we maintain our focus on the Lord, His presence is released and will overpower the enemy. I am not taking away from the power of confrontive, authoritative prayer or rebuking the enemy in the name of Jesus. I am simply making an appeal that, whenever possible, we choose the fights we enter into. Avoid being seduced by lures. Keep your gaze fixed on Jesus.

9. Break the Penalty

By breaking the penalty I mean "closing the door on the backlash of spiritual warfare."

I pulled this gem from the treasure chest of the life of Gideon:

Gideon took ten men of his servants and did as the Lord had spoken to him; and it came about, because he was too afraid of his father's household and the men of the city to do it by day, that he did it by night. When the men of the city arose early in the morning, behold, the altar of Baal was torn down, and the Asherah which was beside it was cut down, and the second bull was offered on the altar which had been built. And they said to one another, "Who did this thing?" And when they searched about and inquired, they said, "Gideon the son of Joash did this thing." Then the men of the city said to Joash, "Bring out your son, that he may die, for he has torn down the altar of Baal, and indeed, he has cut down the Asherah which was beside it." But Joash said to all who stood against him, "Will you contend for Baal, or will you deliver him? Whoever will plead for him shall be put to death by morning. If he is a god, let him contend for himself, because someone has torn down his altar." Therefore on that day he named him Jerubbaal, that is to say, "Let Baal contend against him," because he had torn down his altar.

Judges 6:27–32

Here we find that a penalty—a curse or consequence—was put into place to fall on the one who would tear down the demonic high places. The Scripture does not explicitly say this, but we may infer it by the command the men of the city gave to Gideon's father: "Bring out your son, that he may die" (verse 30). Gideon's father, who owned the altar to Baal, had probably released a demonic stronghold or force to war against whoever who would tear down the altar of false worship to Baal. Now he renamed his son Jerubbaal, "Let Baal contend against him" (see verse 32).

Some spiritual warfare specialists inform us that professional witchcraft practitioners pronounce curses (or penalties) particularly on those who threaten their kingdom. The Old Testament picture from the life of Gideon gives us insight into the necessity of praying a hedge of protection around ourselves and families, and breaking, in the name of Jesus, any curse or penalty that the enemy tries to enforce on God's people when they are confronting darkness.

Notice also God's reward for his valiant warriors: "The Spirit of the LORD came upon Gideon" (Judges 6:34). Literally this means that God's Spirit *clothed* Gideon. He actually took possession of him. So take heart. The reward from God can be awesome!

After engaging in a power encounter with the enemy, which I do in many of my travels and meetings, I offer up a prayer breaking the curse of the enemy—any backlash curse or counterattack—that would try to come against me and my family members, our health, hope, future, calling, finances, possessions, vehicles, pets, etc. The prayer goes like this:

> In the name of Jesus, and by the power of His blood shed on the cross, I command the penalty of the enemy, any word curse that has been pronounced against me and any backlash of the evil one sent against me and my family, to be broken. It shall not prosper as I nullify its effect in Jesus' mighty name. I proclaim a blessing to all that I am, hope to be and put my hand to, and to all that pertains to my life, health, home, finances, ministry and family. I call forth strength, vigor, protection and the supply of the Lord, for the honor and glory of His name. Amen.

Hey, it makes sense. Have *you* blocked the counterattack from coming?

10. The Safety Net: Walking with Others

This is an important part of wisdom. Ecclesiastes 4:9–12 aptly remarks:

> Two are better than one because they have a good return for their labor. For if either of them falls, the one will lift up his companion. But woe to the one who falls when there is not another to lift him up. Furthermore, if two lie down together they keep warm, but how can one be warm

alone? And if one can overpower him who is alone, two can resist him. A cord of three strands is not quickly torn apart.

Look at this more closely. We all have times when we get hit for some reason or another. Isn't it wonderful that the Lord provides others to help us up when we get knocked down?

Check out another aspect of this safety net, too: "Two can resist him." This is an awesome promise to remember, to claim, to proclaim and to kneel on. "Five of you shall chase a hundred, and a hundred of you shall put ten thousand to flight; your enemies shall fall by the sword before you" (Leviticus 26:8, NKJV). A multiplication effect takes place in our power over the devil when we join with others.

Do you have a partner in prayer with whom you walk? Who is watching your backside? The armor of God protects our front side, but we become one another's rear guard. Let's cover one another with godly counsel, fellowship and prayer.

Leaders, too, need the care and cover supplied through the prayers of their followers. This is when others in intercession join together in an organized manner to lift up "the shield of faith" (Ephesians 6:16) for their spiritual leaders.

"Every Finney needs a Father Nash," writes Dick Eastman, "and every preacher needs an intercessor."[3] I believe this, and have given myself to other ministries over the years to be an Aaron or Hur to help hold up their hands through the power of prevailing prayer. And I am grateful today that there are those who stand with Ministry to the Nations in our many endeavors.

There is a precious couple who coordinate the prayer shield for our family and ministry. Ever since we have had this shield in place, fewer attacks of sickness have hit our children. Those who have walked with us and watched and prayed for us regularly have become a safety net for our lives.

May every ministry have a prayer shield raised up for it in Jesus' name!

Whose Battle Is It?

Before we turn the final corner together to peer into the subject of gatekeepers opening the way for God's presence, let me highlight one more thought on the subject of wisdom applications for intercessors: Not every battle is yours. Some are for you; some are for others. Some battles are for today; some are for another day. Some are simply not yours to engage in at all.

Ultimately the devil is not the one to indicate when you are to fight with him. Second Corinthians 2:14 proclaims majestically: "Thanks be to God, who always leads us in His triumph in Christ, and manifests through us the sweet aroma of the knowledge of Him in every place." Where He leads, He always causes us to triumph. Where He does not lead—where we have gone on our own—we do not necessarily have the same safeguards in place, nor do we necessarily triumph. So don't be presumptuous. Seek wisdom. Learn sensitivity to the voice of God. Walk with others. Get confirmation. Then go forth, knowing we have great news.

What is this great news? That where He leads us, He will give us grace and protection and triumph. It is important, as we put our hands to the plow of God's purposes through the arts of prophetic intercession, that we stick with these simple truths.

Here, then, is the bottom-line question: Who is leading me to a particular fight—my soulish zeal, my unsanctified flesh, an enticing spirit or Jehovah-nissi, the Lord our Banner? Remember, the victory of Christ is manifested where Christ leads us. Whose battle is it? The Lord's first and ours second.

Offer with me one of those childhood prayers that the Lord gave me years ago. Maybe you should even join me, like a child, kneeling in humble adoration. Let's kneel on the promises so that wisdom can be ours.

Lord, give me wisdom beyond my years. Father, grant to me the spirit of wisdom and revelation in the knowledge of the glorious Lord Jesus Christ. May I be preserved by Your hand to become a veteran for the next generation, to pass on to them the wonders of Your great love. In Jesus' name. Amen.

PRACTICAL APPLICATIONS—MAKING IT REAL!

- Pray through the book of Proverbs, asking the Father to give you wisdom beyond your years.
- In your times of intercessory prayer, ask the Lord to reveal to you areas of wisdom in which you are lacking and to teach you those things that you should incorporate into your life.
- Gain further wisdom by asking questions from those who have learned in the trenches of prayer. Interview an older believer in Christ.
- Confession of sin is an attitude of humility that draws God's grace onto the scene. Ask the Lord to root out areas of unforgiveness and criticism so you can be a greater channel of blessing to others.
- If you are getting hit spiritually by the fiery darts of the enemy, ask the Holy Spirit to put His finger of conviction on your heart. Confess and repent in order to close any doorways of your life and family to the enemy. Then pray the prayers, in Jesus' name, canceling the penalty against your life, family and ministry.

RECOMMENDED READING

The Spiritual Fight by Pat Gastineau (Word of Love, 1997)

Passion for Jesus by Mike Bickle (Creation House, 1993)

OPENING THE WAY!

The "breakers" are coming! These are the prophetic intercessors who help give birth to the purposes of God for their generation, and they are appearing once again. We need and desire breakthrough in today's society, but there is no breakthrough without a breaker.

Micah 2:13 describes the activity to which in this chapter we will give our attention:

> "The breaker goes up before them; they break out, pass through the gate, and go out by it. So their king goes on before them, and the LORD at their head."

Truly the Lord Jesus Himself is our breaker—the One who has gone before us and broken open the gates of heaven and hell. He has done it all. But today, as in the days of John the Baptist and other strategic breakers, the Holy Spirit is looking for those with a forerunner spirit on them who will go ahead of the pack, pioneer a trail in the spirit and open the way, that the Lord may "pass through the gate" among them.

How I Learned about Breakers

I remember when this verse in Micah was first brought to my attention. I had just returned from the 1987 crusade in Haiti that I mentioned in chapter 4—the meeting in which the 77-year-old grandmother was healed of blindness and I first met Dick Simmons. Mahesh Chavda had met Dick at a campus ministry conference in Virginia and invited him to come and participate with us in our campaign. My heart was joined to this unusual pioneer of intercession as we were brought together for the mission outreach.

After returning home from that crusade, I spent many hours in quietness in my basement office, communing with my Lord and learning, like so many, to practice the presence of Jesus.

While waiting on the Lord one day in February 1988, the voice of the Holy Spirit spoke within my heart: *Where are the breakers who will go before and break open the way for New York City?*

Now that was a strange word for a fellow who grew up in a town of 259 people in rural Missouri! But something stirred within me. I felt I was to write a letter (this was before e-mail days) to my new friend in prayer who lived in Bellingham, Washington. So I penned Dick: "While in prayer today, the Holy Spirit asked me a question that I believe you have something to do with: 'Where are the breakers who will go before and break open the way for New York City?'"

The very day that I wrote this letter, as it turned out, Dick actually prayed from the book of Micah: "Where are the breakers who will go before and break open the way for New York City?" Hard to believe! So when Dick received my letter, he called me immediately and invited me to go with him to the Big Apple.

Off we went through a window filled with divine appointments.

On that trip to New York City I met Richard Glickstein, who was then pastoring One Accord Fellowship in Manhattan. Eventually Richard and one of his close friends, David Fitzpatrick, then pastoring in Michigan, and I became joined at the hip in the trenches of prophetic intercession. (It was during one of our intercessory meetings that I saw the map of the tiny island nation of Bahrain—the vision I described in chapter 6.) Today, more than ten years later, my family lives within two minutes of the Fitzpatricks in Antioch, Tennessee, and Richard and his family reside in Moscow, reaching out to the Jewish people across Central and Eastern Europe. We had no idea what God had in store for us. We were simply attempting to follow the cloud.

In the next eighteen months or so, Dick, Richard, David and I got together every few weeks for days of prayer, to call out before the Lord about many prayer assignments in New York City. This is how I learned about the "breaker anointing." We would cry out to the Lord to release holy, abandoned men and women to the harvest field of this great and needy city. We also found ourselves laboring for God's purposes to be released among the Jewish people worldwide, as we called on the name of the God of Abraham, Isaac and Jacob in the Ukrainian Pentecostal Church building where One Accord Fellowship met.

As we waited on God, He gave us different prayer assignments. Often in 1987 we found ourselves praying that David Wilkerson would return to New York City, the "land of his anointing." We reminded God of His Word in Matthew 9:37–38: "The harvest is plentiful, but the workers are few. Therefore beseech the Lord of the harvest to send out workers into His harvest."

The Lord of the harvest heard our supplications as we knelt on the promises. Within months, as just one example, David Wilkerson sold his ministry property in Lindale, Texas, to Youth With A Mission and moved back to New York City, where he launched Times Square Church.

In this pivotal hour the Holy Spirit continues to look for pioneer, prophetic, intercessory people who will follow after the model of their Messiah and go before others to break open the way for their families, churches, regions, cities, ethnic groups and nations. Could it be that these abandoned, broken warriors who want nothing but the honor and glory of His holy name are already proceeding forth?

Let the breakers arise! Let the breaker anointing be released! Let breakthrough come!

Open Heavens

In reading revival literature, I have found a peculiar term that relates to the concept of breakthrough: *open heavens.* In recent days and months I have found myself pondering the subject of open heavens. Once again I have gone on a search with my Bible. Let me give you a few Scripture passages related to this subject.

Ezekiel 1:1 states that "the heavens were opened and I saw visions of God." As the heavens open, Ezekiel describes a great cloud, sent by God to protect him from His brightness. Can you imagine such a sight? Then Ezekiel sees "fire flashing forth continually" (lightning), bright light, angels and other glorious and fascinating details.

Several other Old Testament passages describe similar experiences in which it appeared that the heavens parted and either heaven came down to earth or else man was somehow caught up into the heavenlies. Consider the transforming visionary experience of Isaiah, in which he was shown the glory of God, the transcendent majesty of His presence, the fire of purification and the message of "Whom shall I send, and who will go for Us?" (Isaiah 6:8). Likewise Daniel, as he received visions in the night, saw the Lord "like a Son of Man" coming through "the clouds of heaven" taking up His throne before the Ancient of Days (Daniel 7:13). Awesome!

Fast forward to the New Testament. At Jesus' very own baptism, as recorded in Matthew 3:16–17, "the heavens were opened" and the Holy Spirit descends on the Son of God in the form of a dove. Then the Father speaks audibly: "This is My beloved Son, in whom I am well-pleased" (verse 17).

In Acts we find Stephen, the flaming deacon, being stoned to death for preaching the Gospel. As this is occurring, he sees "the heavens opened up and the Son of Man standing at the right hand of God" (Acts 7:56). The sky is loosened, the clouds are rolled back and Jesus is standing to receive him. What a sight! What a cost! But what a privilege!

John, the disciple who lays his head on Jesus' heart, has a profound experience recorded in the book of Revelation. John, now imprisoned and eighty years old, is "in the Spirit on the Lord's day" (Revelation 1:10). As he meditates on his Beloved, he sees "a door standing open in heaven" and hears a voice calling him. He is not only able to peer into the heavenly realm, but he is told to "come up here" (Revelation 4:1). As he does, he is shown the One who sits on the throne amid the majesty of His great presence, as the elders, angels and four living creatures all worship radically in the beauty of holiness. As a result John receives many detailed messages from the glorified Lord Jesus Christ.

Psalm 24:7–10 paints poetically a historic time when heaven's choirs of angels release a cry for the gates of heaven to be opened and the ancient doors to be lifted up:

> Lift up your heads, O gates, and be lifted up, O ancient doors, that the King of glory may come in! Who is the King of glory? The LORD strong and mighty, the LORD mighty in battle. Lift up your heads, O gates, and lift them up, O ancient doors, that the King of glory may come in! Who is this King of glory? The LORD of hosts, He is the King of glory.

Even as this psalm records the petition of the heavenly throng to receive its glorious Messiah, so heaven now waits

261

for the inhabitants of earth to cry that the doors and gates from heaven to earth be opened once again.

Openings as Gateways in the Spirit

What are open heavens and how do they occur? Are there any today? This is a subject onto which the Holy Spirit is going to turn His spotlight in the days ahead. Let me give you a possible definition of this phenomenon.

In this kind of visionary experience, a "hole" seems to appear in the immediate sky. The celestial realm is disclosed and heavenly sights of God become visible. Access from man to God and God to man is opened up, or so it seems, and His manifest presence appears.

Some call these portals "thresholds" or "gateways" in the spiritual realm. I believe there are entry points, spiritual hot spots, where God's manifest presence becomes, for a period of time, almost tangible. Remember the lesson concerning those who waited at the pool of Bethesda? At certain seasons an angel of the Lord was released and stirred the water, and the first person to step into the anointed waters was healed (see John 5:1–4). It is my conviction that there are gateways where God's presence seems to invade earthly space and time in a powerful way.

In the natural, gates are used to keep things out and let things in. The elders are to sit at the gates of the city (see Proverbs 31:23) and permit or deny entrance into the regions over which they have been given stewardship. So it is in the spiritual realm. Isaiah 60:18 tells us, "You will call your walls salvation, and your gates praise." Just so, around the life of every believer, and around the perimeter of every church, we need walls of protection. We are told in Psalm 100:4 that we "enter His gates with thanksgiving, and His courts with praise."

Not only are we called to enter the presence of the King through the gate of praise, but we are likewise to overtake the gateways of the enemy. "Upon this rock I will build My church," Jesus said, "and the gates of Hades shall not overpower it" (Matthew 16:18).

A marvelous book by Cindy Jacobs of Generals of Intercession, *Possessing the Gates of the Enemy*, gives us teaching on this point. ("Your seed shall possess the gate of their enemies," Genesis 22:17.) Perhaps now the Holy Spirit is taking us to the flip side of this coin and addressing the reopening of these prophetic gateways of visitation from heaven to earth. The enemy has come along, as he did in the time of Abraham and Isaac, and filled up the wells of salvation. Now the time has come for breakers to redig these ancient wells and allow the waters of God's healing presence once again to flow (see Genesis 26:15–22).

In Genesis 28 we read of Jacob's encounter at Bethel. As he was lying on the hard ground with a stone for a pillow, a ladder between earth and heaven was revealed to him in a dream on which angels were ascending and descending. The Lord stood at the top of the ladder as the communication line between God and man was opened. Jacob declared, "How awesome is this place! This is none other than the house of God, and this is the gate of heaven" (Genesis 28:17).

What had changed? Had God changed His view of the desert land of Beersheeba-Haran? Had the land suddenly changed its appearance and was now a lush, green sight pleasing to the natural eyes?

In Genesis 28:16, when Jacob awoke from his sleep, he stated, "Surely the Lord is in this place, and I did not know it." When the heavens open up over a region, our spiritual eyes are opened and we see with God's eyes. Jacob now saw this appointed place as a Bethel—"house of God"—as the gate of heaven was opened and the manifested presence of God came on down! After all, didn't Jesus teach His disciples to pray, "Thy kingdom come. Thy will be done, on earth as it is in heaven" (Matthew 6:10)? Remember, little keys open big doors, and the keys of holy, bold, persevering prayer are the keys put into heaven's doors that unlock God's resources to come to earth (see Matthew 16:19; 18:18–20).

Isaiah picked up the trumpet and gave us a piercing cry for "opened heavens" to occur:

> Oh, that Thou wouldst rend the heavens and come down, that the mountains might quake at Thy presence—as fire kindles the brushwood, as fire causes water to boil—to make Thy name known to Thine adversaries, that the nations may tremble at Thy presence! When Thou didst awesome things which we did not expect, Thou didst come down, the mountains quaked at Thy presence. For from of old they have not heard nor perceived by ear, neither has the eye seen a God besides Thee, who acts in behalf of the one who waits for Him.
>
> Isaiah 64:1–2

Throughout Church history intercessors have taken these and similar verses and prayed them back to the Father, for openings to occur in the heavens for their generation.

One such example is the historic revival that took place in 1949 in the village of Barvas on the largest island of the Outer Hebrides off the northwest coast of Scotland. Much has been written about the impact of the preaching and meetings of the pastor/evangelist Duncan Campbell as he led the way in the public eye. But little attention has been given the prayer warriors who paved the way before and during that mighty move of God's presence.

Behind the scenes labored two elderly sisters, Peggy Smith, 84 years old and blind, and her sister, Christine Smith, 82 years old and almost doubled over with arthritis. They were unable to attend regular church services, but for months they prayed in their home for God to send revival to Barvas. These two relentless intercessors prayed by name for the people in each cottage along their village streets. They reminded God of His Word in Isaiah 44:3: "I will pour water upon him that is thirsty, and floods upon the dry ground" (KJV). They cried this prophetic promise to the Lord day and night.

Across the village, independent of the Smith sisters, seven young men met three nights a week in a barn to pray for revival. They made a covenant with God and one another, according to Isaiah 62:6–7, that they would give Him no rest until He sent revival their way. Month after month they prevailed in prayer.

One night in particular they prayed with fervency Psalm 24:3–5: "Who shall ascend into the hill of the LORD? or who shall stand in his holy place? He that hath clean hands, and a pure heart. . . . He shall receive the blessing from the LORD" (KJV). Instantly, it seemed, the barn was filled with the glory of God and the young men praying from the Psalms fell prostrate on the floor. An awesome awareness of God overcame them and they were drenched with supernatural power they had never known before.

At that very time, the Lord gave one of the Smith sisters a vision. Peggy Smith saw the churches crowded with people and hundreds being swept into the Kingdom of God. They sent word to their pastor that they had "broken through" and that heaven was about to descend on earth.

And so it did. The whole region seemed saturated with God. Wherever people were—in the workplace, in their homes or on the roads—they were overwhelmed by the presence of almighty God. Water indeed soaked the dry ground as Holy Spirit conviction was poured out in those days. A stream of blessing flowed that brought hundreds to salvation during the days of that historic visitation.[1]

Now let me be vulnerable with you and share a dramatic encounter from my own life that illustrates a gateway of the Spirit.

Encounter at the Lake

It was a quiet Wednesday evening in May 1989. Michal Ann and I had just returned home from a meeting in nearby Kansas City. I was restless and we both knew it. I had to be alone with the Lord; something was up. So Michal Ann blessed me and I got into our car and went on a drive. It was about 9 P.M.

I could hear the still, small voice of the Dove of God speaking in my heart. He would say, *Turn here. Turn right. Go there.* His presence was very near. Eventually I drove up to a manmade, recreational body of water called Longview Lake, not far from our home in South Kansas City. Even the names of the roads leading there seemed prophetic: Longview Road and Highland Drive. And later that night I did experience a long look at a higher place into which Jesus wants to bring His Body.

As I drove, I came to part of the lake that I had never seen before. I parked my car and stepped outside. Immediately to my left I saw a road that looked familiar. I had seen that gravel road earlier that day in a vision. So I proceeded to walk down the narrow road, which led to an arm of land jutting out into the lake. There, at the end of this path, was a concrete block building with a high wire fence around it. It seemed to be some kind of a powerhouse or generator.

Then something—or maybe I should say Someone, that wonderful Guide and discloser of truth, the Holy Spirit—seemed to take over. I heard His gentle voice within me say, *Walk around the powerhouse seven times, praying in the Spirit.*

So I obeyed.

No one was out on the lake that night—no boats, no fishermen. It was a beautiful, serene, still night, even though it had rained recently. I walked around once, praying very quietly with the gift of tongues. I walked around a second and third time. As I continued on my journey of obedience, I found myself praying more loudly with each round. By the time I was walking around for the seventh time, I was praying loudly in the language the Holy Spirit gave me.

When I had completed my seventh trip, I heard His voice again: *Walk around the powerhouse an eighth time, declaring into the heavens.*

Without even pondering what He meant, I headed off. I walked up to the first corner of the fence surrounding the building, stopped, peered into heaven and raised my right arm toward the sky. Out of my mouth came a powerful, unpremeditated declaration: "Open be the way! Open be the way! Open be the way for the beginning of a great visitation."

After releasing this proclamation, I headed off to the next corner, stopped, raised my arm, stared into the sky and again declared, "Open be the way! Open be the way! Open be the way for the beginning of a great visitation."

I proceeded to the third and the fourth corners, doing the same.

When I had completed my fourth proclamation, I thought perhaps that was all I was to do that night, and I started to turn and walk away. But the voice of the Dove came into my heart again: *I want you to go down to the bank of the muddy lake below and strike the waters.*

Well, my human reasoner was turned off and His divine reasoner was turned on. So I mused, *If I'm going to strike the waters, then surely, on whatever path I choose, there will be a branch along the way that I will pick up to strike the waters with.*

Off I went, sauntering through the weeds. Sure enough, along the path I saw a large branch from a tree. I picked it up and Jeremiah 23:5–6 lit up inside me. *There is One who is called the righteous Branch,* I thought as I continued making my way down to the muddy bank of the lake below.

When I arrived there I saw a wood plank resting on the muddy bank of this manmade lake. I stepped onto it.

267

While I stood there, the branch in my hand, the Holy Spirit said, *Another fisherman has stood here before you.* (Hold that thought; I will return to it later.)

Then, as I stood on the wood plank with the branch raised high in the air, I heard these words: *Strike the waters.*

I lowered the branch onto the still water directly in front of me. Then something strange began to take place. Dark, shadowy lines began to form in the middle of the lake, coming toward me. These lines began to take on the shape of waves. I continued to watch as the water swept over my feet on the shore. The atmosphere around me was charged with fear.

"Lord, I'm afraid!" I cried aloud.

At that very moment the waves ceased. Instantly the lake became once again like a sheet of glass. I was startled, amazed and frightened all at the same time.

The persistent Lamb spoke into my being again: *Release a song of love to the Holy Spirit in order to woo the return of His presence.*

I stood on that wood plank and sang out a song of love to the Holy Spirit, inviting His presence to return.

Then I heard it again: *Strike the waters.*

As I lowered the branch the second time onto the water immediately in front of me, dark, shadowy lines again appeared in the middle of the lake and rippled toward me. They grew in intensity, power and thrust. Waves of water began to pound onto the shore and around my feet. This time, however, the atmosphere around me was charged with joy, faith and excitement. I stood there praising the Lord aloud, celebrating and enjoying His presence.

When the waves subsided and the manifest presence of God abated, I decided to start back up the gravel road and head home.

Then He spoke to me for the last time that night: *All I have ever required of My people is two things: that they believe Me and that they do whatever little thing I have commanded them to do.*

Then He personalized it, imprinting His message into my consciousness: *And all I am requiring of you is two things: that you believe Me for the beginning of this great visitation and that you obey whatever little thing I command you to do.*

I walked on up the road, got into my car and drove home. It was late now, and when I arrived home, Michal Ann was already asleep. As I got into bed, the anointing of God's manifest presence began to wear off.

Now what was that? I wondered.

Throwing up one of those feeble "Help me, God!" kinds of prayers, I dozed off.

Interpreting the Encounter

The next day, Thursday, I told Michal Ann about the event. I do not recall relaying it to anyone else.

That Saturday morning I received a phone call from an older Christian gentleman who is a seasoned, prophetically gifted seer named Bob Jones. I will never forget the conversation.

"I saw you in a vision this morning," he remarked. "You and I were walking down a gravel road together. It led to some kind of powerhouse. Then waves of water began coming up on our feet. Does that mean anything to you?"

I sighed and responded quickly, "Yes, it means two things to me. One, I am not crazy, and, two, it confirms the meaning of a profound divine encounter I have just experienced."

I proceeded to explain to Bob what had transpired three days earlier and thanked him for his confirming word. Good old Bob just listened to me—one of the younger, prophetically called people he had taken under his wing at that time. He knew almost all the details, it seemed, before I got them out of my mouth!

What did this unusual encounter mean? First, that the Lord calls forth prophetic intercessors who are "captured," as Elijah was in 1 Kings 18, by a sound in the Spirit that has not yet been heard in the natural. (Remember the lesson from chapter 3: Elijah heard the sound of rain in the spiritual realm before it ever began to drench the earth.) These velvet warriors then begin to kneel on the ground and give birth to their revelation, bringing it into being. They continue until it appears.

Yes, the answers, as in Elijah's day, seem to come first like a cloud the size of a man's hand. But we must never "[despise] the day of small things" (Zechariah 4:10).

Many small, new beginnings of revival and of God's purposes for our generation have erupted in many places and lands in recent years. But we need to discern properly the day of Christ's appearing and not let the fullness of what the Father has planned pass us by. Let's be discerning in these times of His presence, and cultivate and cooperate with the Holy Spirit. Let's keep the fire burning on the altar until the fullness of His purposes has been completed, and not vacate our position before Him in the midst of much activity.

With a word burning within, these priestly breakers look up into the heavens and, like God, "calls things that are not as though they were" (Romans 4:17, NIV). They are captivated by a vision of what is yet to come. Seeing clouds heavy with rain, they take a knife of the Spirit and split the heavens open, calling forth the promised rainfall of His presence.

Thus the cry comes: "Open be the way. Open be the way." This cry is not directed to crowds of men and women but to the balconies of heaven. We must proclaim God's will and Word, pierce the darkness of the hindering powers of the enemy and call out that the gates of heaven be opened up once again. This intercessory cry must persist until the grace of intimacy and communion has opened the way for a time of new beginning.

Remember how I stumbled onto the branch? It represents the work of the cross that each of us is called to carry. The Holy Spirit is seeking those who will lift up the completed work of the cross—only the cross and nothing of themselves. When this righteous Branch is lifted up, Jesus draws all men to Himself (see John 12:32).

Yes, let's lift up Jesus. The primacy of our message is not that of movements and streams and denominations. In fact, our message is not even the preaching of the Church. It is Christ Jesus crucified and risen from the dead (see 1 Corinthians 2:2; 2 Corinthians 4:5; Galatians 6:14). There is no deeper message than the simple, "foolish" preaching of the cross (see 1 Corinthians 1:18–25). Let's extravagantly lift up Jesus!

The Two Waves

Just as I lowered the branch two times onto the water at Longview Lake, followed by two releases of waves, so I am convinced that there are two great waves of God's manifest presence and glory coming to the Church in this generation.

First is a wave of His presence restoring the fear of the Lord. Oh, how we need this fragrance of the perfume of God splashed onto the contemporary Church! It has been a missing ingredient in a generation that has sought the hand of God (His blessing) at times, but not the face of God Himself.

This magnificent first wave of grace will be followed, I believe, by an extraordinary surge upon surge of power evangelism flowing across the nations. As the fear of the Lord is restored to the bride of Christ, the power of God will flow as rarely seen since the days of the book of Acts. We could be on the verge of a tidal wave of His presence.

The combination of these two great movements will usher in a great end-time harvest for the Lord's glory. O Lord, let it come!

A Few Simple Words

The first time I described my experience at Longview Lake publicly (I told you I would come back to this), a man came up to me at the end of the church service who had never been to that church before.

"I know that wood plank you were talking about," he told me. "I was the fisherman who stood there before you."

The spot, it turned out, was his favorite fishing hole. He had stood on that wood plank before I ever knew it existed.

I got to pray with this man to accept Jesus as his Savior that very morning. This codger of a real-life fisherman gave his heart to Jesus.

Yes, the Lord will indeed make us fishers of men!

The reality of my experience at Longview Lake comes down to a few simple words: *All I have ever required of My people is two things: that they believe Me and that they do whatever little thing I have commanded them to do.*

How many of us are waiting for God to tell us some "big" thing to do? *Sell all you have and go to the tribal peoples of Nepal.* That might be a true, authentic word for certain believers, but do you get my point? Even if you feel that something God is asking you to do is silly or insignificant, obey the impression and watch the Holy Spirit move.

Many of us are waiting for a huge word of commissioning to come, when He has already told us in His Word to love our neighbors or feed the poor right in our own backyards. I have no doubt that as we do something with the power of His presence we have already received, we will get more.

But how many of us receive words as suggestions and not commands? What are the "little" things God has commanded you to do? Did you hear these commands? Does it sound as though the Man Upstairs thinks He is God and has come to rule your life? He has. He has come to take over. The good news is that His will is good. Our little acts of kindness can be a big token of God's love to someone else.

Let's do our little stuff, then, so He can do His big stuff. May a passionate generation of violent, broken, obedient warriors arise and lay hold of the Word of God as the God of His Word lays hold of us.

It Is Time for the Breakers

It is time for the breakers to come forth for this generation. Time to turn on the light as our means of confronting the darkness. Time for the gatekeepers of His presence to insert the little keys of agreeing prayer into heaven's big doors and open up the way, so that the King of glory will pass before us. Open be the way for the beginning of a great visitation! It is time for the watchmen on the walls and the elders at the gates to walk together to prepare for breakthrough for this generation.

The breakers are coming to open the way. A generation of authentic, apostolic men and women, boys and girls, old and young, will walk in these principles and see "the knowledge of the glory of the LORD" cover the earth "as the waters cover the sea" (Habakkuk 2:14).

Right now you might be feeling your heart beat more loudly within you as you read these very lines. "What is this strange thing happening to me?" you may be asking. Your heart is coming into a greater rhythm with God's as you have pondered the words of this strange book. Do you sense Him drawing near? It is the Holy Spirit calling you to be one of the drums that God, the Chief of all warriors, wants to beat upon. He is calling you to be a breaker. Will you answer the call?

Stop right here. Tell Him that with all that lies within you, you want Him to be honored and glorified. Volunteer to be a watchman on the walls—a priestly, prophetic intercessor. This is what you were created for. Offer yourself anew to Christ and His purposes. Tell your gracious Father that you want His rule in your life. Don't wait. Tell Him now.

But I sense one last question lingering and rumbling around in your soul: "What if that is not my calling—this thing you keep calling prophetic intercession?"

Let me shed some light on that question, right here at the end of this book, by asking you a question in return: Where in the Bible is prayer, praise, worship or intercession called a special spiritual gift? Yes, I know the Levites in the Old Testament were a tribe set aside to minister to the Lord. I am also aware that there are gifts of faith, discerning of spirits, evangelism and so on. But where in the Book is prayer, praise, worship or intercession called a special gift?

I will give you the answer: Nowhere. Do you know why? Because these activities are the right of every priest. If you are a believer in Jesus, they are exactly what you are called to do. Your birth certificate in the Kingdom of God comes with a job description: *Priest and prophet to the Lord.*

"Wait a minute, Jim," you say. "Priest I can maybe accept, but prophet?"

Remember what Moses said when Joshua urged him to restrain Eldad and Medad prophesying in the camp: "Would that all the LORD's people were prophets, that the LORD would put His Spirit upon them!" (Numbers 11:29). God is answering Moses' prayer. He is going to put the awesome spirit of wisdom and revelation on you, too. He said it and I believe it. In fact, I think I hear someone joining in with me: "We'll pray it and then we'll see it."

Now you have it! The intimate place of hearing His voice and the passionate place of intercession—this is not for an elite little crew; it is for you, my friend. So take your place, prophetic priest, and do that for which you were created.

One Last Shot

In this book I have tried to establish a biblical grounding for prophetic, priestly intercession, relate it to Church history and offer glimpses of my own personal journey—all with the intent of cultivating in you a heart for prayer and the prophetic, giving birth to God's purposes in our generation. I have pondered this material for well over two decades. I have wanted to write this book for years. Now that I have done it, it seems right, yet feels inadequate. All I have brought forth, I realize, is really just the first chapter in the book of a lifetime in the treasury of prayer.

So what can I leave you with? What else can I give you, my new friend and comrade in this road less traveled? What is my one last shot?

There is indeed one more bullet left in my arsenal. If there is one thing I would love to infect you with, it is a heart that hungers for God. I wish for you a heart ever hungry for its Maker. I trust that you will become so overwhelmed with the loveliness of Christ Jesus that you cannot help but fall on your face before His majestic grace. He is a Lover. He is the Prince of life. He is the great I AM. He is the reason for living. He is life indeed. He is our magnificent obsession and our transcendent majesty.

To close out the blessed privilege of composing a book called *Kneeling on the Promises*, I have decided to pray a prophetic blessing for you in my own, sometimes romantic words. Bear with me if it seems too intimate or lofty or strange. I just want the Holy Spirit to unveil to you the splendor of the wonderful God and King who has taken up residence among and within us.

Any kind of prayer, you see, is more than a methodology; it is the means by which we relate to our Father God through His only Son, Jesus Christ our Lord. So let the following be a personal prophetic prayer of blessing:

> Father, my Father, my holy and awesome Maker and Creator, I bow in my heart before Your majesty and presence. How glorious, how beautiful, how magnificent is the wonder of Your dear Son! How I love the courts of Your presence as I come offering this sacrifice of thanksgiving and praise to Your great and honorable name! May Your name be exalted in the earth as it is in the heavens.

Holy Father, through Christ Jesus and Him alone I bring before You these Your children who are hungering and longing to know Your ways. As though I were walking with them hand in hand, I present them before You right now. May they be sanctified by Your living Word and washed by the power of the blood of the cross of Christ. May their consciences be cleansed from dead works in order to serve the living God.

Would You write their names down to be enrolled in Your school of prayer? Enlist them to be Your end-time velvet warriors. Now, even now, may Your Holy Spirit come upon them and fill them with the knowledge of Your great love. May they be filled with the compassionate heart of Your Son, their loving Messiah. May His heart beat more loudly and in greater union with theirs. May their hearts pulsate with the rhythm of heaven. Anoint these ones to be priests ministering in Your presence.

As they stand in Your majestic light, put Your prophetic graces upon and within them. Overshadow them with the revelatory knowledge of Your glorious Son and King. Give to them the Spirit of wisdom and revelation of this one Man Christ Jesus. Lay Your hand upon them now and release a revelation of Your ravished heart for them. This is my plea.

Surround them with the fear of the Lord and let them know the jealousy You have toward and for them. May these ones be servants to You as prophetic, warring priests, offering back to You anointed prayers from hearts in union with Yours. Now, by the authority and power of the name of Christ Jesus, may they be set apart to kneel on the promises and fulfill their destinies for the glory of His name in the earth.

I ask You, Father, to impart the power of Your great and brilliant presence to them. May they smell like the sweet fragrance of Your Son and be thrust forth into the world to release His fragrance and to do exploits for the glory of Your name in the earth. In Jesus' mighty name. Amen.

Yes, We're Kneeling!

I know this might sound corny, but thanks for taking the time to read this book. I am grateful to the Lord for the privilege He has given me of ruining other people's lives for heaven's sake!

As I composed these last few words, I found myself weeping for you. May these tears fall, in turn, on your heart and undo you with His invitation to change history at His throne.

I am inviting you to continue with me on the journey to be one of those kneeling on the promises for such a time as this. May you see Jesus and the kindness of His face. And as you do, look through His eyes and see what He sees. See a dying generation—lost, broken, sick and wandering far from God and His ways. Then, for the love of Christ, let this compassion erupt in you until all you can do is help give birth to His purposes by kneeling on the promises.

> Kneeling, kneeling,
> Kneeling on the promises of God my Savior;
> Kneeling, kneeling,
> I'm kneeling on the promises of God.

By now you have caught the tune. In fact, I think I just heard you singing with me. May a choir of voices arise that will usher the King home.

PRACTICAL APPLICATIONS—MAKING IT REAL!

- God is looking for pioneer prophetic intercessors who will go before others to break open the way for their families, churches, regions and nations. Will you arise and join the ranks? Set aside a time to come aside before the Lord and ask Him to ignite the fires of pioneering such a call.
- Read books on Church history and revival. Go visit a historic site where God poured out His presence in times past and call forth the redigging of that ancient well.

- Visit a location where revival is taking place today—where there seems to be an open heaven or gateway in the Spirit through which His presence is being manifested.
- Meditate and ask what little thing God last commanded you to do. Come before Him with fresh passion to fulfill what He has called you to.

RECOMMENDED READING

Revival Fire by Wesley L. Duewel (Zondervan, 1995)

Welcoming a Visitation of the Holy Spirit by Wesley Campbell (Creation House, 1996)

Digging the Wells of Revival by Lou Engle (Destiny Image, 1998)

SCRIPTURE PROMISES FOR REMINDING GOD

1. Prophetic Promises of Restoration

Acts 3:21 tells us that Jesus will not come again "until the period of restoration of all things" promised by the holy prophets of old. What exactly are these promises spoken by the holy prophets? Isaiah 62:6–7 tells us, speaking specifically about Jerusalem, that these watchmen are to remind the Lord of promises and appointments not yet met and fulfilled (see chapter 8 for more details).

The following is a compilation—from all sixteen prophets, from Isaiah to Malachi—of many of these promises of restoration or revival. My understanding is that they are promises to be fulfilled both by physical, natural Israel (the Jewish people and their land by covenant) and by spiritual Israel (the Church). See Romans 2:28–29; 4:11–17; 9:6–8; Galatians 3:28–29; 4:29; and Hebrews 12:22–23.

This list of Scripture promises has been adapted by permission of the teaching ministry of Mike Bickle, senior pastor of Metro Christian Fellowship and director of Friends of the Bridegroom, Grandview, Missouri.

A. Isaiah
1. Isaiah 4:2–6: God will purify His people, and Jesus in the Church will be glorious.
2. Isaiah 5:16: God will remove sin and demonstrate His power.
3. Isaiah 27:6: Revival will cover the earth in that day (i.e., in the end times).
4. Isaiah 28:5: God's reigning power will be demonstrated.
5. Isaiah 29:14, 17–24: Revival includes signs and wonders, with many children (new converts).
6. Isaiah 30:18–26: God wants to give grace; when prayer is offered, revival will come.
7. Isaiah 32:12–20: Pray and beat your breasts in mourning until revival comes.
8. Isaiah 33:13–14: The conviction of the Word will greatly increase.
9. Isaiah 33:21–24: Healing for all will come like a river.
10. Isaiah 34:16–17: God declares it will happen according to His Word.
11. Isaiah 35:1–10: Revival will come with power and miracles and with grace to make the Church holy.
12. Isaiah 37:14–20: Example of prayer for deliverance from opposition (Assyrians = the enemy of God).
13. Isaiah 40:30–31: God will anoint people who pray, wait on God.
14. Isaiah 41:8–20: God has chosen us to destroy the devil and to bring rivers of anointing to the afflicted.
15. Isaiah 42:6–9: God said we will see healing and that a new thing will spring forth.
16. Isaiah 43:5–7: There will be worldwide revival with protection from evil (see verses 1–2).
17. Isaiah 43:18–21: This new move of God will come with rivers of anointing.
18. Isaiah 44:1–5: The rivers of anointing will flow on a thirsty Church.
19. Isaiah 45:8: God intercedes for the Church and nation of Israel.
20. Isaiah 45:22–25: God will raise up Jesus' name and save many souls (see verse 14).
21. Isaiah 46:8–11: God will do it.
22. Isaiah 46:13: God's glory and salvation will come to physical and spiritual Israel.
23. Isaiah 49:4: God will show justice on behalf of Jesus' death and resurrection.
24. Isaiah 49:6: Jesus' light and salvation through the Church will cover the earth.
25. Isaiah 49:7–13: Kings will bow to Jesus as His people restore the land by the Spirit.

26. Isaiah 49:14–26: God will not forget us, there will be many new converts and our enemy will be defeated.
27. Isaiah 51:3–6: God's power will be demonstrated.
28. Isaiah 51:9–11: Isaiah asks God to awaken and do now what He did through Moses.
29. Isaiah 51:14–16: Those in sin and sickness will be delivered by the anointing on the Church.
30. Isaiah 52:13–15: Jesus' name will be exalted in this city.
31. Isaiah 53:10–12: Jesus' Church will prosper and divide the spoil.
32. Isaiah 54:4–17: Revival will come through God's sure love.
33. Isaiah 58:6–12: God's light and glory will come in revival if we give to the poor.
34. Isaiah 59:19–21: He will be like a mighty rushing stream through us.
35. Isaiah 60:1; 62:12: Here is a picture of revival. (Ask God for specific verses to pray back to Him.)
36. Isaiah 63:7–14: Isaiah reminded the people and God of His glorious deeds as seen in Exodus through Moses. For us it refers to the deeds done by Peter and Paul as recorded in the book of Acts.
37. Isaiah 63:15; 64:12: Isaiah leads in intercessory prayer for revival.
38. Isaiah 65:1–7: God answers 64:12, in effect, with, "No, I will not restrain or withhold Myself toward praying people since I answered those who did not even seek Me."

B. Jeremiah
  1. In the book of Jeremiah
    a. Jeremiah 1:12: God says He will watch over His Word (promises of restoration) to perform it.
    b. Jeremiah's intercessory burdens
      i. Jeremiah 8:18
      ii. Jeremiah 10:19
      iii. Jeremiah 13:17
      iv. Jeremiah 14:17
      v. Jeremiah 23:9
    c. Jeremiah 14:7–9, 19–22: Jeremiah offers intercessory prayer for revival.
    d. Jeremiah 17:12–18: Jeremiah expresses personal worship and prayer.
    e. Jeremiah 23:29: God's Word under the anointing is like a fire and a hammer.
    f. Jeremiah 24:6–7: Revival takes place as God's people return to Him.
    g. Jeremiah 29:10–14: Revival will come through prayer.

      h. Jeremiah 30:3, 9–11, 16–22: Sin will be conquered and blessing will flow.

      i. Jeremiah 30:24: God's wisdom will be released in the end times.

      j. Jeremiah 31:1–14, 17, 20–26, 31–40: Revival promises are given for physical and spiritual Israel.

      k. Jeremiah 32:17–25: Jeremiah offers intercessory prayer for revival.

      l. Jeremiah 33:3: Prayer is the key to revival.

      m. Jeremiah 33:6–26: Blessing and power will come when God restores His people.

      n. Jeremiah 50:4–7, 17–20, 33–34: We will be forgiven and restored to where the saints were in the book of Acts.

      o. Jeremiah 51:20–23: God will make us His weapon.

  2. In the book of Lamentations. Here the Church of Jesus without revival mourns for the fullness of God. The enemy is a picture of the devil. The mourning is for more power and grace. Zion is the Church. The key verses: Lamentations 2:18–20.

      a. Lamentations 1:9, 11, 16

      b. Lamentations 2:12–13

      c. Lamentations 2:18–20

      d. Lamentations 3:20–26

      e. Lamentations 3:31–33

      f. Lamentations 5:1–22

C. Ezekiel

  1. Ezekiel 11:14–21: God will gather from the whole world to redeem.

  2. Ezekiel 16:60–63: God will restore, and never again will we backslide into shame.

  3. Ezekiel 33:1–9: We have a responsibility to say what God says, despite opposition.

  4. Ezekiel 34:11–16: Revival will affect both the physical and spiritual realms.

  5. Ezekiel 34:25–31: Restoration comes; God shepherds His people.

  6. Ezekiel 36:8–15: New converts are drawn and all find success in the Holy Spirit over enemies.

  7. Ezekiel 36:22–32: God will exalt Jesus' name in our sight.

  8. Ezekiel 36:33–38: The heathen will see God's blessing on us.

  9. Ezekiel 37:24–28: God's covenant and blessings will be manifested in unity and power.

  10. Ezekiel 39:25–29: We will know God is in our midst in power.

  11. Ezekiel 47:1–9: Rivers from the heavenly Temple will flow on us.

D. Daniel
   1. Daniel 7:18–27: Saints will prevail over the devil through God's grace.
   2. Daniel 9:1–19: Daniel, the premier intercessor, records his prayer that released Israel from captivity into revival.
E. Hosea
   1. Hosea 1:7, 10: Grace will deliver us and we will be called sons of God.
   2. Hosea 2:19–23: We will be joined intimately to God's grace; rain and new wine will flow.
   3. Hosea 3:5: Jews will be saved in the end-time revival.
   4. Hosea 5:15; 6:3: As we seek God, He will not withhold but will come as the rain.
   5. Hosea 6:11: God will fully restore the Church.
   6. Hosea 10:12: Righteousness will rain on our hearts.
   7. Hosea 11:1, 3–4, 8–11: We are to remind God of these facts, of His love for Israel.
   8. Hosea 12:10: Remind God. He gave numerous visions, even under the old covenant.
   9. Hosea 14:4–7: God will heal freely and His Church will blossom.
F. Joel
   1. Joel 2:17: Here is Joel's call to intercessory prayer.
   2. Joel 2:18–20: God will be zealous.
   3. Joel 2:23–29: God will bring about a worldwide revival of power.
   4. Joel 3:1: God will restore.
   5. Joel 3:17–20: The Church will be holy and established by God.
G. Amos. Amos 9:11–15: God will rebuild the Tabernacle of David and restore worship in the Spirit.
H. Obadiah. Obadiah 1:17–21: The Church will experience power and will prevail against all sin (Esau).
 I. Micah
   1. Micah 2:12: Israel and the Church will be restored.
   2. Micah 2:13: The "breaker" anointing opens the way.
   3. Micah 4:12–13: God will thresh and pulverize opposition through the Church.
   4. Micah 5:3–4: God will return to His people in power to shepherd them.
   5. Micah 5:7–9: Blessings from heaven will fall.
   6. Micah 7:7–20: Here is Micah's intercessory prayer for revival.
J. Habakkuk
   1. Habakkuk 2:14: The earth will be filled with God's glory; worldwide revival.
   2. Habakkuk 3:2: Here is Habakkuk's intercessory prayer.
K. Zephaniah
   1. Zephaniah 3:9: Holiness and unity will come.

      2. Zephaniah 3:12–20: The purified and prosperous Church will rejoice.

  L. Haggai. Haggai 2:4, 9: God will be with us to make His end-time Church more glorious than the first-century Church (see also Isaiah 61:7; Zechariah 9:12). We will have a double portion.

  M. Zechariah

      1. Zechariah 1:3: God will return to us with power and grace as we return to Him.

      2. Zechariah 1:12: The angel of the Lord offers a prayer for revival.

      3. Zechariah 1:12–17: God is jealous and will return to this people.

      4. Zechariah 2:4–5: Glory will protect the Church.

      5. Zechariah 2:9–13: Revival comes through God's presence in our midst.

      6. Zechariah 6:12–15: Jesus will build His Church with great authority.

      7. Zechariah 8:2–3: God will be jealous for revival in the Church.

      8. Zechariah 8:7–13: God will treat His people with favor.

      9. Zechariah 8:20–23: Revival will be worldwide.

     10. Zechariah 9:11–17: Here is a picture of revival.

     11. Zechariah 10:1: Ask God for rain (that is, anointing).

     12. Zechariah 10:3, 5: The saints will be mighty in God.

     13. Zechariah 10:6–9: Revival comes as God brings back His people.

     14. Zechariah 10:12: The people will be strengthened by grace (see also Ephesians 3:16).

     15. Zechariah 12:3–11: Revival will be attended by fire and power and the Spirit of grace and prayer.

     16. Zechariah 13:1–4, 9: During revival the Lord gathers His people.

     17. Zechariah 14:9: His name alone will be exalted on earth.

  N. Malachi

      1. Malachi 1:11: Jesus' name will be great in all the earth.

      2. Malachi 3:1: Jesus will suddenly visit His people.

      3. Malachi 3:7, 10–12: He will supply until there is no more need.

      4. Malachi 4:2–3: Jesus will be exalted with healing.

      5. Malachi 4:5–6: Elijah is coming with great power.

2. New Testament Apostolic Prayers for the Corporate Church

  A. Prayers for the release of the gifts, fruit and wisdom of the Holy Spirit to the corporate Body

      1. Ephesians 1:17–19: The spirit of wisdom and revelation is expressed through release of revelation and power gifts, the spirit of conviction on the preaching of the Word and a release of wisdom for the corporate direction of the Church and her ministries.

2. Colossians 1:9–11; 4:12; James 1:5: These prayers are to make known God's will and Word to us. This also occurs by the release of the gifts, conviction and wisdom.

3. Ephesians 3:16–19: This prayer asks for strength in the inner man of the saints. It will be fulfilled by the release of God's presence within. This includes the release of the gifts of the Spirit, the power of conviction and the release of wisdom.

4. 2 Thessalonians 2:17; 3:5; Hebrews 13:9: These verses speak of strengthening the heart. The release of God's power, conviction and wisdom will do this.

5. Philippians 1:9–11; 1 Thessalonians 3:12; 2 Thessalonians 3:5: These prayers ask that our hearts grow in love by the impartation of the Spirit. We, too, will grow in love as the Spirit of conviction reveals carnality and unbrokenness in us. We are able to express love to others by the release of the gifts of the Spirit. Also, God will grant wisdom to reveal how to walk in love more specifically and effectively.

6. 1 Corinthians 1:8; 2 Corinthians 13:9; 1 Thessalonians 3:10; Hebrews 13:20–21: These are prayers for the Church to be established, confirmed and made complete. She will be made complete by the release of gifts, by the release of conviction that leads to the fruit of the Holy Spirit and by receiving wisdom in our personal and corporate lives.

7. John 17:20–23; Romans 15:5–6: These are prayers for unity in the Church, especially for her leadership. This will also occur by the release of gifts, conviction and wisdom in our midst.

8. Romans 15:13; 2 Thessalonians 2:16–17; 3:16: These are prayers to release peace, joy and hope (see also Acts 9:31; Romans 14:17).

9. John 17:11–12, 15; Romans 16:20; 2 Thessalonians 3:3; James 4:7: These are prayers to overcome and resist Satan, the evil one.

10. Acts 4:29–31; Ephesians 6:19: These are prayers to release boldness in the saints of God. Boldness is a specific manifestation of the Holy Spirit that is released through prayer.

11. John 17:11–17; 2 Corinthians 13:7–9; Philippians 1:9; 1 Thessalonians 3:10–13; 5:23: These are prayers to bring the Church into purity, love and sanctification. The release of the Spirit of conviction and revelation will produce this in the lives of the saints. The release of power and gifts will greatly aid in this (see also Acts 5:1–11; 1 Corinthians 5:1–5; 2 Corinthians 10:4–6).

12. Matthew 9:37–38; Luke 10:2: These are prayers to the Father to release anointed laborers. Only those anointed with gifts, conviction and wisdom will fully answer this prayer.

13. 2 Thessalonians 3:1–2: The increase of the Word will come only by the release of gifts, conviction and wisdom (see also Acts 6:7; 12:24; 13:48; 19:20).
14. Acts 14:1–28; Colossians 4:3–4: Doors are opened for the Gospel by miracles.
15. 2 Thessalonians 1:11–12: Prayer is given for the Body to be mature by experiencing grace and being found worthy to fulfill its sovereign calling.
16. Ephesians 3:18–19; 2 Thessalonians 3:5: Revelation of God's love comes by the Spirit of revelation and conviction. God's love is experienced by the power of the Holy Spirit.
17. Colossians 1:11; 2 Thessalonians 3:5: The Church is called to grow in patience, endurance and steadfastness.

B. Prayers for the salvation of sinners
1. Acts 13:12, 48; 19:20; 2 Thessalonians 3:1–2: Prayers for the Word to increase
2. Colossians 4:3–4: Prayers for a door for the Gospel to open
3. Romans 10:1: Prayers for salvation of sinners
4. Matthew 9:37–38: Prayers for labors to be anointed with power and conviction

C. Prayers for individuals, especially for traveling ministries
1. 2 Corinthians 1:11; Ephesians 6:18; Philippians 1:19; 1 Thessalonians 5:25; Hebrews 13:18: Prayers for others
2. Acts 12:5, 12; Romans 15:31; 2 Thessalonians 3:2; Philemon 22: Prayers for protection
3. Colossians 4:3: Prayers for anointing (opening a door of power)
4. Matthew 6:31; Luke 22:31–32; 2 Corinthians 13:7: Prayers for deliverance from temptation and evil
5. Philippians 4:7, 19: Prayers for personal needs
6. Ephesians 6:19: Prayers for boldness
7. Colossians 4:3, 12: Prayers for wisdom
8. 2 Timothy 1:16–18: Prayers for mercy on a house
9. James 5:14–15: Prayers regarding sickness
10. 2 Timothy 4:14–15: Prayers to be on guard

D. Prayers for Israel: Psalm 79; 80; 83; 85; 86; 122:6–7; Isaiah 62:1–2, 6–7; Jeremiah 31:7; Romans 10:1; 11:26–27. (More on this subject in Appendix 2.)

E. Prayer for those in secular authority: 1 Timothy 2:1–3

F. Prayers to avenge and deliver from persecution of the Body: Psalm 7; 54–59; 94; 109; Revelation 6:10

G. Prayers for personal visitations of God to us as individuals and as a corporate body: Acts 1:8; 2:1–4; 26:13–18; Galatians 1:12–17. (See also Matthew 17:21 regarding prayer that helps us grow in faith and prevail over sickness and demons.)

H. Prayers to magnify or vindicate Jesus' name in our cities: Psalm 2:7–9; 110; Isaiah 45:22–25; 52:13–15; Ezekiel 36:22–32, 37

I. Other intercessory prayers: Ezra 9:5–15; Nehemiah 1:4–11; Isaiah 63:15–64:12; Daniel 9; Habakkuk 3:2

3. Prayers in the Psalms

A. Praise to God for His great blessings: Psalm 45:3–5; 65; 67; 85; 86; 90:13–17; 102:12–22; 110:1–5; 132
B. For times of personal defeat and need for help against enemies: Psalm 6; 13; 25; 44; 51; 69; 80; 83; 88; 137
C. For times of personal devotion: Psalm 25; 26; 27; 40; 41; 42; 43; 45; 63; 65; 69; 84; 86; 88; 130; 138
D. Pray through the Psalms and categorize them for you personally. Ask God to make Psalms 5–10 special for you. (Note: In interpreting the Psalms for prayer purposes, the word *enemy* can refer to the power of sin, sickness and Satan in the Church. The word *nations* can refer to geographic regions, ethnic groups or even the unbelievers in a given society. Anger, wrath and judgment in the Psalms can refer to the withholding of the fullness of grace in the Church or of God's anger against an ungodly city, nation, etc.)

4. Threefold Grace of God (1 Thessalonians 1:2, 5)

"We give thanks to God always for all of you, making mention of you in our prayers; . . . for our gospel did not come to you in word only, but also in power and in the Holy Spirit and with full conviction; just as you know what kind of men we proved to be among you for your sake."

This one general prayer request may be broken down into the following three aspects of gifts, fruit and wisdom of the Holy Spirit:
A. The gifts of the Spirit—the power of God in our lives
  1. 1 Corinthians 12:7–9: Nine gifts are named.
  2. Matthew 17:21; Luke 9:1: The Body is given a special measure of anointing over demons.
  3. Acts 2:1–4: There is a corporate release of Holy Spirit power.
  4. Acts 2:17: The Spirit of revelation is poured out.
  5. Acts 8:18: The Holy Spirit falls on those we lay hands on.
  6. Hebrews 1:14: The ministry of angels is released to the Body.
B. The fruit of the Spirit—the character of God in our lives
  1. The Body is called to pray for the release of conviction that results in godly character in those who hear. John 16:8 explains that Jesus brings the conviction or revelation of sin, righteousness and judgment.
  2. The Body is called to pray for the release of the fear of God, righteousness, peace and joy (the comfort) of the Holy Spirit. See Acts 9:31; Romans 14:17; 15:13; 2 Corinthians 1:3–4; 2 Thessalonians 2:16–17; 3:16.

3. See Acts 2:37–41. The Body is also to pray for the power of the Word upon the hearers:

a. Psalm 45:5: In the arrow that pierces the hearts of hearers.

b. Isaiah 33:13–14: In the fire that consumes the hearts of hearers.

c. Jeremiah 23:29: In the hammer that shatters the hearts of hearers.

d. Hebrews 4:12: In the sword that pierces the hearts of hearers (see Acts 2:37–41).

C. The wisdom of God—the administration of God's purposes

1. John 14:16, 26; 16:13–15, 26–27: The Body will receive the teaching ministry of the Holy Spirit.

2. Ephesians 1:17; 3:9–10: The corporate Church will receive the administration of God's purposes.

3. Colossians 1:9–10; 4:12: The Body can pray for direction for a specific church or ministry.

4. Psalm 25:5; 43:3–4; James 1:5: Individuals can receive personal direction.

5. Revelation 3:18: God gives eyesalve that the Body may see.

SCRIPTURES FOR PRAYING FOR ISRAEL

I appreciate the help of Avner Boskey of Final Frontier Ministries in Beersheva, Israel, for his consultation in the preparation of this teaching outline.

1. Seven Scriptural Reasons to Pray for Israel

A. Israel is still the apple of God's eye and His inheritance, close to His heart.
   1. Deuteronomy 32:9–11: "'The Lord's portion is His people; Jacob is the allotment of His inheritance. . . . He encircled him, He cared for him, He guarded him as the pupil of His eye. . . . He spread His wings and caught them, He carried them on His pinions.'"
   2. Psalm 33:11–12: "The counsel of the Lord stands forever, the plans of His heart [proceed] from generation to generation. Blessed [are] . . . the people whom He has chosen for His own inheritance."
   3. Psalm 148:14: "He has lifted up a horn for His people, praise for all His godly ones; even for the sons of Israel, a people near to Him."

4. Zechariah 2:8: "'He who touches you, touches the apple of His eye.'"
5. Romans 11:29: "The gifts and the calling of God are irrevocable."

B. God says that His servants should pray with compassion over Israel's condition. Psalm 102:13–14: "'Thou wilt arise and have compassion on Zion; for it is time to be gracious to her, for the appointed time has come. Surely Thy servants find pleasure in her stones, and feel pity for her dust." (See also verses 15–17.)

C. God commands us to give Him and ourselves no rest until He establishes Jerusalem and makes her the praise of the earth. Isaiah 62:1, 6–7: "For Zion's sake I will not keep silent, and for Jerusalem's sake I will not keep quiet, until her righteousness goes forth like brightness, and her salvation like a torch that is burning. . . . On your walls, O Jerusalem, I have appointed watchmen; all day and all night they will never keep silent. You who remind the Lord, take no rest for yourselves; and give Him no rest until He establishes and makes Jerusalem a praise in the earth."

D. God's heart will travail through us for Israel's salvation.
1. Romans 9:2–3: "I [Paul] have great sorrow and unceasing grief in my heart."
2. Romans 10:1: "My heart's desire and my prayer to God for them is for their salvation." (See also verse 14.)

E. God commands us to seek the spiritual and physical good of the Israeli people and to pray for the peace of Jerusalem.
1. Psalm 122:4, 6–7, 9: "[Jerusalem] To which the tribes go up, even the tribes of the Lord—an ordinance for Israel. . . . Pray for the peace of Jerusalem: 'May they prosper who love you. May peace be within your walls, and prosperity within your palaces.' . . . For the sake of the house of the Lord our God I will seek your good."
2. Romans 1:16: "I am not ashamed of the gospel, for it is the power of God for salvation to every one who believes, to the Jew first and also to the Greek."
3. Romans 2:9–11: "There will be tribulation and distress . . . glory and honor and peace . . . to the Jew first and also to the Greek. For there is no partiality with God."
4. Romans 15:25–27: "I am going to Jerusalem serving the saints. For Macedonia and Achaia have been pleased to make a contribution for the poor among the saints in Jerusalem. Yes, they were pleased to do so, and they are indebted to them. For if the Gentiles have shared in their spiritual things, they are indebted to minister to them also in material things."

F. The Jewish people's acceptance of Messiah Jesus will lead to life from death—worldwide revival of unprecedented magnitude.

1. Isaiah 27:6: "In the days to come Jacob will take root, Israel will blossom and sprout; and they will fill the whole world with fruit."
2. Romans 11:15: "If their rejection be the reconciliation of the world, what will their acceptance be but life from the dead?"

G. Jesus linked His second coming to Israel's national turning to Him: Matthew 23:39: "'I say to you, from now on you shall not see Me until you say, "Blessed is He who comes in the name of the Lord!"'"

2. Eight Biblical Intercessors and Their Prayers for Israel

A. Moses
1. Exodus 32:11–13, 32: Moses cries to the Lord based on His reputation and covenant, as well as for His glory's sake.
2. Numbers 14:13–19: Moses' intercession is followed by an intense cry for pardon according to God's great lovingkindness.
3. Deuteronomy 9:18–19, 25–29: Moses fasts for forty days for God's intervention in a time of great crisis.
4. Deuteronomy 30:1–10: The proclamation of restoration is taught to the sons.

B. Solomon. 1 Kings 8:46–53: Solomon offers a prayer to God to forgive as He has done before.

C. Nehemiah. Nehemiah 1:4–11: Nehemiah gives a compassionate plea for the forgiveness of his people.

D. Asaph and the sons of Korah
1. Psalm 44: A plea is offered for God to rise up and redeem His people.
2. Psalm 74: An appeal is made against the devastation of the land by the enemy.
3. Psalm 79: A lament is given over the destruction of Jerusalem and a cry for help made.
4. Psalm 80: God is implored to rescue His people.
5. Psalm 83: A prayer is offered for the Lord to confound their enemies.
6. Psalm 85: A prayer is offered for God's mercy on the nation.

E. Isaiah
1. Isaiah 58:1: "Cry loudly," says the Lord through the prophet, "do not hold back."
2. Isaiah 62:1, 6: Those who intercede are to pray day and night for Jerusalem's sake.
3. Isaiah 63:15–19; 64: Isaiah offers a desperate prayer for mercy and help.

F. Jeremiah
1. Jeremiah 9:1: His intercessor's heart yearns to weep day and night.

2. Jeremiah 14:7–9, 17–22: Jeremiah acknowledges his people's many sins and implores the Lord to act for His name's sake.
3. Jeremiah 15:5: A plea comes in the midst of judgment.
4. Lamentations 3:43–51: Jeremiah says his eyes pour down tears unceasingly until the Lord looks down and sees from heaven.
5. Lamentations 5:19–22: Jeremiah offers a prayer for mercy that his people may be restored.

G. Daniel. Daniel 9:1–19: Daniel offers a prayer of confession on behalf of his people.

H. Joel
1. Joel 1:8, 13–14: Joel calls the people to a solemn assembly.
2. Joel 2:12–17: Joel calls the people to gather and give an intercessory cry to God to spare His people.

3. Journey in Prayer for Israel

A. The scattering and regathering
1. Jeremiah 31:8–10: "'Behold, I am bringing them from the north country, and I will gather them from the remote parts of the earth, among them the blind and the lame, the woman with child and she who is in labor with child, together; a great company, they shall return here. With weeping they shall come, and by supplication I will lead them; I will make them walk by streams of waters, on a straight path in which they shall not stumble; for I am a father to Israel, and Ephraim is My first-born.' Hear the word of the Lord, O nations, and declare in the coastlands afar off, and say, 'He who scattered Israel will gather him, and keep him as a shepherd keeps his flock.'"
2. Hosea 1:10: "The number of the sons of Israel will be like the sand of the sea, which cannot be measured or numbered; and it will come about that, in the place where it is said to them, 'You are not My people,' it will be said to them, 'You are the sons of the living God.'"

B. Scriptures for *aliyah*—the return to the land. Note that from 1989 to 1991 some 400,000 Jews made *aliyah* from the land of the north. From 1991 to 1998 approximately another 300,000 have come to Israel. Russian is now the second leading spoken language in Israel.
1. Isaiah 11:11–12: "It will happen on that day that the Lord will again recover the second time with His hand the remnant of His people, who will remain, from Assyria, Egypt, Pathros, Cush, Elam, Shinar, Hamath and from the islands of the sea. And He will lift up a standard for the nations, and will assemble the banished ones of Israel, and will gather the dispersed of Judah from the four corners of the earth."

Scriptures for Praying for Israel

2. Isaiah 43:5–6: "'Do not fear, for I am with you; I will bring your offspring from the east, and gather you from the west. I will say to the north, "Give them up!" And to the south, "Do not hold them back." Bring My sons from afar, and My daughters from the ends of the earth.'"

3. Jeremiah 16:14–15: "'Behold, days are coming,' declares the Lord, 'when it will no longer be said, "As the Lord lives, who brought up the sons of Israel out of the land of Egypt," but, "As the Lord lives, who brought up the sons of Israel from the land of the north and from all the countries where He had banished them." For I will restore them to their own land which I gave to their fathers.'"

4. Jeremiah 23:7–8: "'Behold, the days are coming,' declares the Lord, 'when they will no longer say, "As the Lord lives, who brought up the sons of Israel from the land of Egypt," but, "As the Lord lives, who brought up and led back the descendants of the household of Israel from the north land and from all the countries where I had driven them." Then they will live on their own soil.'"

C. Our scriptural response. The three scriptural keys we are to put into the door as prophetic intercessors are *proclaiming*, *praising* and *praying*. Then God's promises will be unlocked and fulfilled.

1. Jeremiah 30:3: "'Behold, days are coming,' declares the Lord, 'when I will restore the fortunes of My people Israel and Judah.' The Lord says, 'I will also bring them back to the land that I gave to their forefathers, and they shall possess it.'"

2. Jeremiah 31:7: "For thus says the Lord, 'Sing aloud with gladness for Jacob, and shout among the chiefs of the nations; proclaim, give praise, and say, "O Lord, save Thy people, the remnant of Israel."'"

NOTES

Chapter 1: On Bended Knee

1. R. Kelso Carter, "Standing on the Promises," *The Methodist Hymnal* (Nashville: Methodist Publishing House, 1964), pp. 221–222.

2. Dick Eastman, *No Easy Road* (Grand Rapids: Baker, 1971), p. 123.

3. Joseph L. Garlington, *Worship: The Pattern of Things in Heaven* (Shippensburg, Pa.: Destiny Image, 1997), p. 5.

4. W. E. Vine, *An Expository Dictionary of New Testament Words* (Old Tappan, N.J.: Fleming H. Revell, 1966), p. 235.

Chapter 3: The Desperate Prayer of the Heart

1. R. A. Torrey, *How to Pray* (Chicago: Moody, 1900), pp. 33–34.

2. Charles G. Finney, *Principles of Prayer* (Minneapolis: Bethany, 1980 edition), p. 71.

3. E. M. Bounds, *The Necessity of Prayer* (New York: Revell, 1920), p. 56.

4. William Booth quoted in Eastman, *No Easy Road*, p. 92.

5. Stephen Hill, *Time to Weep* (Foley, Ala.: Together in the Harvest, 1996), p. 234.

6. Ibid., p. 240.

7. Ibid., p. 237.

8. Ibid., p. 252.

9. Paul Cain, *The Gift of Tears* (Kansas City, Mo.: Shiloh, 1997), pp. 1–2.

10. Wesley L. Duewel, *Mighty, Prevailing Prayer* (Grand Rapids: Zondervan, 1990), pp. 221–222.

Notes

11. Ibid., p. 222.
12. Ibid., p. 222.
13. W. E. Vine, *An Expository Dictionary of New Testament Words* (Old Tappan, N.J.: Fleming H. Revell, 1966), p. 182.

Chapter 4: Travail: The Prayer That Brings Birth

1. Leonard Ravenhill, *Why Revival Tarries* (Minneapolis: Bethany, 1982), p. 138.
2. Charles G. Finney, *Lectures on Revival* (Minneapolis: Bethany, 1988 edition), p. 46.
3. Quoted by Philip E. Howard Jr., *The Life and Diary of David Brainerd* (Chicago: Moody Bible Institute, 1949, 1995), pp. 172–173.
4. Wesley L. Duewel, *Mighty, Prevailing Prayer* (Grand Rapids: Zondervan, 1990), pp. 210–211.

Chapter 5: Wanted: A Generation of Prophetic People

1. David Pytches, *Spiritual Gifts in the Local Church* (Minneapolis: Bethany, 1985), p. 79.
2. Dick Iverson, *The Holy Spirit Today* (Portland: BT Publications, 1976), p. 155.
3. Rodney M. Howard-Browne, *The Touch of God* (Louisville: R.H.B.E.A., 1992), p. vi.

Chapter 6: The Prophetic Intercessory Task

1. Bryn Jones, *Prophetic Intercession in the Final Generation*, U.S.A. PRAY! Training Manual (Reston, Va.: Intercessors for America, 1989), p. 43.
2. Norman Stone, *They're Killing My Children* (Spokane, Wash.: Walk Across America for Life, 1983).
3. Andrew Gowers, *Financial Times* (Wednesday, September 23, 1987), p. 1.
4. Jack Hayford, *Did God Not Spare Nineveh?* (Van Nuys, Calif.: Church On The Way, 1980).

Chapter 7: Calling All Watchmen

1. Rick Joyner, *The Prophetic Ministry* (Charlotte, N.C.: MorningStar, 1997), p. 199.
2. Ibid., p. 202.

Chapter 8: Reminding God of His Word

1. Jack Deere has written *Surprised by the Power of the Spirit* (Zondervan, 1993) and *Surprised by the Voice of God* (Zondervan, 1996).
2. Andrew Murray, *With Christ in the School of Prayer* (Springdale, Pa.: Whitaker, 1981), pp. 161–162.
3. This story was told in R. Edward Miller's book *Thy God Reigneth* (Mar del Plata, Argentina: Argentine Bible Assemblies, n.d.). I heard him

tell the account on a video as well. This out-of-print book, according to the jacket, "tells of the beginning of the outflow of God's river of revival to Argentina and its flowing from 1949–1954."

4. Murray, *School of Prayer*, p. 167.

Chapter 9: Israel: God's Prophetic Calendar

1. Tom Hess, *Let My People Go!* (Washington, D.C.: Progressive Vision, 1987), pp. 118–120.

2. Ramon Bennett, *When Day and Night Cease* (Jerusalem: Arm of Salvation, 1992), pp. 122–123.

3. Ibid., p. 123.

4. Louis Rapoport, *The Jerusalem Post*, June 1, 1991, p. 1.

5. Associated Press, *News Messenger* (Marshall, Tex.), May 26, 1991, p. 1.

Chapter 10: Crisis Intervention through Intercession

1. Doris M. Ruscoe, *The Intercession of Rees Howells* (Fort Washington, Pa.: Christian Literature Crusade, 1983), p. 27.

Chapter 11: Wisdom Issues for Intercessors

1. Ken Blue, *The Authority to Heal* (Downers Grove, Ill.: InterVarsity, 1987), p. 76.

2. Terry Crist, *Interceding against the Powers of Darkness* (Tulsa: Terry Crist Ministries, 1990), p. 19.

3. Dick Eastman, *No Easy Road* (Grand Rapids: Baker, 1971), p. 61.

Chapter 12: Opening the Way!

1. This story is told in chapter 40, "The Revival in the Hebrides Islands," from the book *Revival Fire* by Wesley L. Duewel (Grand Rapids: Zondervan, 1995), pp. 306–318.

GLOSSARY

OF TERMS

I hope this simple glossary of terms will help clarify the meaning of a few terms used throughout this book. By no means is it a thorough and comprehensive professional dictionary. Rather, I have simply defined these terms in my own words. I trust it will be of help to you.

Aliyah. The Hebrew word for the return of the Jews to their homeland in Israel.

Anointing. The presence and power of God manifested—or the manifested presence of God—working in, on or through an individual or corporate group, enabling them to do the works of Christ.

Apostle. One called and sent by Christ to have the spiritual authority, character, gifts and abilities to reach and establish people in Kingdom truth and order, especially through founding and overseeing local churches.

Baptism in the Holy Spirit. The receiving and continued infilling of the power and life of the Holy Spirit, enabling and enduing believers in Christ with power and life to be His witnesses.

Breakers. Those called to break open the way for the Lord to come forth (see Micah 2:13). They are forerunners like John the Baptist, who prepared the way for the coming of the King.

Cessationism. A theological belief system stating that the gifts of the Holy Spirit ceased when the canon of Scripture was closed with the completion of the New Testament. Cessationists do not accept that the gifts of the Spirit are valid or necessary for today.

Charismatic. Coming from the Greek word *charis* for "grace," a term coined in the 1960s to describe those who believe that the gifts of the Holy Spirit are active today.

Crisis intercession. Petitioning the Father intensely for either His mercy to be extended in the midst of prevailing circumstances or for His judgment to be withheld.

Curse. A word spoken with some form of spiritual power and authority for evil. This sets into motion a power that will probably extend from generation to generation.

Dark night of the soul. A state of being in which an individual is abandoned to terrible dryness and darkness of the soul, and in which he finds little joy or sweetness. Through this season God purifies, prepares and subdues the individual's nature to unite him with His Spirit. The depriving of God's light causes the individual to cease operating from his own strength and prepares him for union with God.

Day of Atonement. The most holy day for the Jews, an annual day of fasting, penitence and sacrifice for sin. Before the destruction of the Temple, the High Priest would enter the Holy of Holies on the tenth day of the seventh month of the Hebrew calendar and offer sacrifices for the sanctuary, the priests and the people. This foreshadowed the entrance of Jesus, the great High Priest, who offered Himself as our eternal sacrifice once for all, having purchased for us eternal salvation. This day, also known as Yom Kippur, is observed today with fasting and confession of sins.

Deliverance. A Holy Spirit encounter by which an individual is set free in the name of Jesus from the oppression of evil spirits, and also from circumstances that oppress from without.

Demonization. The state of being under the influence or control of a demonic power.

Diaspora. A dispersion of the Jews from their homeland, such as the Jewish people being sent into Egypt in the time of Moses.

Despot. An absolutely tyrannical ruler.

Dream. The inspired pictures and impressions given to the heart while one is sleeping. These are given by the Holy Spirit in order to teach, exhort, reveal, warn, cleanse or heal.

Evangelicals. Christians who believe in the inerrancy of Scripture and the classic doctrines of the Church—including the deity of Jesus Christ, His atoning death and His bodily ascension and return—with evangelistic zeal.

Gatekeepers. The elders of a city or church who have the authority to open or close the gates of a city as alerted by the watchmen.

Gift of discerning of spirits. Supernatural perception given by God to enable believers to distinguish the motivating spirit behind words or deeds, and to discern the source of operation as human, demonic or the Holy Spirit.

Gift of prophecy. The supernatural ability to hear the voice of the Holy Spirit and speak God's mind or counsel. Given for the purpose of edifying, exhorting, comforting, convicting, instructing, imparting and testifying of and from Jesus.

Gifts of the Spirit. The expression of God's power at work, given by the Holy Spirit, to be used at special times for special occasions. Such gifts as recorded in 1 Corinthians 12:4–11 are the attestation of the empowering of the Holy Spirit and are vital in the "signs and wonders" ministry.

Healing evangelist. One who heralds the Good News with signs, wonders, miracles and healings following.

Humility. A true knowledge of God and oneself. It means to declare and confess that the Lord is great and exceedingly to be praised, and to declare that before Him we are nothing.

Intercession. The act of making a request to a superior, or expressing a deep-seated yearning to our one and only superior, God.

Intercessor. One who reminds God of His promises and appointments yet to be fulfilled; who takes up a case of injustice before God on behalf of another; who makes up the "hedge" (that is, builds up the wall in time of battle); and who stands in the gap between God's righteous judgments and the people's need for mercy.

Manifested presence of God. While God is omnipresent, or everywhere, He nevertheless reveals or manifests His presence strategically and locationally.

No common ground. Every spiritual warrior must allow the Holy Spirit to prepare him before battle through purification. The reason Jesus could stand in such power and authority, and deal so effectively with the wicked oppressor, was that He had no ground in common with His adversary.

Open heaven or portal. A hole, opening or portal between heaven and earth through which the manifested presence of God is poured forth over those under that vicinity.

Open vision. A kind of vision in which the natural eyes are open and the believer is seeing and perceiving realities in the spiritual world.

Penalty. See *curse.*

Pentecostal. Christian who emphasizes the baptism in the Holy Spirit with the accompanying gift of speaking in tongues; generally connected with one of several Pentecostal denominations.

Petition. An earnest request or plea before God.

Power evangelism. The response to the spontaneous direction of the Holy Spirit to minister the power of the Gospel for salvation (as opposed to following a planned program to evangelize).

Power healing. Holy Spirit demonstrations in which one is set free and healed physically, emotionally or spiritually from the chains of captivity.

Prayer of groanings. Sighing or praying nonverbally with grief, groans and even indignation, as directed by the Holy Spirit to bring release and liberty.

Priest. One who pleads the needs of the people before God. In the Old Testament a special tribe, the Levites, was set apart for this purpose. In the New Testament each believer in Christ is a priest unto the Lord.

Priestly intercession. An intercessory task in which the priest not only represents himself before the Lord but, like priests of old, carries the twelve stones of Israel on his heart—the burdens, needs and cares of others—before the great High Priest.

Prophet/prophetess. A man or woman who represents the interests of God to the people. Having stood in the council of God, the prophet releases a clarion call to the people of what is in God's heart at the moment. Some refer to this as one of the fivefold ministry gifts listed in Ephesians 4:11.

Prophetic destiny. The revelatory promise of God portraying His purposes, plans and pursuits for an individual, group, city or nation.

Prophetic intercession. The act of waiting before God in order to hear or receive His burden—His word, concern, warning, condition, vision or promise—and responding back to Him and the people with appropriate actions.

Prophetic priests. Individuals in whom are united the Old Testament offices of prophet and priest with New Testament applications for today. They not only hear from the Lord the pronouncements from His throne but pray the promises back to the Father.

Prophetic song of the Lord. An inspired revelatory song sung by an individual or group declaring the heart of the Lord for that specific setting. It is hearing the voice of God and singing His heart.

Prophetic unction/anointing. When one is impressed by the Holy Spirit to speak, sing or act out what has been revealed by the special enduement of grace.

Seer. An individual gifted as a "receptor" of God, operating in visions and revelatory gifts to "see" and describe what is received from the Lord.

Spirit of revelation. The unfolding or unveiling of God's will to the eyes of the heart. The revelation of truth otherwise unknown can come through impressions, prophecy, dreams, visions, trances and messages from the Lord.

Spiritual warfare. The confrontation of the kingdom of darkness by the power of the Kingdom of God to displace the works of darkness and elevate His Son Jesus.

Supplication. To entreat, seek, implore or beseech God in earnest prayer.

Trance. A visionary state in which revelation is received from God. In this rapturous state an individual is no longer limited to natural consciousness and volition. He is "in the spirit" where full consciousness of the natural may be temporarily transcended.

Travail. The prayer that brings forth a birthing in the spirit, which creates or enlarges an opening for an increased dimension of the Kingdom of God.

Velvet warriors. Those who come forth in brokenness, on bended knee, in unity, resolved in their hearts to take territory for the King.

Vision. A sight disclosed supernaturally to the spiritual eyes.

Visionary revelation. The grace of the Holy Spirit enabling a Christian to experience such manifestations as visions, dreams and trances.

Visitation. A supernatural experience in which a distinct sense of the presence of God is accompanied by fear of the Lord. This may come in the form of an angelic visitation, as in the book of Acts, or by other biblical means.

Waiting. A posture of stillness before the Lord but attentiveness to His Spirit moving.

Watch of the Lord. A gathering in Jesus' name (see Matthew 24; Mark 13; Luke 21) to watch, pray and be vigilant for the life of a church, city or nation. It is also a position on the wall of the Lord in order to see outside the city, in order to alert the gatekeepers of approaching enemies or envoys from the King; and inside the city to recognize and confront disorderly, unlawful activity of the enemy within.

Watchmen. Those who serve in the position of watching. See *watch of the Lord.*

Witchcraft. Any spirit other than the Holy Spirit in which people operate to manipulate and control others.

Word of knowledge. Supernatural revelation by the Holy Spirit that discloses the truth He wishes to make known about a person or situation.

Worship. Posturing one's heart in awe and reverence before God; to bow down before Him.

RECOMMENDED READING

Alves, Elizabeth. *The Mighty Warrior.* Bulverde, Tex.: Intercessors International, 1987.

Austin, Dorothea. *The Name Book.* Minneapolis: Bethany, 1982.

Bacovcin, Helen, trans. *The Way of a Pilgrim* and *The Pilgrim Continues His Way: Spiritual Classics from Russia.* New York: Doubleday/Image, 1992.

Bennett, Ramon. *When Day and Night Cease.* Jerusalem: Arm of Salvation, 1992.

Bickle, Mike. *Passion for Jesus.* Lake Mary, Fla.: Creation House, 1993.

———. *A Personal Prayer List.* Kansas City, Mo.: Metro Christian Fellowship, 1988.

——— with Michael Sullivant. *Growing in the Prophetic.* Lake Mary, Fla.: Creation House, 1995.

Billheimer, Paul E. *Destined for the Throne.* Minneapolis: Bethany, 1975.

Blomgren, David. *Prophetic Gatherings in the Church: The Laying on of Hands and Prophecy.* Portland: BT Publishing, 1979.

———. *Song of the Lord.* Portland: BT Publishing, 1978.

Bounds, E. M. *The Complete Works of E. M. Bounds on Prayer.* Grand Rapids: Baker, 1990.

Bradshaw, Paul F. *Two Ways of Praying.* Nashville: Abingdon, 1995.

Bullinger, Ethelbert W. *Numbers in Scripture.* Grand Rapids: Kregel, 1967.

Cain, Paul. *The Gift of Tears.* Kansas City, Mo.: Shiloh, 1997.

Campbell, Wesley. *Welcoming a Visitation of the Holy Spirit.* Lake Mary, Fla.: Creation House, 1996.

Castro, David A. *Understanding Supernatural Dreams according to the Bible.* Brooklyn: Anointed Publications, 1994.

Chavda, Mahesh. *Only Love Can Make a Miracle.* Ann Arbor, Mich.: Servant, 1990.

Chevreau, Guy. *Pray with Fire: Interceding in the Spirit.* Toronto: HarperPerennial/HarperCollins, 1995.

Conner, Kevin J. *Interpreting the Symbols and Types.* Portland: BT Publications, 1980.

———. *Today's Prophets.* Portland: BT Publications, 1989.

——— and Ken Malmin. *Interpreting the Scriptures.* Portland: BT Publications, 1983.

Cooke, Graham. *Developing Your Prophetic Gifting.* Kent, Sussex: Sovereign World, 1994.

Cornwall, Judson. *Praying the Scriptures.* Lake Mary, Fla.: Creation House, 1990.

Crist, Terry. *Warring according to Prophecy.* Springdale, Pa.: Whitaker, 1989.

———. *Interceding against the Powers of Darkness.* Tulsa: Terry Crist Ministries, 1990.

Damazio, Frank. *Developing the Prophetic Ministry.* Portland: Trilogy, 1983.

Dawson, Joy. *Intimate Friendship with God.* Old Tappan, N.J.: Chosen, 1986.

Deere, Jack. *Surprised by the Power of the Spirit.* Grand Rapids: Zondervan, 1993.

———. *Surprised by the Voice of God.* Grand Rapids: Zondervan, 1996.

Duewel, Wesley L. *Mighty, Prevailing Prayer.* Grand Rapids: Francis Asbury/Zondervan, 1990.

———. *Revival Fire.* Grand Rapids: Zondervan, 1995.

———. *Touch the World through Prayer.* Grand Rapids: Zondervan, 1986.

Eastman, Dick. *Change the World School of Prayer.* Studio City, Calif.: World Literature Crusade, 1976.

———. *The Hour That Changes the World: A Practical Plan for Personal Prayer.* Grand Rapids: Baker, 1978.

———. *Love on Its Knees.* Old Tappan, N.J.: Chosen, 1989.

———. *No Easy Road: Inspirational Thoughts on Prayer.* Grand Rapids: Baker, 1971.

Engle, Lou. *Digging the Wells of Revival.* Shippensburg, Pa.: Destiny Image, 1998.

de Fenelon, François. *The Seeking Heart.* Beaumont, Tex.: SeedSowers, 1992.

Finney, Charles G. *Lectures on Revival.* Minneapolis: Bethany, 1988.

Forsyth, P. T. *The Soul of Prayer.* Salem, Oh.: Schmul, 1986.

Foster, Glenn. *The Purpose and Use of Prophecy.* Glendale, Calif.: Sweetwater, 1988.

Foster, Richard J. *Prayer: Finding the Heart's True Home.* San Francisco: HarperSanFrancisco, 1992.

—— and James Bryant Smith. *Devotional Classics: Selected Readings for Individuals and Groups.* San Francisco: HarperSanFrancisco, 1993.

Frangipane, Francis. *The House of the Lord.* Lake Mary, Fla.: Creation House, 1991.

Gardiner, Gordon P. *Radiant Glory: The Life of Martha Wing Robinson.* Brooklyn: Bread of Life, 1962.

Gastineau, Pat. *Modes of Prayer.* Roswell, Georgia: Word of Love, 1997.

——. *The Spiritual Fight.* Roswell, Georgia: Word of Love, 1997.

Goll, Jim W. *The Lost Art of Intercession.* Shippensburg, Pa.: Destiny Image, 1997.

—— and Michal Ann Goll. *Encounters with a Supernatural God.* Shippensburg, Pa.: Destiny Image, 1998.

Grubb, Norman. *Rees Howells, Intercessor.* Fort Washington, Pa.: Christian Literature Crusade, 1987.

Grudem, Wayne. *The Gift of Prophecy in the New Testament Church and Today.* Westchester, Ill.: Crossway, 1988.

Guyon, Jeanne. *Experiencing God through Prayer.* Ed. Donna C. Arthur. Springdale, Pa.: Whitaker, 1984.

Hagin, Kenneth E. *The Art of Intercession: Handbook on How to Intercede.* Tulsa: Kenneth Hagin Ministries, 1987.

——. *Concerning Spiritual Gifts.* Tulsa: Faith Library, 1974.

——. *The Gift of Prophecy.* Tulsa: Faith Library, 1982.

——. *The Holy Spirit and His Gifts.* Tulsa: Faith Library, 1974.

——. *The Ministry of a Prophet.* Tulsa: Faith Library, 1981.

Hamon, Bill. *Prophets and Personal Prophecy.* Vol. 1, *God's Prophetic Voice Today.* Shippensburg, Pa.: Destiny Image, 1987.

——. *Prophets and the Prophetic Movement.* Point Washington, Fla.: Christian International, 1990.

——. *Prophets, Pitfalls, and Principles.* Shippensburg, Pa.: Destiny Image, 1991.

Hawthorne, Steve, and Graham Kendrick. *Prayer-Walking: Praying on Site with Insight.* Lake Mary, Fla.: Creation House, 1993.

Hayford, Jack W. *Prayer Is Invading the Impossible.* S. Plainfield, N.J.: Bridge, 1995.

Recommended Reading

————. *Did God Not Spare Nineveh?* Van Nuys, Calif.: Church On The Way, 1980.

Hess, Tom. *The Watchmen.* Charlotte, N.C.: MorningStar, 1998.

Hill, Stephen. *Time to Weep.* Foley, Ala.: Harvest, 1996.

Howard, Philip E. *The Life and Diary of David Brainerd.* Jonathan Edwards, ed. Chicago: Moody Bible Institute, 1949, 1995.

Intercessors for America, *USA Pray! Training Manual.* Reston, Va.: Intercessors for America, 1989.

Isleib, Mary Alice. *Effective, Fervent Prayer.* Minneapolis: Mary Alice Isleib Ministries, 1991.

————. *The Holy Spirit Today.* Portland: BT Publications, 1976.

Jacobs, Cindy. *Possessing the Gates of the Enemy.* Tarrytown, N.Y.: Chosen, 1991.

Jacobsen, Wayne. *A Passion for God's Presence.* Eugene, Ore.: Harvest House, 1991.

Joyner, Rick. *The Prophetic Ministry.* Charlotte, N.C.: MorningStar, 1997.

————. *The World Aflame: The Welsh Revival and Its Lessons for Our Time.* Charlotte, N.C.: MorningStar, 1993.

Keating, Thomas. *Open Mind, Open Heart.* New York: Continuum, 1986.

Kelsey, Morton T. *Companions on the Inner Way: The Art of Spiritual Guidance.* New York: Crossroad, 1983.

————. *God, Dreams, and Revelation.* Minneapolis: Augsburg, 1974.

Lawrence, Brother, and Frank Laubach. *Practicing His Presence.* Auburn, Mass.: Christian Books, 1973.

Lindsay, Gordon. *Prayer and Fasting: The Master Key to the Impossible.* Dallas: Christ for the Nations, 1979.

Lloyd-Jones, Martyn. *Enjoying the Presence of God.* Ann Arbor, Mich.: Servant, 1991.

Mumford, Bob. *Take Another Look at Guidance.* S. Plainfield, N.J.: Logos, 1971.

Murray, Andrew. *Absolute Surrender.* Springdale, Pa.: Whitaker, 1982.

————. *Like Christ.* Springdale, Pa.: Whitaker, 1981.

————. *Waiting on God.* Springdale, Pa.: Whitaker, 1981.

————. *With Christ in the School of Prayer.* Springdale, Pa.: Whitaker, 1981.

Nori, Don. *The Power of Brokenness.* Shippensburg, Pa.: Destiny Image, 1997.

————. *Secrets of the Most Holy Place.* Shippensburg, Pa.: Destiny Image, 1992.

Nouwen, Henri J. M. *The Way of the Heart.* New York: Ballantine, 1983.

————. *Making All Things New.* New York: Ballantine, 1983.

Patterson, Ben. *Waiting: Finding Hope When God Seems Silent.* Downers Grove, Ill.: InterVarsity, 1989.

Prince, Derek. *Blessing or Curse: You Can Choose!* Old Tappan, N.J.: Chosen, 1990.

————. *Fasting.* Fort Lauderdale: Derek Prince Ministries, 1986.

————. *How to Fast Successfully.* Fort Lauderdale: Derek Prince Ministries, 1976.

————. *How to Judge Prophecy.* Fort Lauderdale: Derek Prince Ministries, 1971.

————. *The Last Word on the Middle East.* Lincoln, Va.: Chosen, 1978.

————. *Praying for the Government.* Fort Lauderdale: Derek Prince Ministries, 1970.

————. *Shaping History through Prayer and Fasting.* Old Tappan, N.J.: Spire, 1973.

———— and Ruth Prince. *Prayers and Proclamations.* Fort Lauderdale: Derek Prince Ministries, 1990.

Pytches, David. *Prophecy in the Local Church: A Practical Handbook and Historical Overview.* London: Hodder & Stoughton, 1993.

————. *Spiritual Gifts in the Local Church.* Minneapolis: Bethany, 1985.

Randolph, Larry. *User-Friendly Prophecy.* Shippensburg, Pa.: Destiny Image, 1998.

Ravenhill, Leonard. *Revival Praying.* Minneapolis: Bethany, 1962.

————. *A Treasury of Prayer: The Best of E. M. Bounds on Prayer in a Single Volume.* Minneapolis: Bethany, 1981.

————. *Why Revival Tarries.* Minneapolis: Bethany, 1959, 1982.

Riffel, Herman H. *Dream Interpretation: A Biblical Understanding.* Shippensburg, Pa.: Destiny Image, 1993.

————. *Dreams: Wisdom Within.* Shippensburg, Pa.: Destiny Image, 1989.

Runcorn, David. *A Center of Quiet: Hearing God When Life Is Noisy.* Downers Grove, Ill.: InterVarsity, 1990.

Ruscoe, Doris M. *The Intercession of Rees Howells.* Fort Washington, Pa.: Christian Literature Crusade, 1983.

St. Teresa of Avila, *Interior Castle.* Trans. and ed. E. Allison Peers. New York: Image/Doubleday, 1961, 1989.

Sandford, John and Paula. *The Elijah Task.* Tulsa: Victory House, 1977.

Scott, Martin. *Prophecy in the Church.* Altamonte Springs, Fla.: Creation House, 1993.

Shaw, Gwen. *Redeeming the Land.* Jasper, Ark.: Engeltal, 1987.

Sheets, Dutch. *Intercessory Prayer.* Ventura, Calif.: Regal, 1996.

Silvoso, Ed. *That None Should Perish: How to Reach Entire Cities for Christ through Prayer Evangelism.* Ventura, Calif.: Regal, 1994.

Simpson, A. B. *The Life of Prayer.* Camp Hill, Pa.: Christian Publications, 1989.

Sjoberg, Kjell. *Winning the Prayer War.* Chichester, W. Sussex, U.K.: New Wine, 1991.

Sorge, Bob. *In His Face.* Canandaigua, N.Y.: Oasis, 1994.

Swope, Mary Ruth, *Listening Prayer.* Springdale, Pa.: Whitaker, 1987.

Thomas, Benny. *Exploring the World of Dreams.* Springdale, Pa.: Whitaker, 1990.

Tompkins, Iverna, with Judson Cornwall. *On the Ash Heap with No Answers.* Altamonte Springs, Fla.: Creation House, 1992.

Virkler, Mark and Patti. *Communion with God.* Shippensburg, Pa.: Destiny Image, 1990.

———. *Counseled by God.* Woy Woy, Australia: Peacemakers, 1986.

———. *Dialogue with God.* S. Plainfield, N.J.: Bridge, 1986.

Wagner, C. Peter. *Engaging the Enemy: How to Fight and Defeat Territorial Spirits.* Ventura, Calif.: Regal, 1991.

———. *Warfare Prayer.* Ventura, Calif.: Regal, 1992.

Wallis, Arthur. *God's Chosen Fast.* Fort Washington, Pa.: Christian Literature Crusade, 1968.

Willard, Dallas. *The Spirit of the Disciplines.* San Francisco: HarperSanFrancisco, 1991.

Wilson, Walter. *Wilson's Dictionary of Bible Types.* Grand Rapids: Eerdmans, 1950.

Yocum, Bruce. *Prophecy.* Ann Arbor, Mich.: Servant, 1976.

Willhite, B. J. *Why Pray?* Lake Mary, Fla.: Creation House, 1988.

Wimber, John. *Power Healing.* SanFrancisco: Harper & Row, 1987.

SUBJECT INDEX

SCRIPTURE INDEX

Scripture Index

10:3 285
10:5 285
10:6–9 285
10:12 285
12:3–11 285
12:10 51, 130, 202
13:1–4 285
13:9 285
14:9 285

Malachi

1:11 286
3:1 286
3:7 286
3:10–12 286
3:17 170
4:2–3 286
4:5–6 286

Matthew

3:16–17 261
6:10 263
6:13 155
6:31 288
8:2–3 23
9:18–19 24
9:23–25 24
9:37–38 259, 287, 288
11:12 79
12:43–45 143
15:22 24
15:25 24
15:28 24
16:18 263
16:19 264
17:21 288, 289
18:18–20 264
18:19 164
21:16 243
23:39 293
24 306
24:42 141
24:42–44 156
25:1–13 156
26:40–41 155
26:41 141

Mark

6:48 145
11:24 55
13 306
13:33–37 141
14:38 141

Luke

1:7–13 86
1:57 86
2:36–37 122
2:38 123
9:1 289
10:2 287
18:1–8 165
18:4–5 165
19:41 63, 64
21 306
21:36 141
22:31–32 288

John

4:23 23
5:1–4 262
10:10 143
11:4 71
11:11 70
11:21 71
11:32 71
11:33 73
11:33–42 72
12:32 271
14:16 290
14:26 290
14:30 247
15:7 162
16:8 290
16:13–15 290
16:26–27 290
17:11–12 287
17:11–17 287
17:15 287
17:20–23 287

Acts

1:8 288
2:1–4 288, 290
2:17 110, 290
2:19–20 110
2:37–41 290
2:39 110
3:1 146

3:21 279
4:29–31 287
5:1–11 287
6:7 287
7:56 261
8:18 290
9:31 287, 290
12:5 288
12:12 288
12:24 287
13:1–3 23
13:12 288
13:48 287, 288
14:1–28 287
16:25 23
16:25–26 243
19:20 287, 288
20:31 63
26:13–18 288

Romans

1:16 203, 292
2:9–11 293
2:28–29 280
4:11–17 280
4:17 270
5:9 170, 244
8:15 170
8:22 92
8:26 68
8:26–27 67
8:27 68
9:2–3 292
9:6–8 280
10:1 203, 288, 292
10:14 292
10:17 98, 173
11:6 188
11:15 293
11:26–27 288
11:29 292
14:17 287, 290
15:5–6 287
15:13 287, 290
15:25–27 293
15:31 288
16:20 287

1 Corinthians

1:8 286
1:18–25 271

2:2 271
5:1–5 287
12:7–9 289
12:10 132
14:1 119
14:1–4 132
14:3 104
14:8 153
14:15–16 132
14:40 108, 109
15:46 33
28:11–19 151

2 Corinthians

1:3–4 290
1:11 288
2:4 63
2:10–11 240, 241
2:11 143, 248
2:14 243, 253
4:5 271
10:4–6 287
13:7 288
13:7–9 287
13:9 286

Galatians

1:12–17 288
3:28–29 280
4:19 92
4:29 280
5:19–25 108
6:14 271

Ephesians

1:7 170, 244
1:15–19 112, 119
1:17 111, 290
1:17–19 286
1:18 113
2:6 130
3:9–10 290
3:14 21
3:16 285
3:16–19 286
3:18–19 288
3:20 68
4:11 105, 305
5:25–27 236
5:27 156

Jim Goll and his wife, Michal Ann, are founders of Ministry to the Nations, an organization based in Antioch, Tennessee, dedicated to releasing God's presence through prophetic intercession, missions and training.

After pastoring for thirteen years, Jim was thrust forth in 1987 into an itinerant role of equipping leaders and churches. He has traveled extensively across North and Central America, Europe, Asia, the former Soviet Union, Israel and the Caribbean, teaching and imparting the power of intercession, prophetic ministry and life in the Holy Spirit. The author of two additional books and numerous study materials, he was a teacher in the School of the Spirit of the Grace Training Center, Kansas City, Missouri, and a dean of Christian Leadership University, Buffalo, New York.

He and Michal Ann have been married for 23 years and have four children.

For more information:

Jim W. Goll
Ministry to the Nations
P.O. Box 338
Antioch, TN 37011-0338
Office Phone: (615) 365-4401
Office Fax: (615) 365-4408
e-mail: info@ministrytothenations.org
Web site: http://www.ministrytothenations.org